HARROW

◄ ◆ ABANDONED ◆ ►

COUNTY

HARROW

⤙ ABANDONED ⤚

COUNTY

™

Script
CULLEN BUNN

Art, chapters 1–2
CARLA SPEED McNEIL

Colors, chapters 1–2
JENN MANLEY LEE

Art, chapters 3–4
TYLER CROOK

Cover art, chapter breaks, and letters
TYLER CROOK

DARK HORSE BOOKS

President and Publisher
MIKE RICHARDSON

Editor
DANIEL CHABON

Assistant Editor
CARDNER CLARK

Designer
KEITH WOOD

Digital Art Technician
CHRISTIANNE GOUDREAU

NEIL HANKERSON Executive Vice President · TOM WEDDLE Chief Financial Officer · RANDY STRADLEY Vice President of Publishing
MATT PARKINSON Vice President of Marketing · DAVID SCROGGY Vice President of Product Development · DALE LAFOUNTAIN Vice President
of Information Technology · CARA NIECE Vice President of Production and Scheduling · NICK MCWHORTER Vice President of Media Licensing
MARK BERNARDI Vice President of Digital and Book Trade Sales · KEN LIZZI General Counsel · DAVE MARSHALL Editor in Chief
DAVEY ESTRADA Editorial Director · SCOTT ALLIE Executive Senior Editor · CHRIS WARNER Senior Books Editor · CARY GRAZZINI Director
of Specialty Projects · LIA RIBACCHI Art Director · VANESSA TODD Director of Print Purchasing · MATT DRYER Director of Digital Art and Prepress
SARAH ROBERTSON Director of Product Sales · MICHAEL GOMBOS Director of International Publishing and Licensing

Published by Dark Horse Books
A division of Dark Horse Comics, Inc.
10956 SE Main Street
Milwaukie, OR 97222

First edition: May 2017
ISBN 978-1-50670-190-5

International Licensing: (503) 905-2377 · Comic Shop Locator Service: (888) 266-4226

Harrow County Volume 5: Abandoned

This volume collects *Harrow County* #17–#20.

10 9 8 7 6 5 4 3 2 1
Printed in China

DarkHorse.com

Library of Congress Cataloging-in-Publication Data

Names: Bunn, Cullen, author. | Crook, Tyler, artist, letterer. | Lee, Jenn
  Manley, colourist.
Title: Harrow County, Volume 5, Abandoned / script, Cullen Bunn ; art,
  chapters 1-2 Carla Speed McNeil ; colors, chapters 1-2 Jenn Manley Lee ;
  art, chapters 3-4 Tyler Crook ; cover art, chapter breaks, and letters,
  Tyler Crook.
Other titles: Abandoned
Description: First edition. | Milwaukie, OR : Dark Horse Books, 2017. | "This
  volume collects Harrow County #17-#20"
Identifiers: LCCN 2016053726 | ISBN 9781506701905 (paperback)
Subjects: LCSH: Comic books, strips, etc. | BISAC: COMICS & GRAPHIC NOVELS /
  Horror. | COMICS & GRAPHIC NOVELS / Fantasy.
Classification: LCC PN6727.B845 H39 2017 | DDC 741.5/973--dc23
LC record available at https://lccn.loc.gov/2016053726

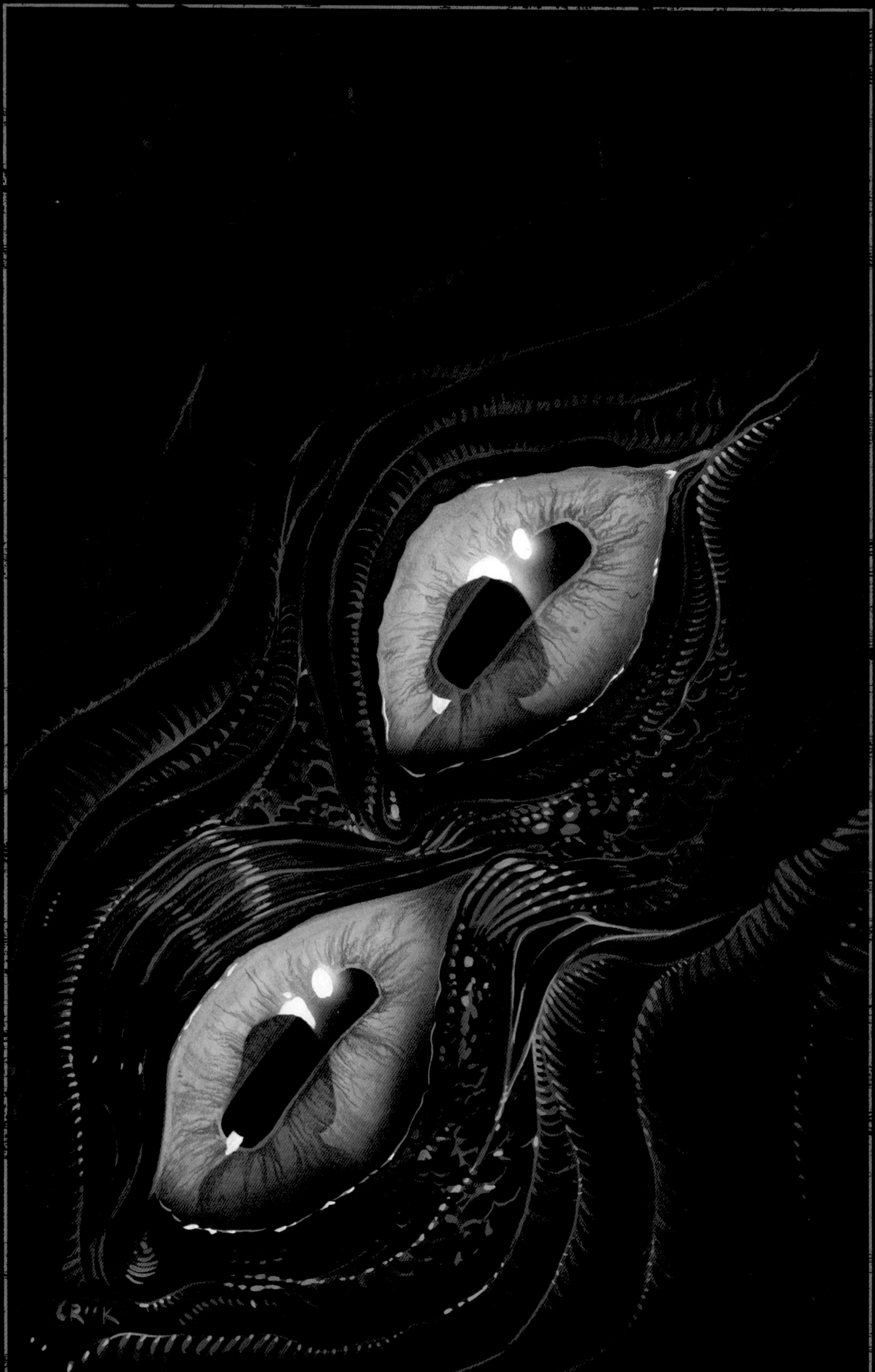

ONE

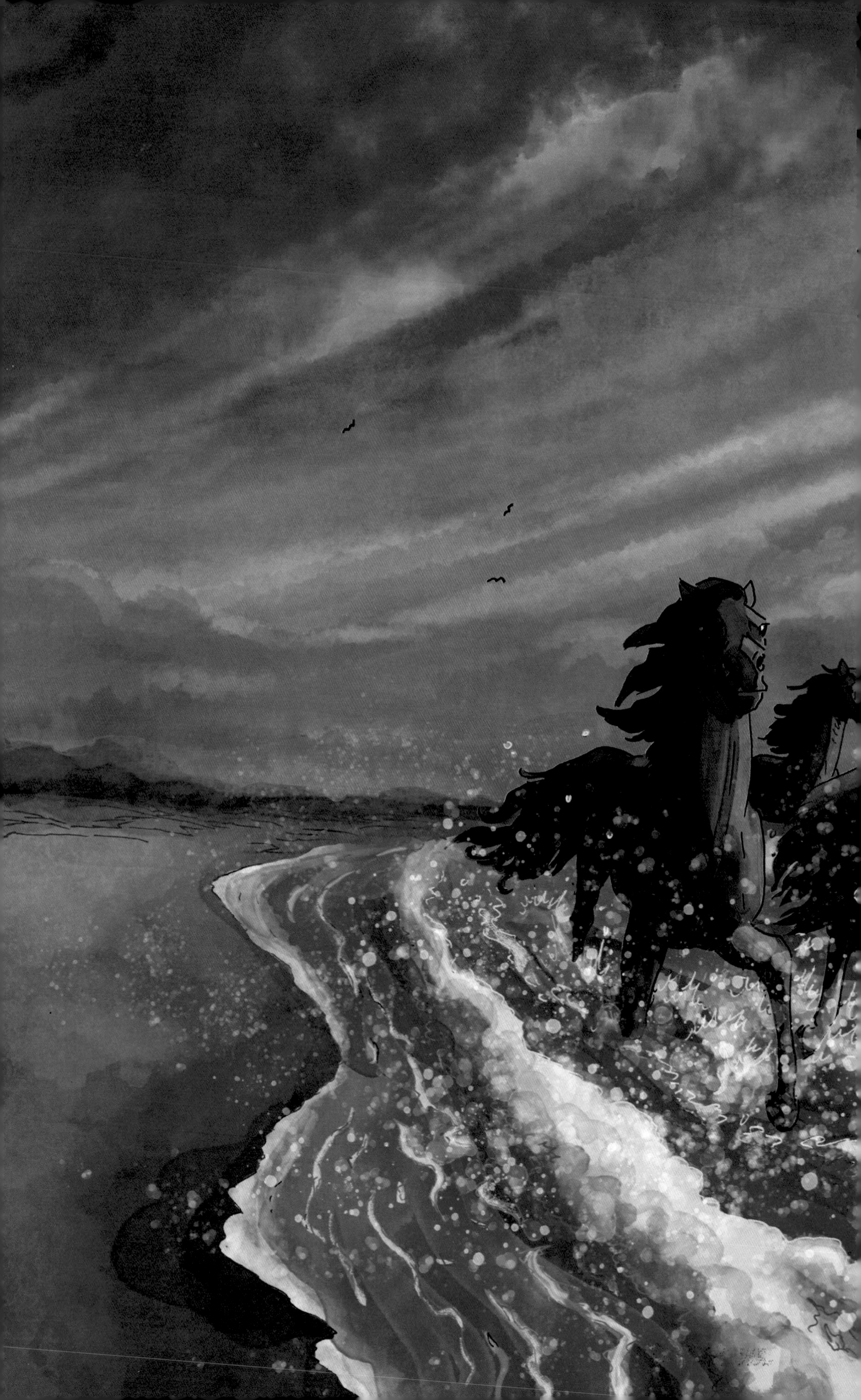

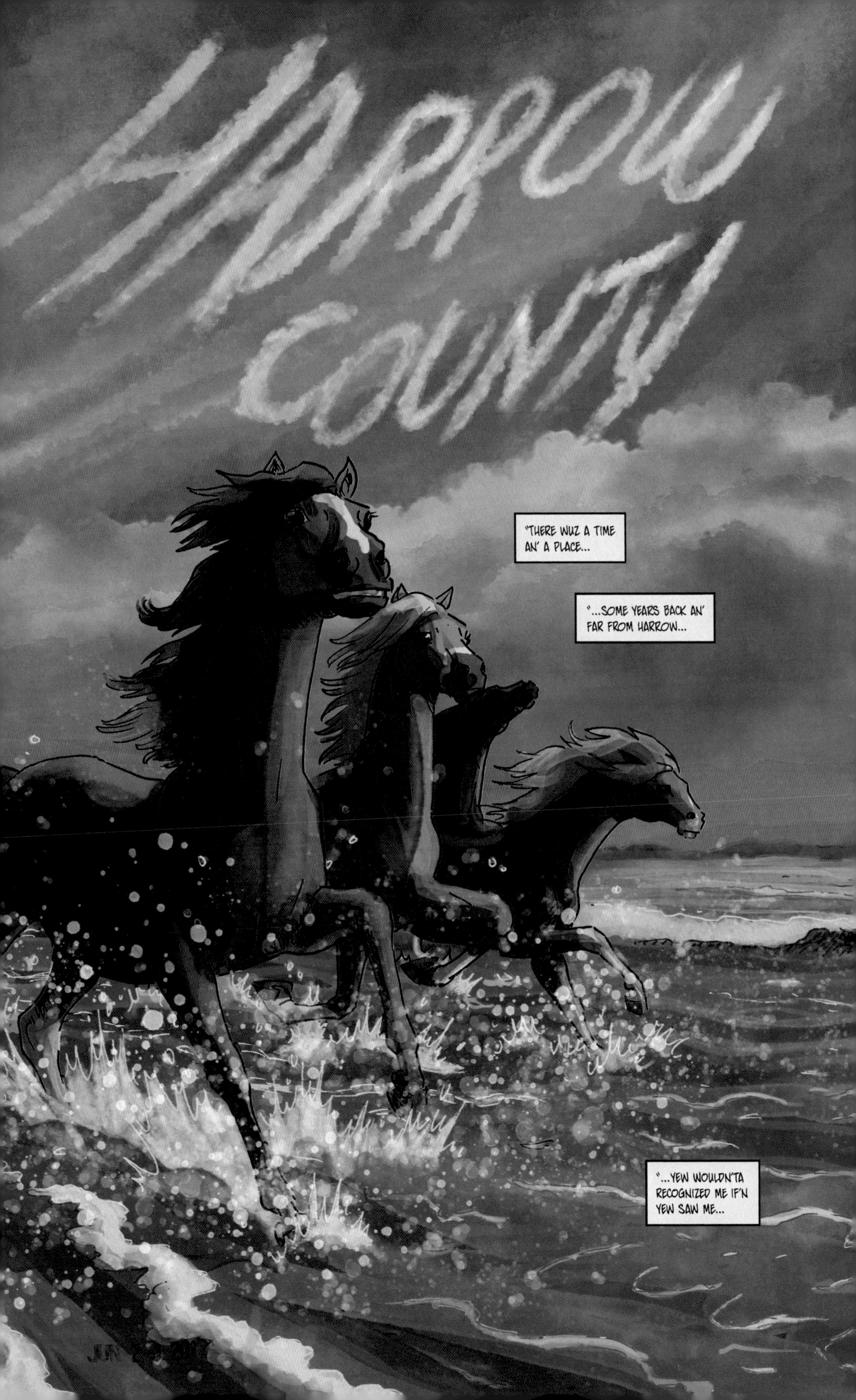
HARROW COUNTY
"THERE WUZ A TIME AN' A PLACE...
"...SOME YEARS BACK AN' FAR FROM HARROW...
"...YEW WOULDN'TA RECOGNIZED ME IF'N YEW SAW ME...

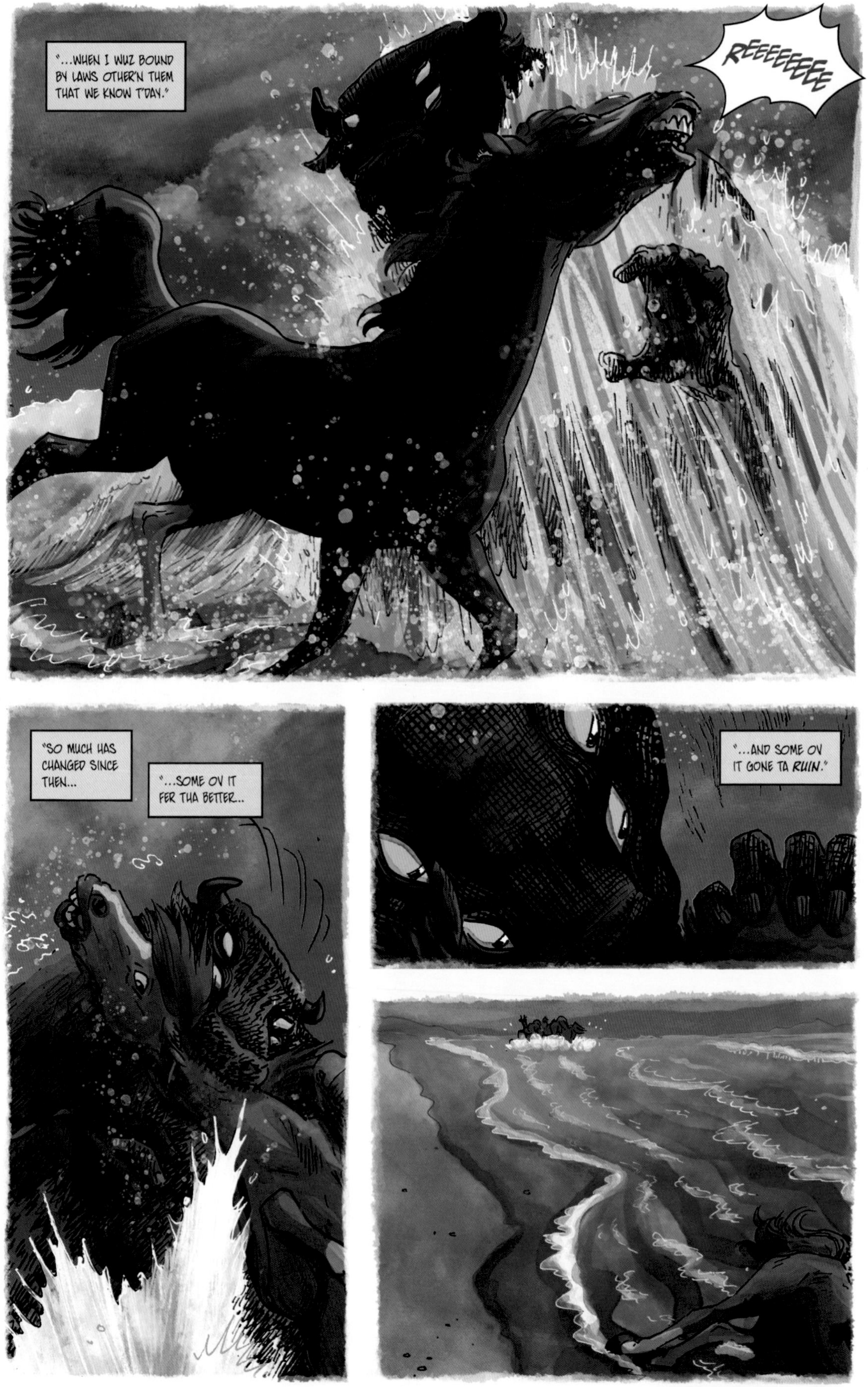
"...WHEN I WUZ BOUND BY LAWS OTHER'N THEM THAT WE KNOW T'DAY."
REEEEEEEE
"SO MUCH HAS CHANGED SINCE THEN...
"...SOME OV IT FER THA BETTER...
"...AND SOME OV IT GONE TA *RUIN*."

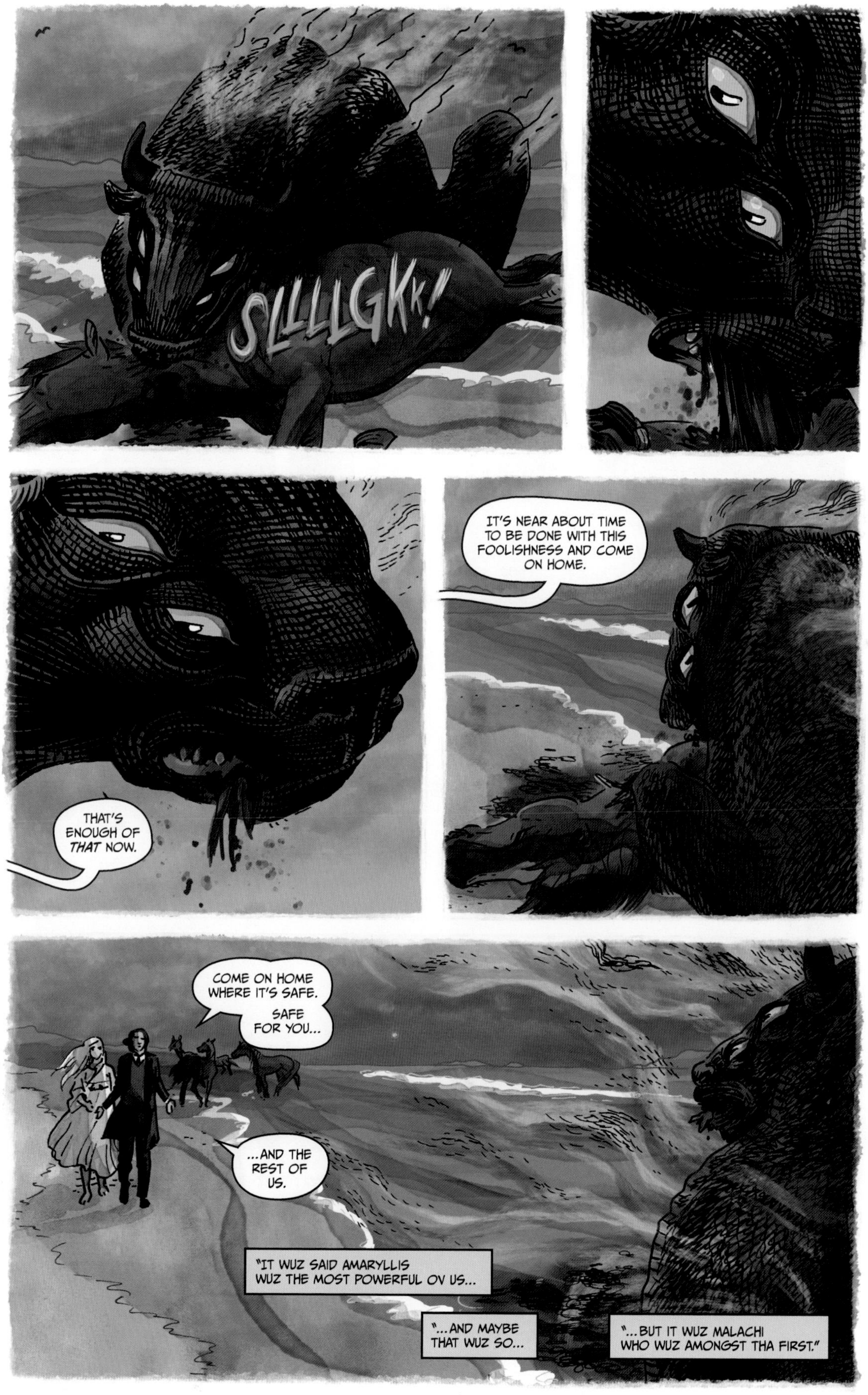
SLLLLGKK!
THAT'S ENOUGH OF *THAT* NOW.
IT'S NEAR ABOUT TIME TO BE DONE WITH THIS FOOLISHNESS AND COME ON HOME.
COME ON HOME WHERE IT'S SAFE.
SAFE FOR YOU...
...AND THE REST OF US.
"IT WUZ SAID AMARYLLIS WUZ THE MOST POWERFUL OV US...
"...AND MAYBE THAT WUZ SO...
"...BUT IT WUZ MALACHI WHO WUZ AMONGST THA FIRST."

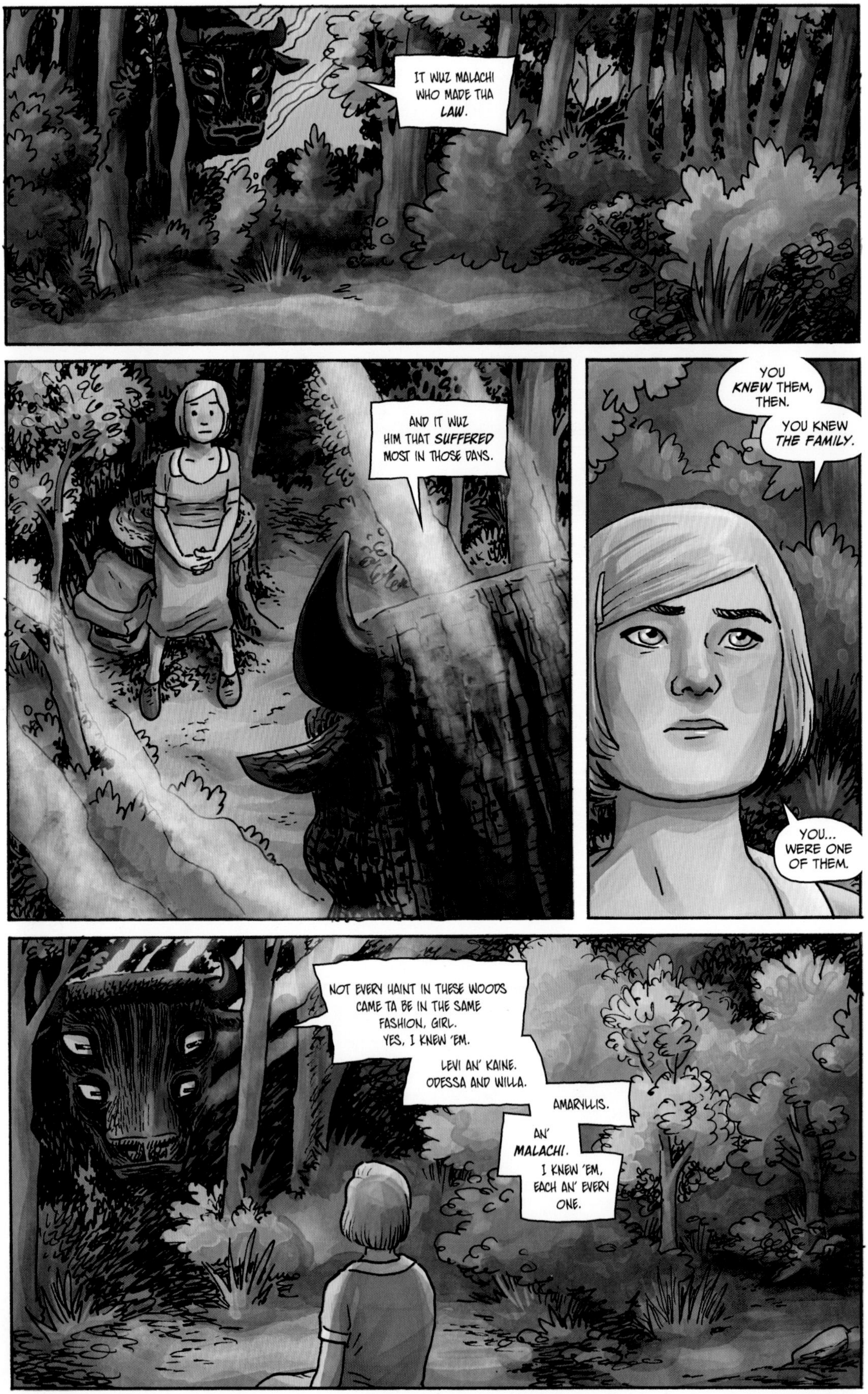
IT WUZ MALACHI WHO MADE THA LAW.
AND IT WUZ HIM THAT SUFFERED MOST IN THOSE DAYS.
YOU KNEW THEM, THEN.
YOU KNEW THE FAMILY.
YOU... WERE ONE OF THEM.
NOT EVERY HAINT IN THESE WOODS CAME TA BE IN THE SAME FASHION, GIRL. YES, I KNEW 'EM.
LEVI AN' KAINE. ODESSA AND WILLA.
AMARYLLIS.
AN' MALACHI.
I KNEW 'EM, EACH AN' EVERY ONE.

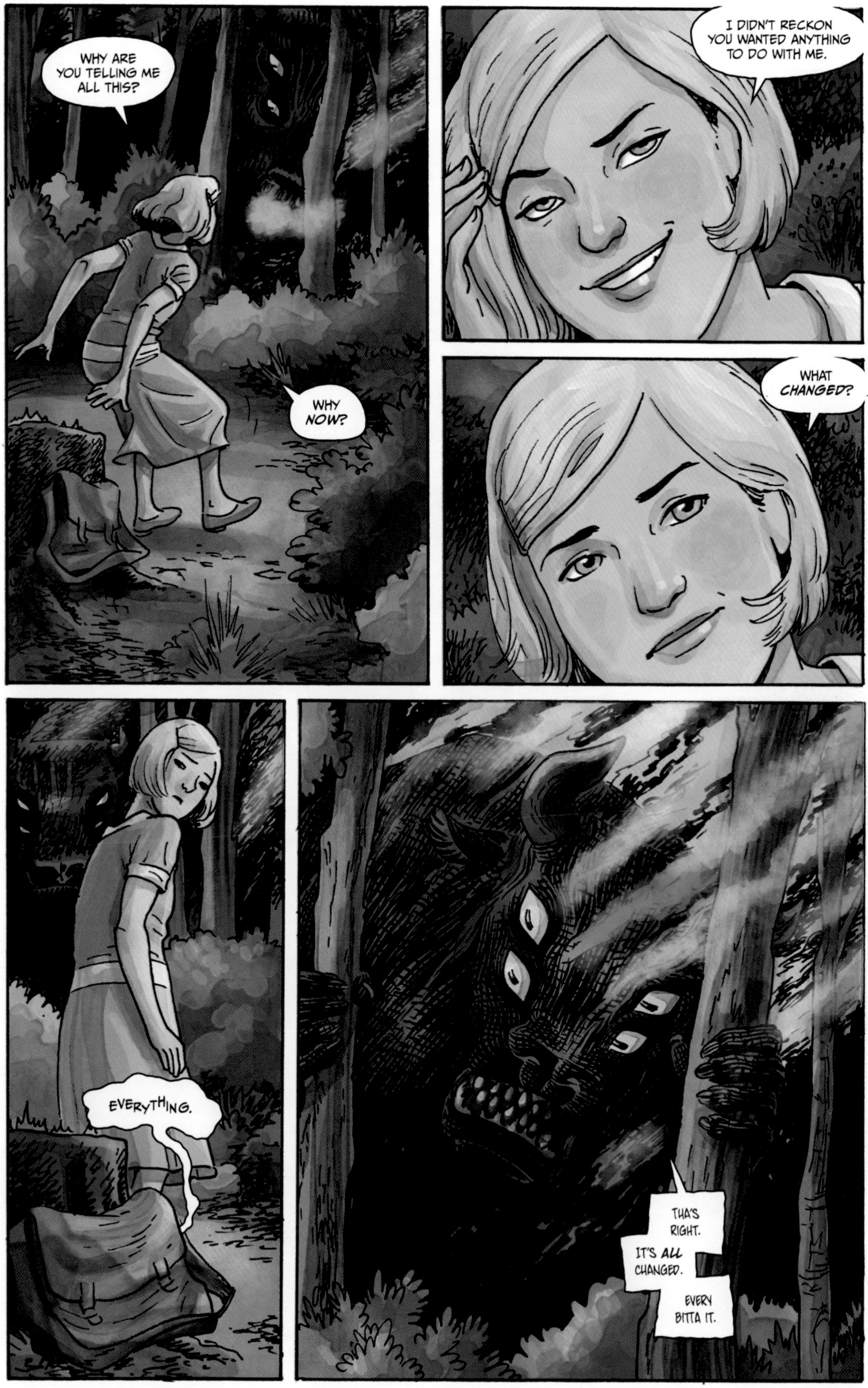
WHY ARE YOU TELLING ME ALL THIS?
WHY NOW?
I DIDN'T RECKON YOU WANTED ANYTHING TO DO WITH ME.
WHAT CHANGED?
EVERYTHING.
THA'S RIGHT.
IT'S ALL CHANGED.
EVERY BITTA IT.

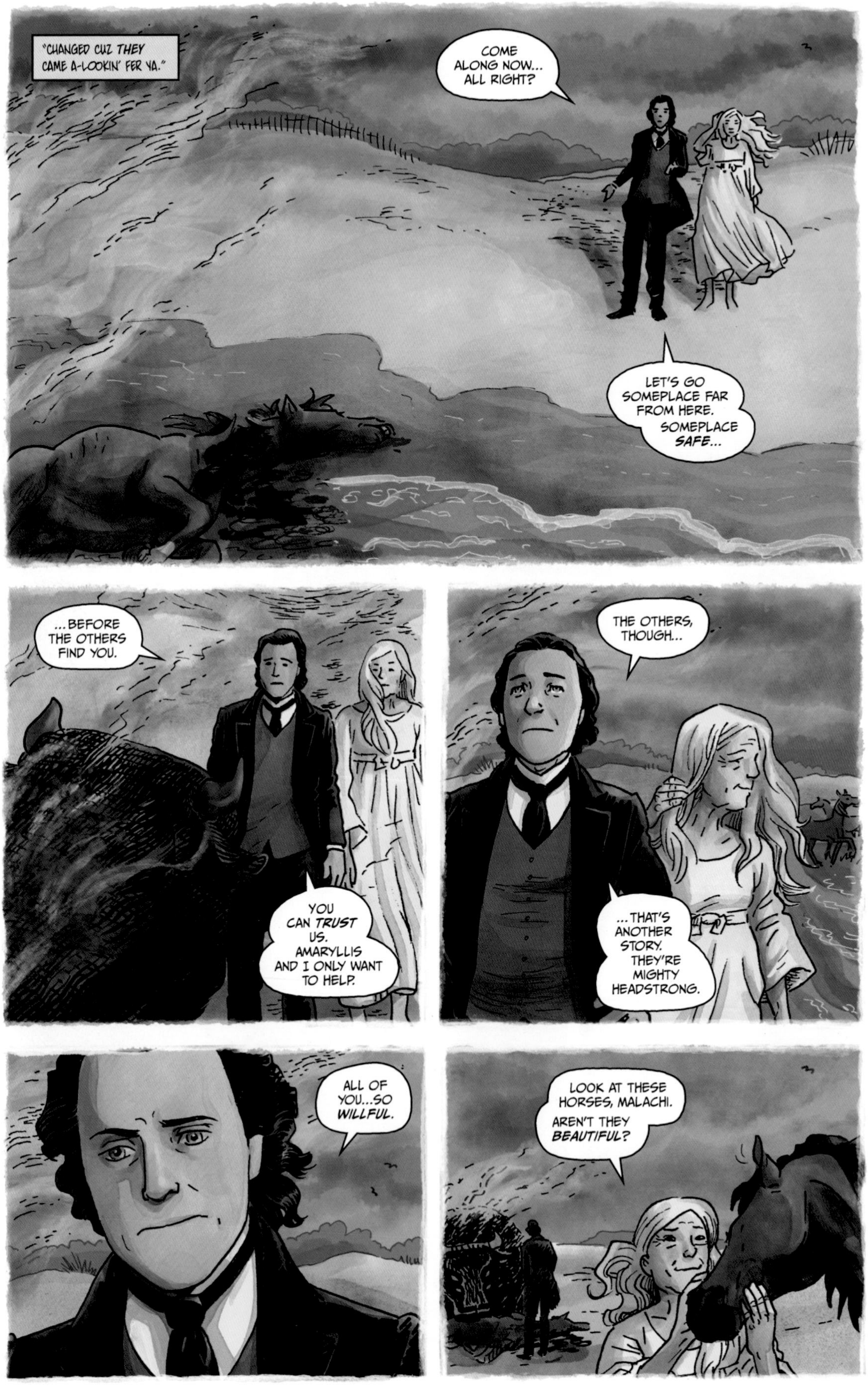
"CHANGED CUZ THEY CAME A-LOOKIN' FER YA."
COME ALONG NOW... ALL RIGHT?
LET'S GO SOMEPLACE FAR FROM HERE. SOMEPLACE SAFE...
...BEFORE THE OTHERS FIND YOU.
YOU CAN TRUST US. AMARYLLIS AND I ONLY WANT TO HELP.
THE OTHERS, THOUGH...
...THAT'S ANOTHER STORY. THEY'RE MIGHTY HEADSTRONG.
ALL OF YOU...SO WILLFUL.
LOOK AT THESE HORSES, MALACHI.
AREN'T THEY BEAUTIFUL?

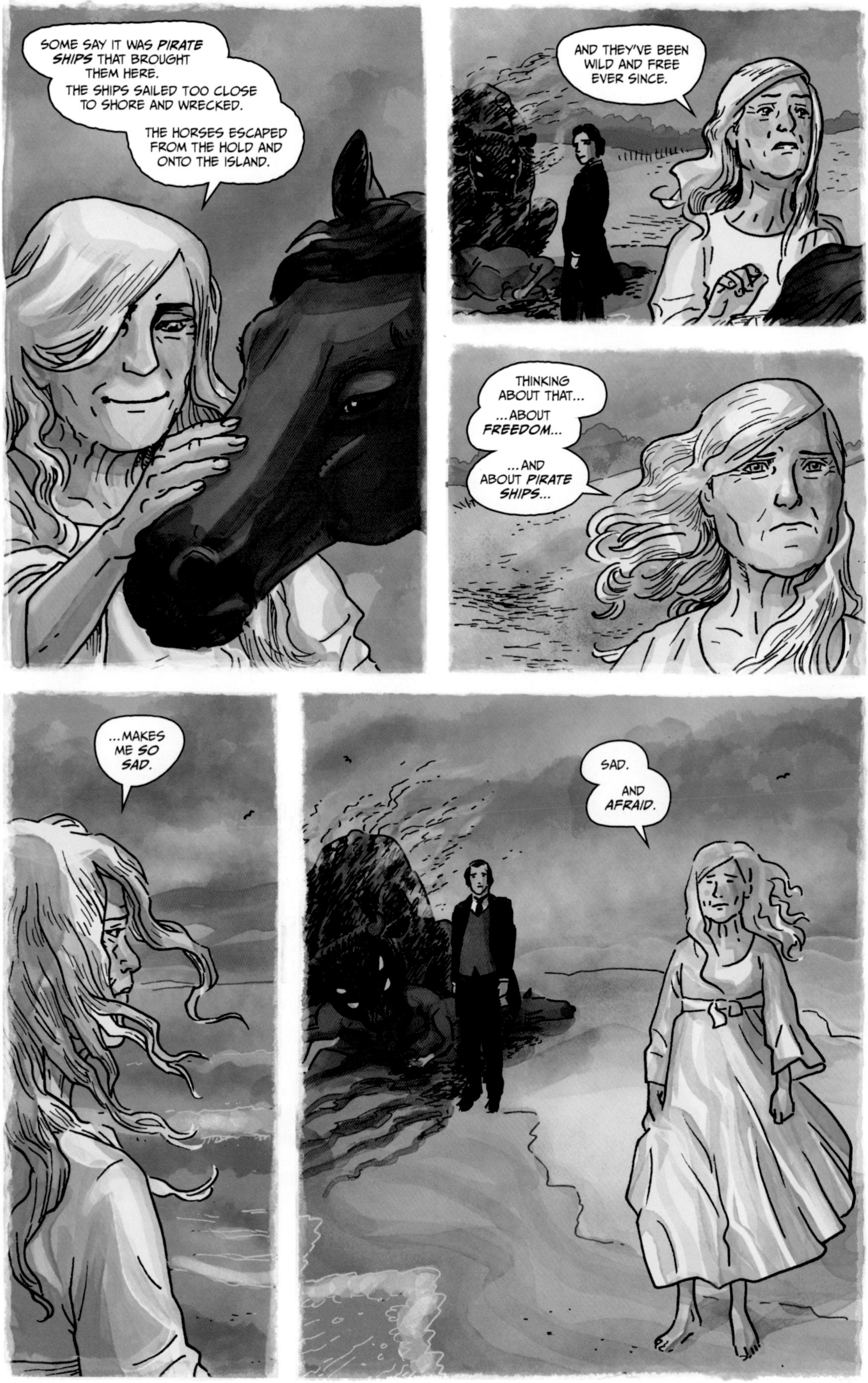
SOME SAY IT WAS *PIRATE SHIPS* THAT BROUGHT THEM HERE.
THE SHIPS SAILED TOO CLOSE TO SHORE AND WRECKED.
THE HORSES ESCAPED FROM THE HOLD AND ONTO THE ISLAND.
AND THEY'VE BEEN WILD AND FREE EVER SINCE.
THINKING ABOUT THAT...
...ABOUT *FREEDOM*...
...AND ABOUT *PIRATE SHIPS*...
...MAKES ME *SO SAD*.
SAD.
AND *AFRAID*.

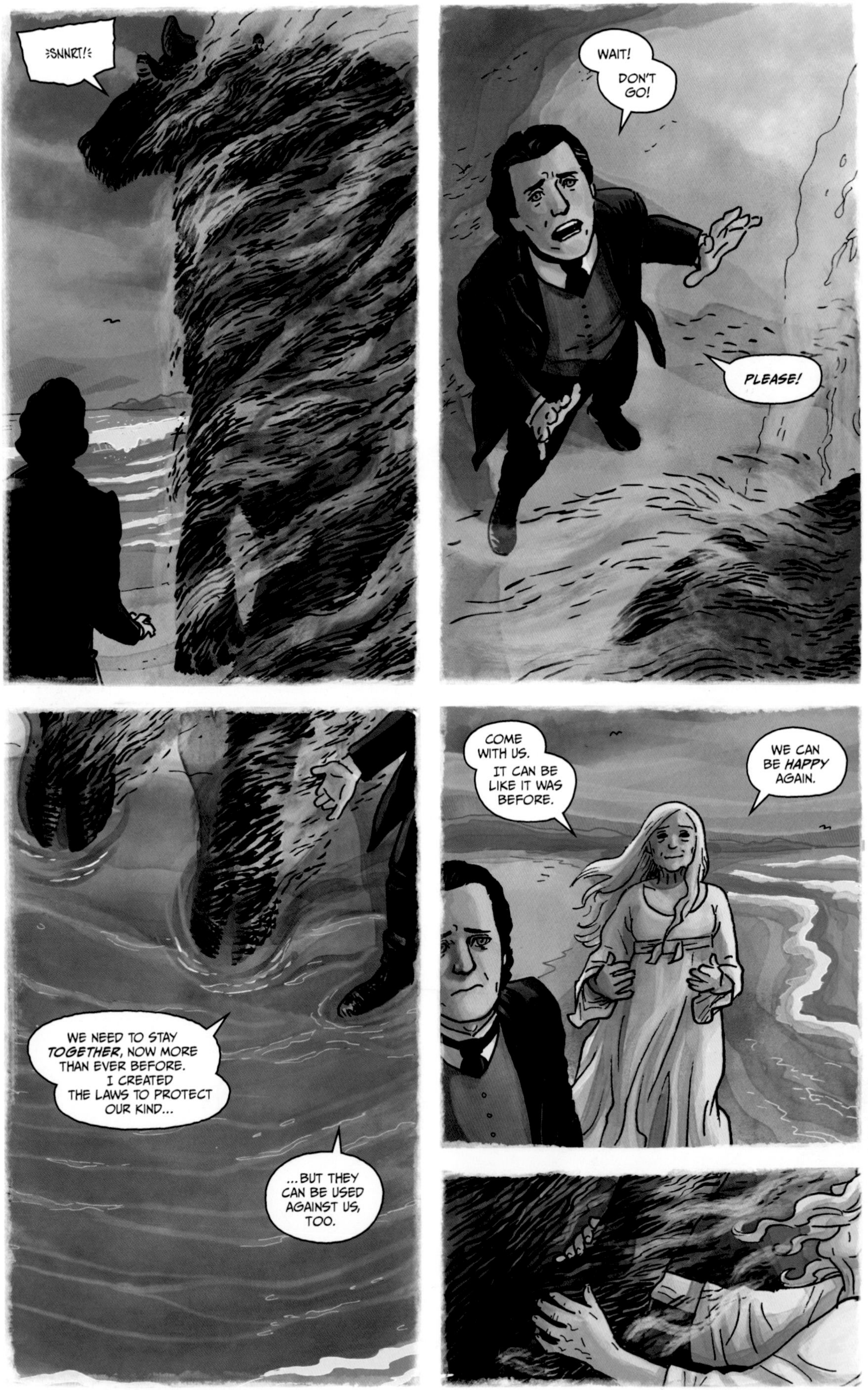

SNNRT!
WAIT!
DON'T GO!
PLEASE!
WE NEED TO STAY TOGETHER, NOW MORE THAN EVER BEFORE. I CREATED THE LAWS TO PROTECT OUR KIND...
...BUT THEY CAN BE USED AGAINST US, TOO.
COME WITH US. IT CAN BE LIKE IT WAS BEFORE.
WE CAN BE HAPPY AGAIN.

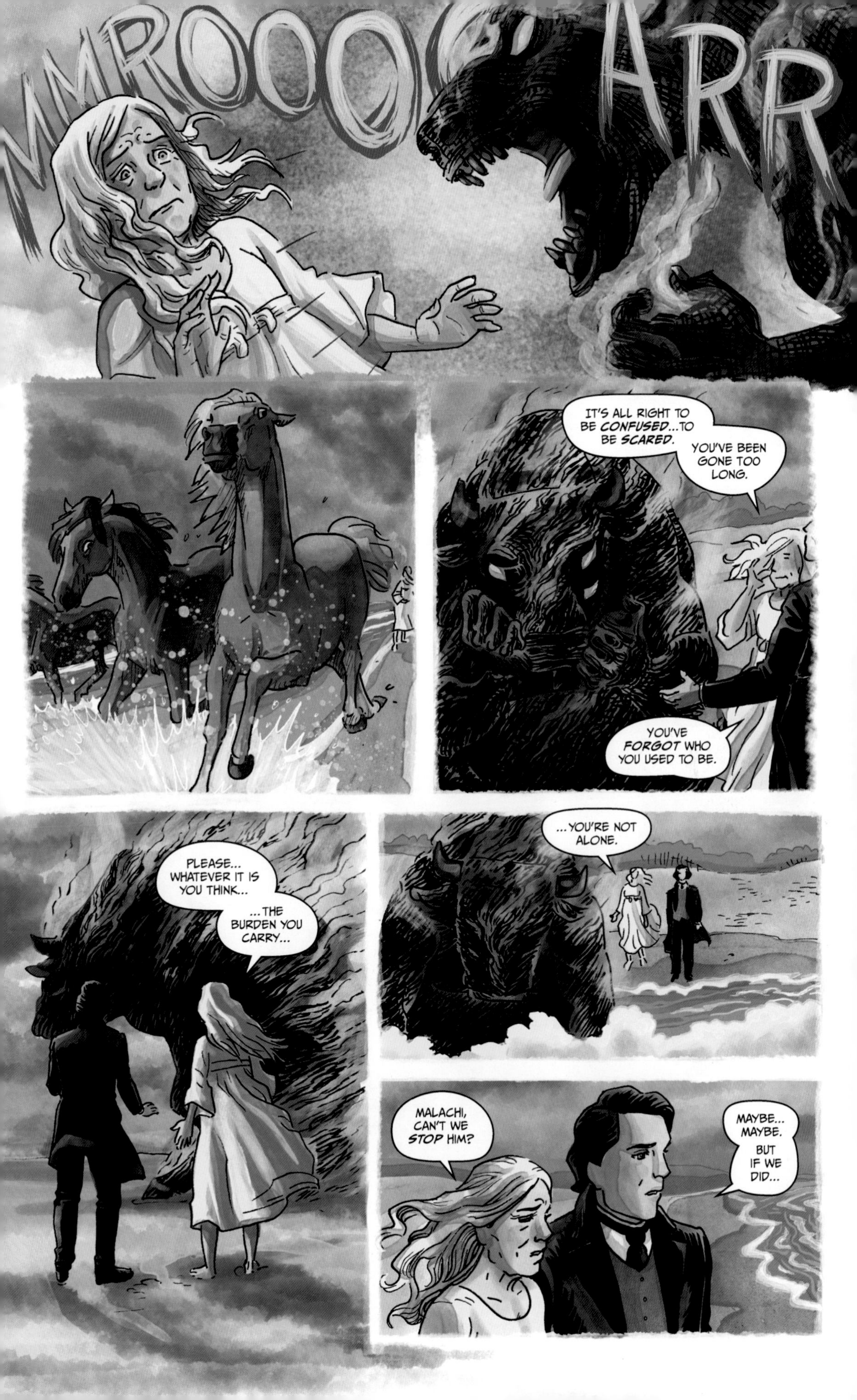
MMROOOO' ARR
IT'S ALL RIGHT TO BE CONFUSED...TO BE SCARED.
YOU'VE BEEN GONE TOO LONG.
YOU'VE FORGOT WHO YOU USED TO BE.
PLEASE... WHATEVER IT IS YOU THINK...
...THE BURDEN YOU CARRY...
...YOU'RE NOT ALONE.
MALACHI, CAN'T WE STOP HIM?
MAYBE... MAYBE.
BUT IF WE DID...

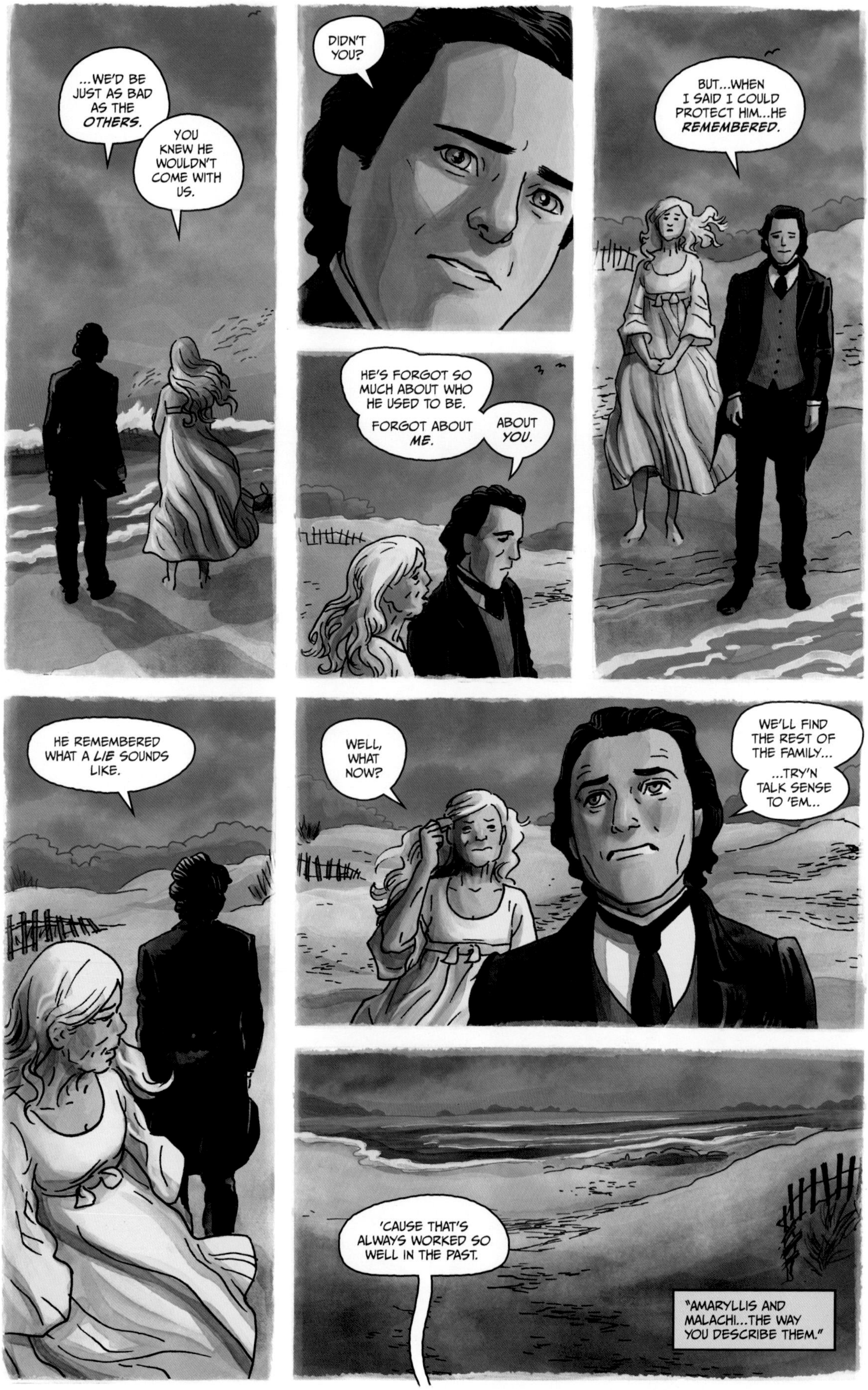
...WE'D BE JUST AS BAD AS THE *OTHERS*.
YOU KNEW HE WOULDN'T COME WITH US.
DIDN'T YOU?
HE'S FORGOT SO MUCH ABOUT WHO HE USED TO BE.
FORGOT ABOUT *ME*.
ABOUT *YOU*.
BUT...WHEN I SAID I COULD PROTECT HIM...HE *REMEMBERED*.
HE REMEMBERED WHAT A *LIE* SOUNDS LIKE.
WELL, WHAT NOW?
WE'LL FIND THE REST OF THE FAMILY...
...TRY'N TALK SENSE TO 'EM...
'CAUSE THAT'S ALWAYS WORKED SO WELL IN THE PAST.
"AMARYLLIS AND MALACHI...THE WAY YOU DESCRIBE THEM."

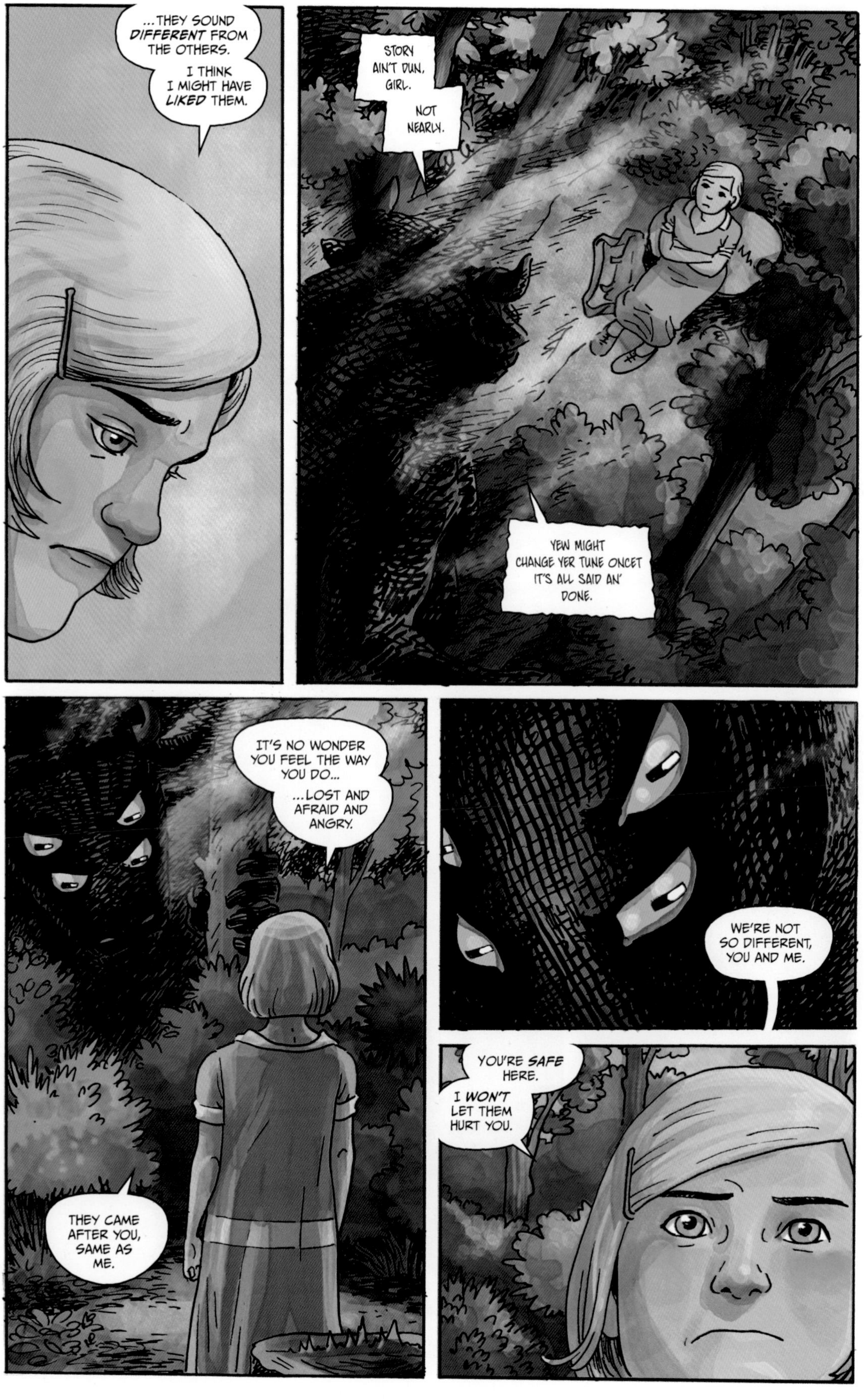
...THEY SOUND *DIFFERENT* FROM THE OTHERS.
I THINK I MIGHT HAVE *LIKED* THEM.
STORY AIN'T DUN, GIRL.
NOT NEARLY.
YEW MIGHT CHANGE YER TUNE ONCET IT'S ALL SAID AN' DONE.
IT'S NO WONDER YOU FEEL THE WAY YOU DO...
...LOST AND AFRAID AND ANGRY.
THEY CAME AFTER YOU, SAME AS ME.
WE'RE NOT SO DIFFERENT, YOU AND ME.
YOU'RE *SAFE* HERE.
I *WON'T* LET THEM HURT YOU.

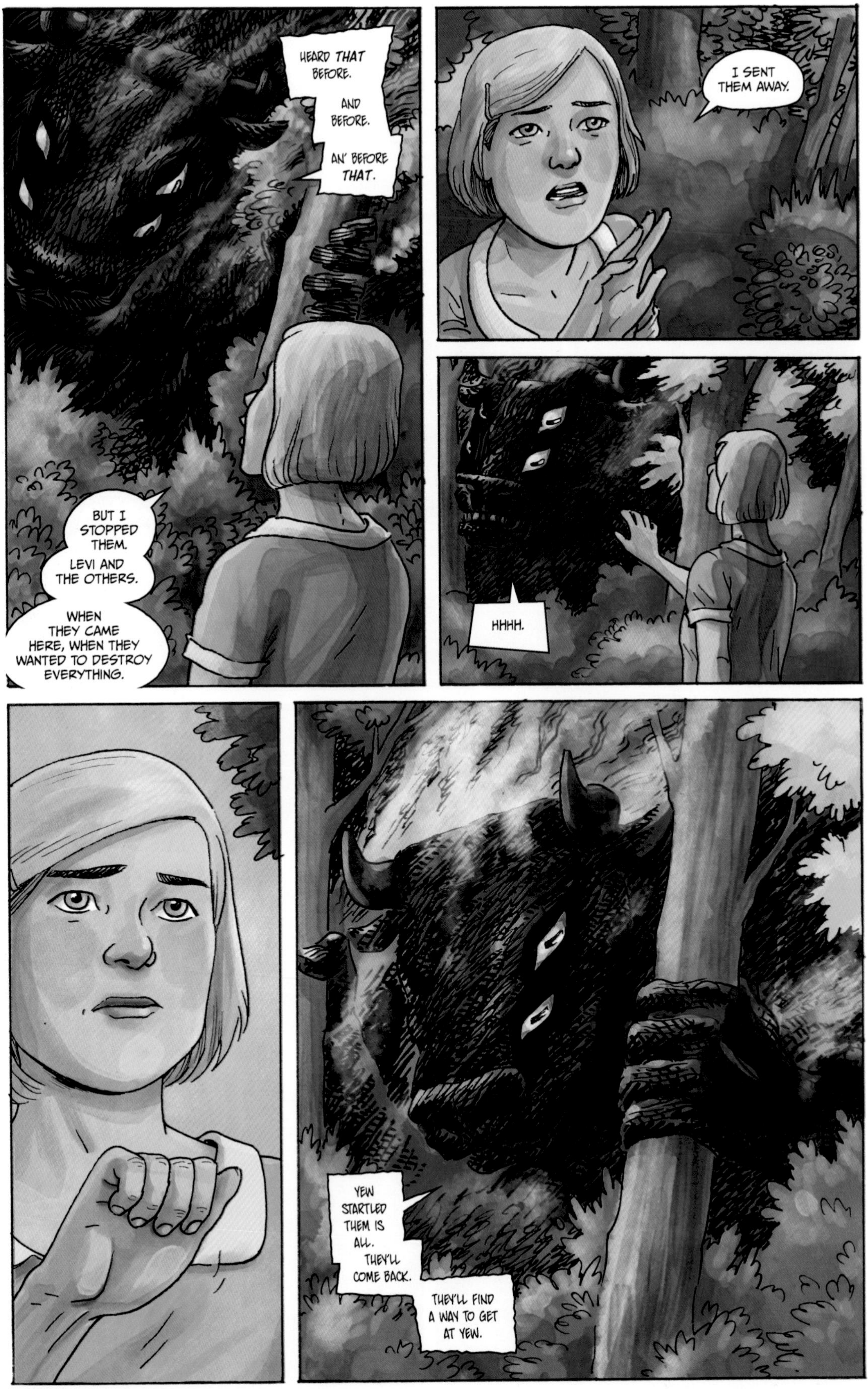
HEARD THAT BEFORE.
AND BEFORE.
AN' BEFORE THAT.
BUT I STOPPED THEM.
LEVI AND THE OTHERS.
WHEN THEY CAME HERE, WHEN THEY WANTED TO DESTROY EVERYTHING.
I SENT THEM AWAY.
HHHH.
YEW STARTLED THEM IS ALL.
THEY'LL COME BACK.
THEY'LL FIND A WAY TO GET AT YEW.

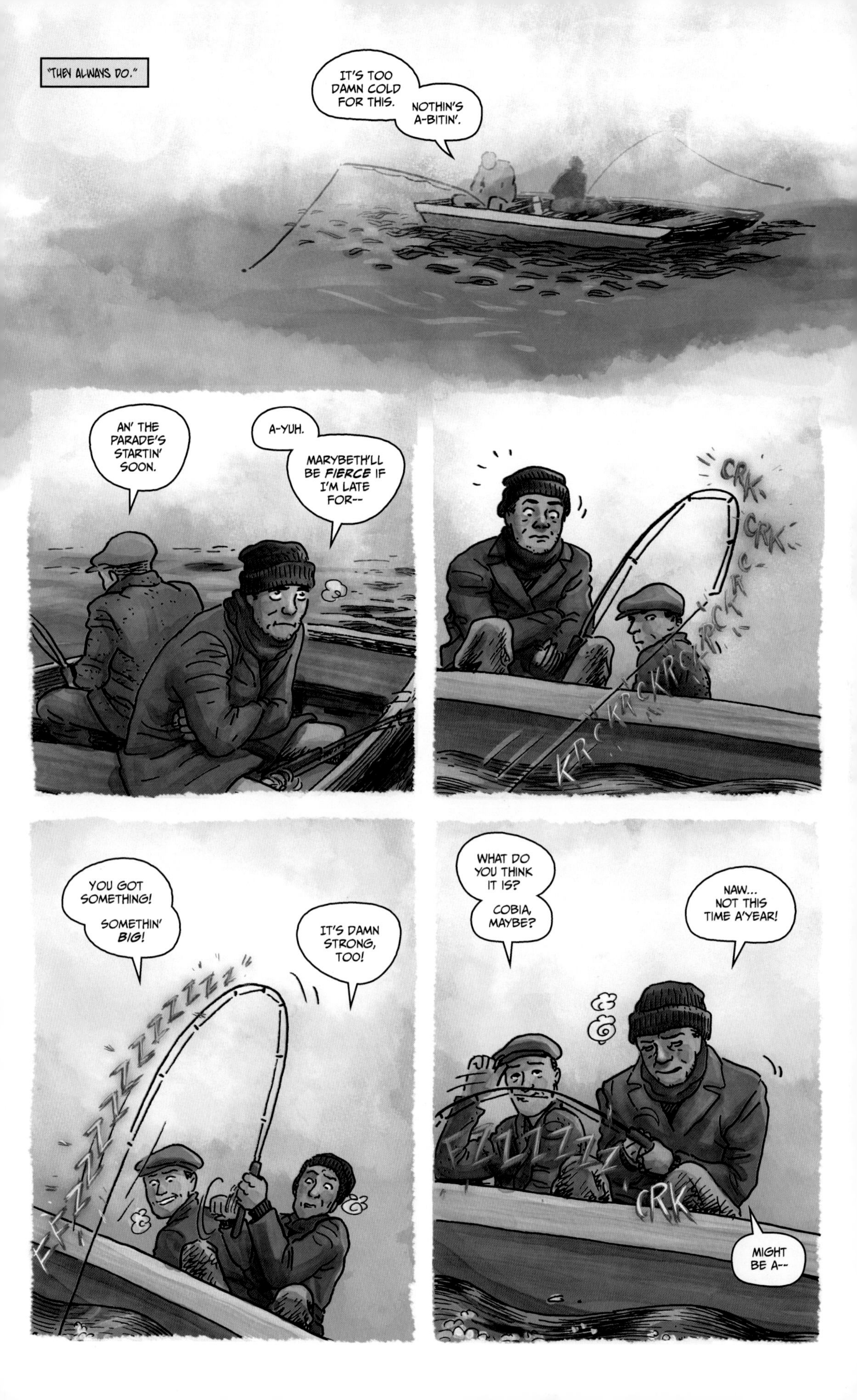
"THEY ALWAYS DO."
IT'S TOO DAMN COLD FOR THIS.
NOTHIN'S A-BITIN'.
AN' THE PARADE'S STARTIN' SOON.
A-YUH.
MARYBETH'LL BE *FIERCE* IF I'M LATE FOR--
CRK CRK
KRCKRCKRCKRCKRC
YOU GOT SOMETHING!
SOMETHIN' *BIG*!
IT'S DAMN STRONG, TOO!
FFZZZZZZZZZZZZ
WHAT DO YOU THINK IT IS?
COBIA, MAYBE?
NAW... NOT THIS TIME A'YEAR!
FZZZZZZZ
CRK
MIGHT BE A--

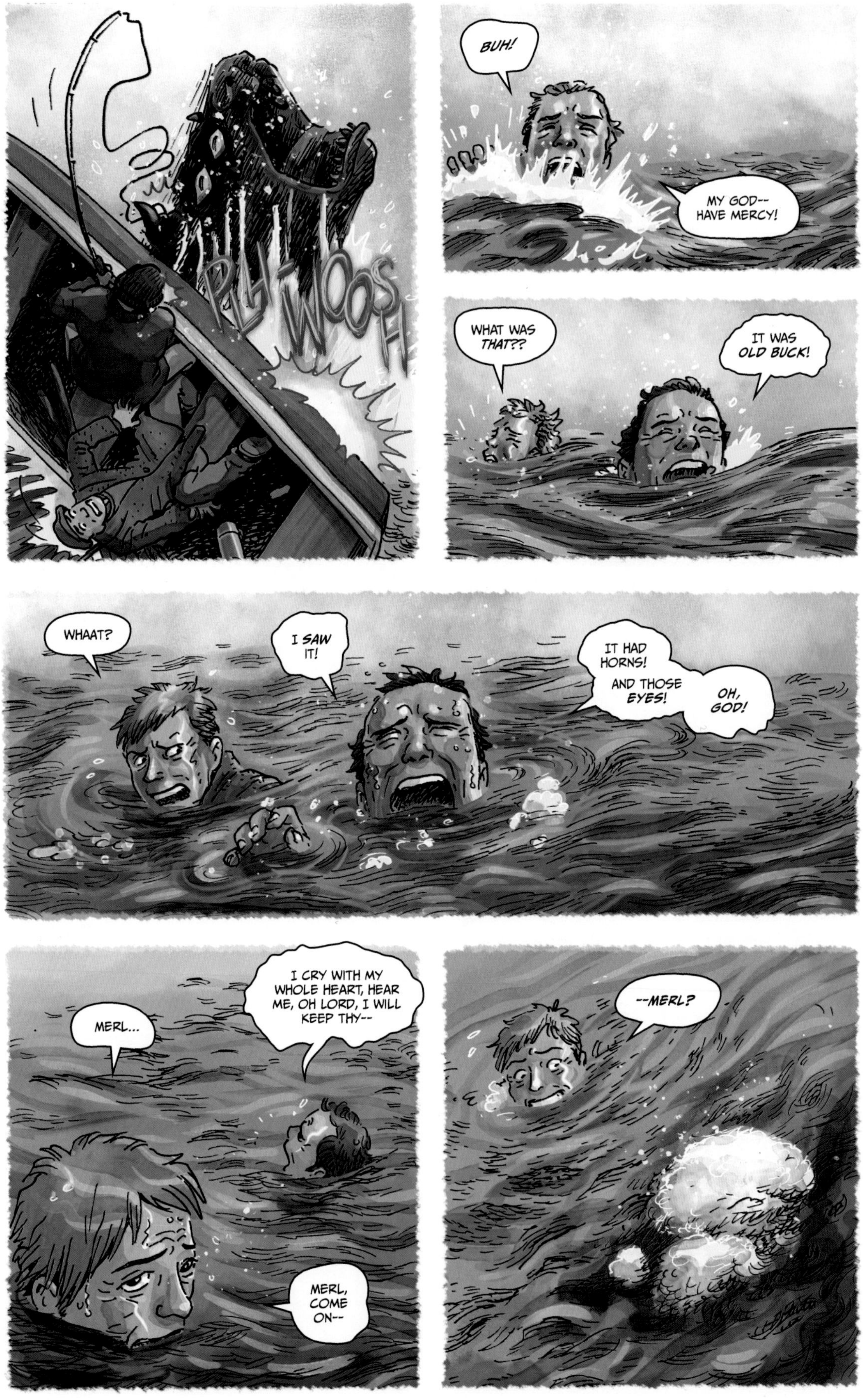
PLH-WOOSH
BUH!
MY GOD-- HAVE MERCY!
WHAT WAS THAT??
IT WAS OLD BUCK!
WHAAT?
I SAW IT!
IT HAD HORNS!
AND THOSE EYES!
OH, GOD!
MERL...
I CRY WITH MY WHOLE HEART, HEAR ME, OH LORD, I WILL KEEP THY--
MERL, COME ON--
--MERL?

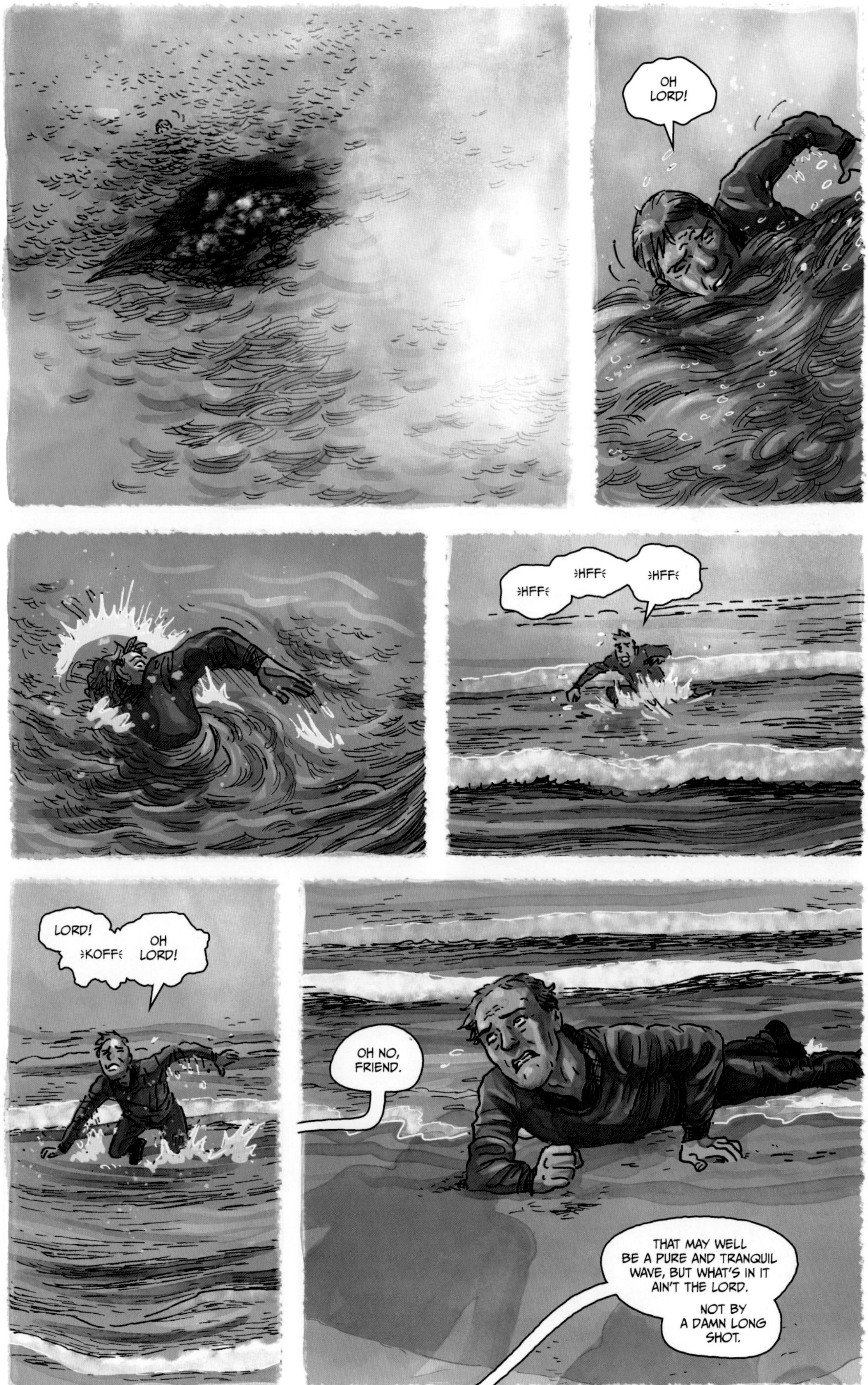
OH LORD!
HFF HFF HFF
LORD! KOFF OH LORD!
OH NO, FRIEND.
THAT MAY WELL BE A PURE AND TRANQUIL WAVE, BUT WHAT'S IN IT AIN'T THE LORD.
NOT BY A DAMN LONG SHOT.

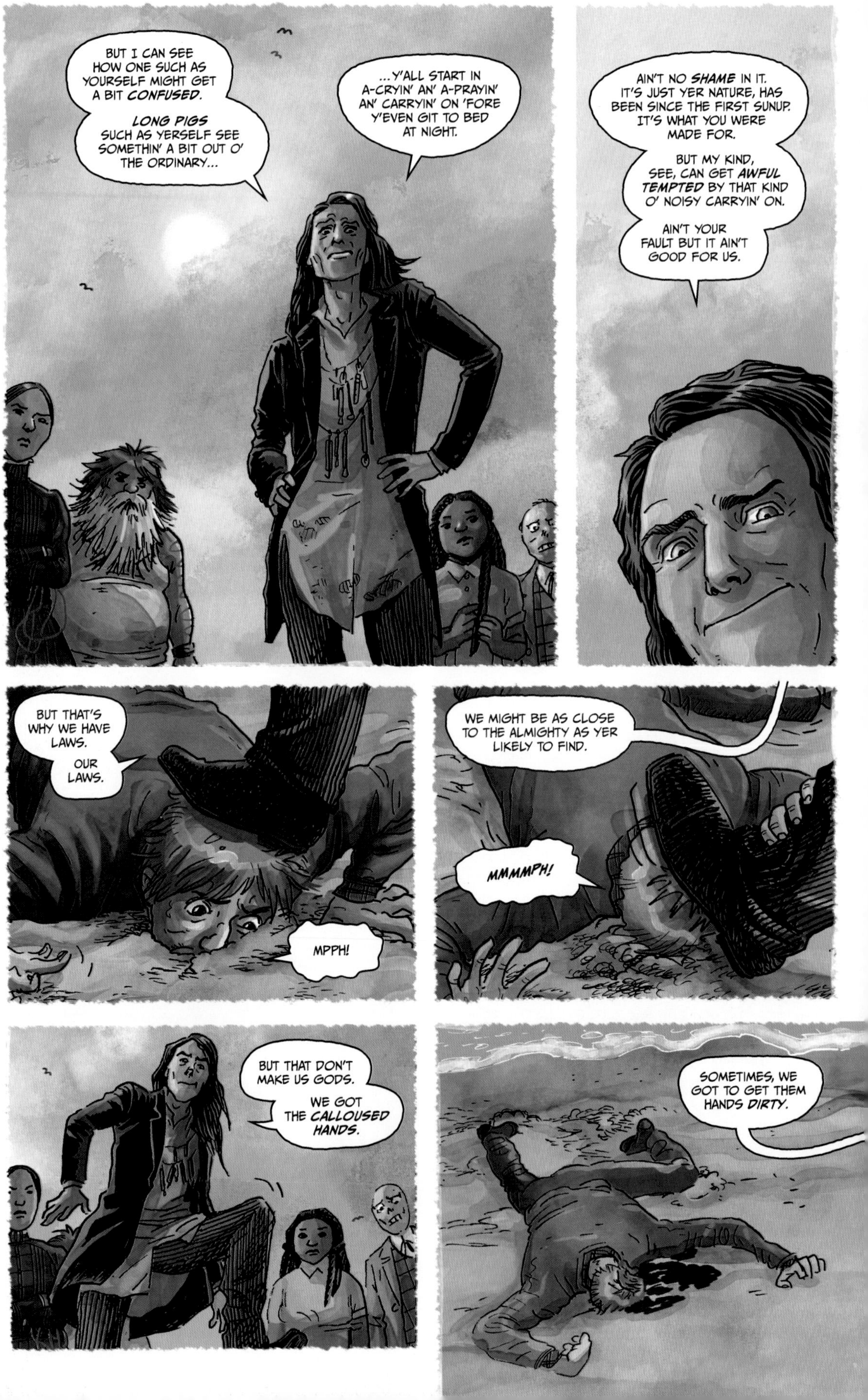
BUT I CAN SEE HOW ONE SUCH AS YOURSELF MIGHT GET A BIT CONFUSED.
LONG PIGS SUCH AS YERSELF SEE SOMETHIN' A BIT OUT O' THE ORDINARY...
...Y'ALL START IN A-CRYIN' AN' A-PRAYIN' AN' CARRYIN' ON 'FORE Y'EVEN GIT TO BED AT NIGHT.
AIN'T NO SHAME IN IT. IT'S JUST YER NATURE, HAS BEEN SINCE THE FIRST SUNUP. IT'S WHAT YOU WERE MADE FOR.
BUT MY KIND, SEE, CAN GET AWFUL TEMPTED BY THAT KIND O' NOISY CARRYIN' ON.
AIN'T YOUR FAULT BUT IT AIN'T GOOD FOR US.
BUT THAT'S WHY WE HAVE LAWS.
OUR LAWS.
MPPH!
WE MIGHT BE AS CLOSE TO THE ALMIGHTY AS YER LIKELY TO FIND.
MMMMPH!
BUT THAT DON'T MAKE US GODS.
WE GOT THE CALLOUSED HANDS.
SOMETIMES, WE GOT TO GET THEM HANDS DIRTY.

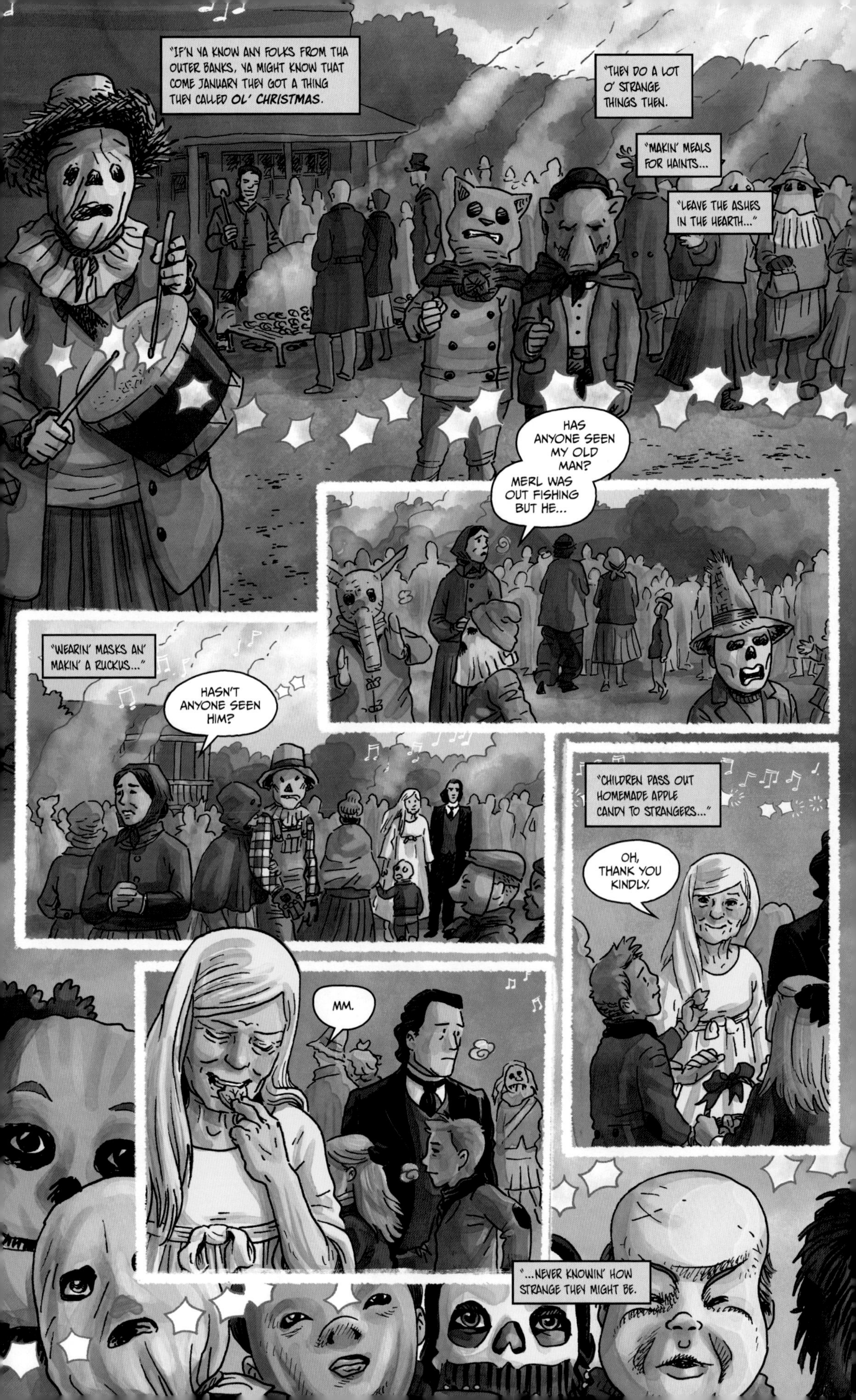
"IF'N YA KNOW ANY FOLKS FROM THA OUTER BANKS, YA MIGHT KNOW THAT COME JANUARY THEY GOT A THING THEY CALLED OL' CHRISTMAS.
"THEY DO A LOT O' STRANGE THINGS THEN.
"MAKIN' MEALS FOR HAINTS...
"LEAVE THE ASHES IN THE HEARTH..."
HAS ANYONE SEEN MY OLD MAN?
MERL WAS OUT FISHING BUT HE...
"WEARIN' MASKS AN' MAKIN' A RUCKUS..."
HASN'T ANYONE SEEN HIM?
"CHILDREN PASS OUT HOMEMADE APPLE CANDY TO STRANGERS..."
OH, THANK YOU KINDLY.
MM.
"...NEVER KNOWIN' HOW STRANGE THEY MIGHT BE.

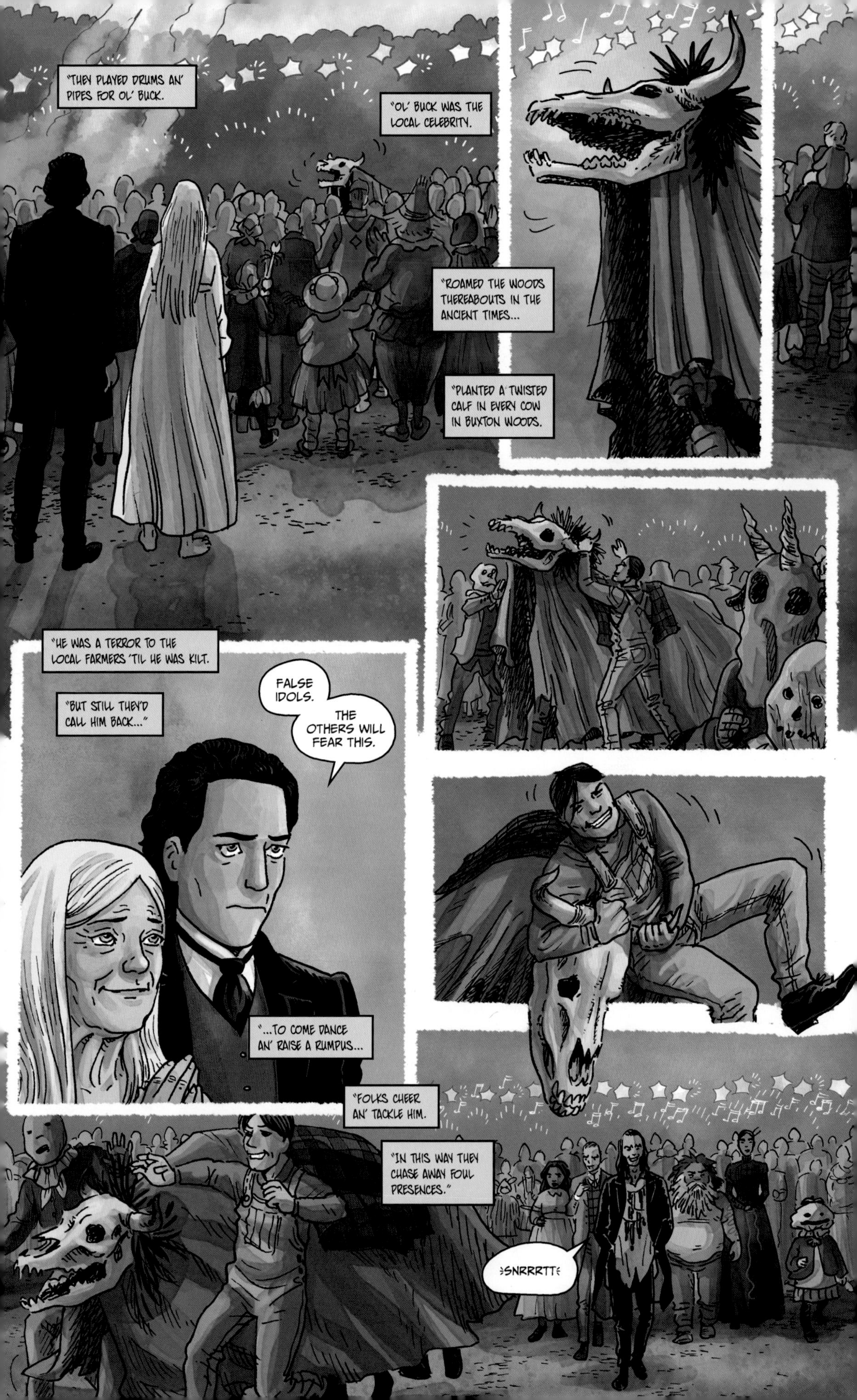
"THEY PLAYED DRUMS AN' PIPES FOR OL' BUCK.
"OL' BUCK WAS THE LOCAL CELEBRITY.
"ROAMED THE WOODS THEREABOUTS IN THE ANCIENT TIMES...
"PLANTED A TWISTED CALF IN EVERY COW IN BUXTON WOODS.
"HE WAS A TERROR TO THE LOCAL FARMERS 'TIL HE WAS KILT.
"BUT STILL THEY'D CALL HIM BACK..."
FALSE IDOLS.
THE OTHERS WILL FEAR THIS.
"...TO COME DANCE AN' RAISE A RUMPUS...
"FOLKS CHEER AN' TACKLE HIM.
"IN THIS WAY THEY CHASE AWAY FOUL PRESENCES."
SNRRRTT

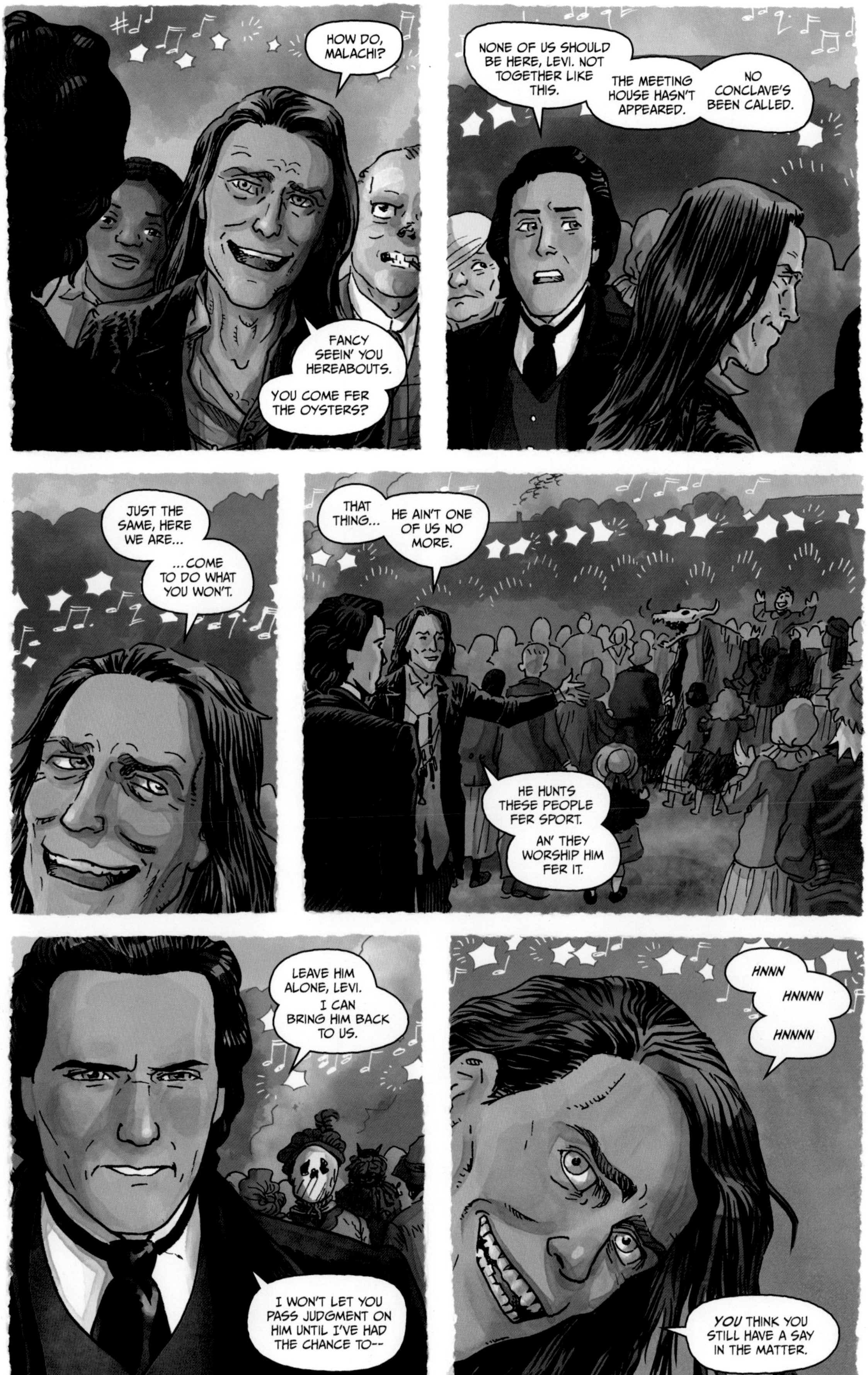
HOW DO, MALACHI?
FANCY SEEIN' YOU HEREABOUTS.
YOU COME FER THE OYSTERS?
NONE OF US SHOULD BE HERE, LEVI. NOT TOGETHER LIKE THIS.
THE MEETING HOUSE HASN'T APPEARED.
NO CONCLAVE'S BEEN CALLED.
JUST THE SAME, HERE WE ARE...
...COME TO DO WHAT YOU WON'T.
THAT THING...
HE AIN'T ONE OF US NO MORE.
HE HUNTS THESE PEOPLE FER SPORT.
AN' THEY WORSHIP HIM FER IT.
LEAVE HIM ALONE, LEVI.
I CAN BRING HIM BACK TO US.
I WON'T LET YOU PASS JUDGMENT ON HIM UNTIL I'VE HAD THE CHANCE TO--
HNNN
HNNNN
HNNNN
YOU THINK YOU STILL HAVE A SAY IN THE MATTER.

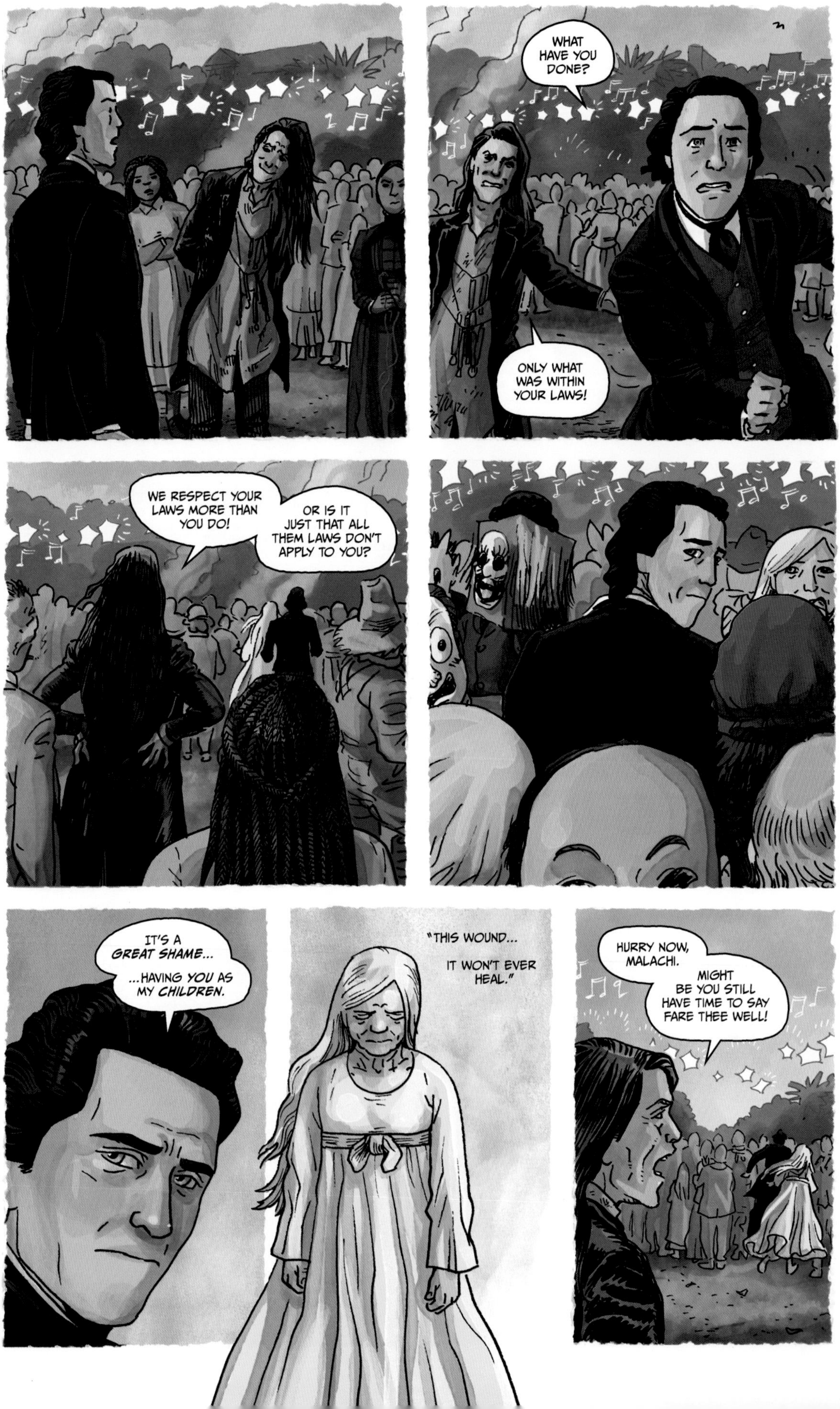
WHAT HAVE YOU DONE?
ONLY WHAT WAS WITHIN YOUR LAWS!
WE RESPECT YOUR LAWS MORE THAN YOU DO!
OR IS IT JUST THAT ALL THEM LAWS DON'T APPLY TO YOU?
IT'S A GREAT SHAME...
...HAVING YOU AS MY CHILDREN.
"THIS WOUND...
IT WON'T EVER HEAL."
HURRY NOW, MALACHI.
MIGHT BE YOU STILL HAVE TIME TO SAY FARE THEE WELL!

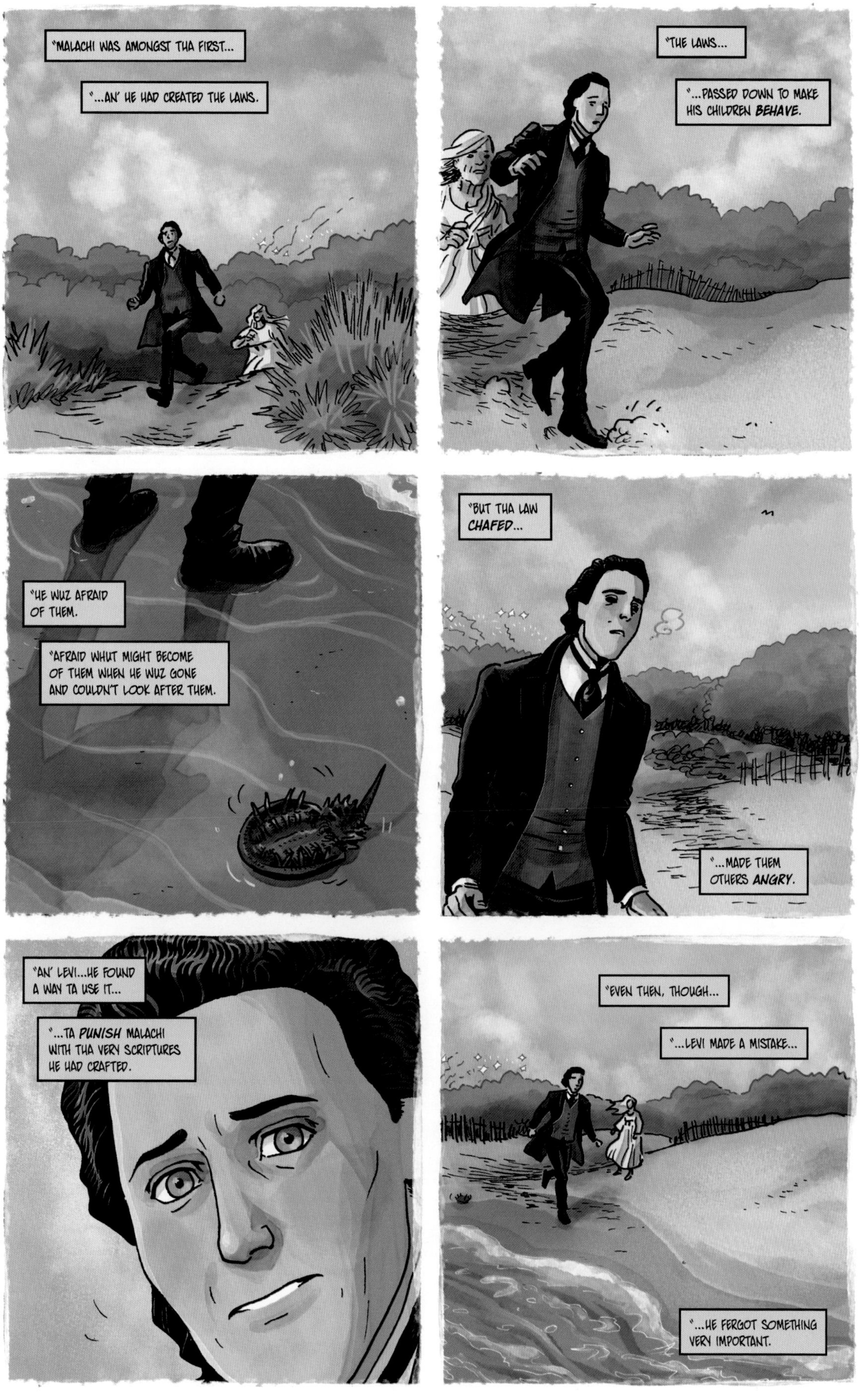
"MALACHI WAS AMONGST THA FIRST...
"...AN' HE HAD CREATED THE LAWS.
"THE LAWS...
"...PASSED DOWN TO MAKE HIS CHILDREN **BEHAVE**.
"HE WUZ AFRAID OF THEM.
"AFRAID WHUT MIGHT BECOME OF THEM WHEN HE WUZ GONE AND COULDN'T LOOK AFTER THEM.
"BUT THA LAW **CHAFED**...
"...MADE THEM OTHERS **ANGRY**.
"AN' LEVI...HE FOUND A WAY TA USE IT...
"...TA ***PUNISH*** MALACHI WITH THA VERY SCRIPTURES HE HAD CRAFTED.
"EVEN THEN, THOUGH...
"...LEVI MADE A MISTAKE...
"...HE FERGOT SOMETHING VERY IMPORTANT.

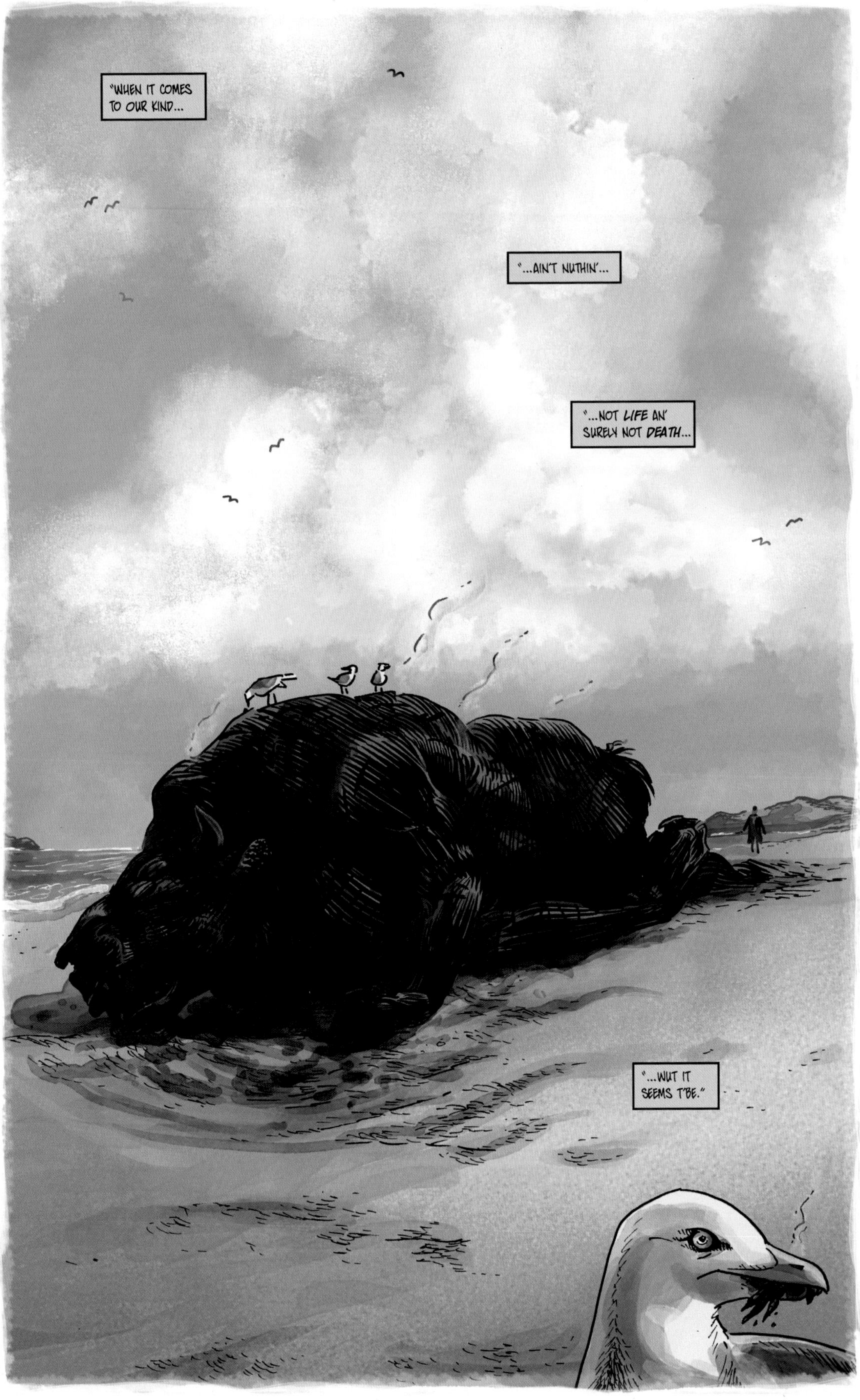
"WHEN IT COMES TO OUR KIND...
"...AIN'T NUTHIN'...
"...NOT LIFE AN' SURELY NOT DEATH...
"...WUT IT SEEMS T'BE."

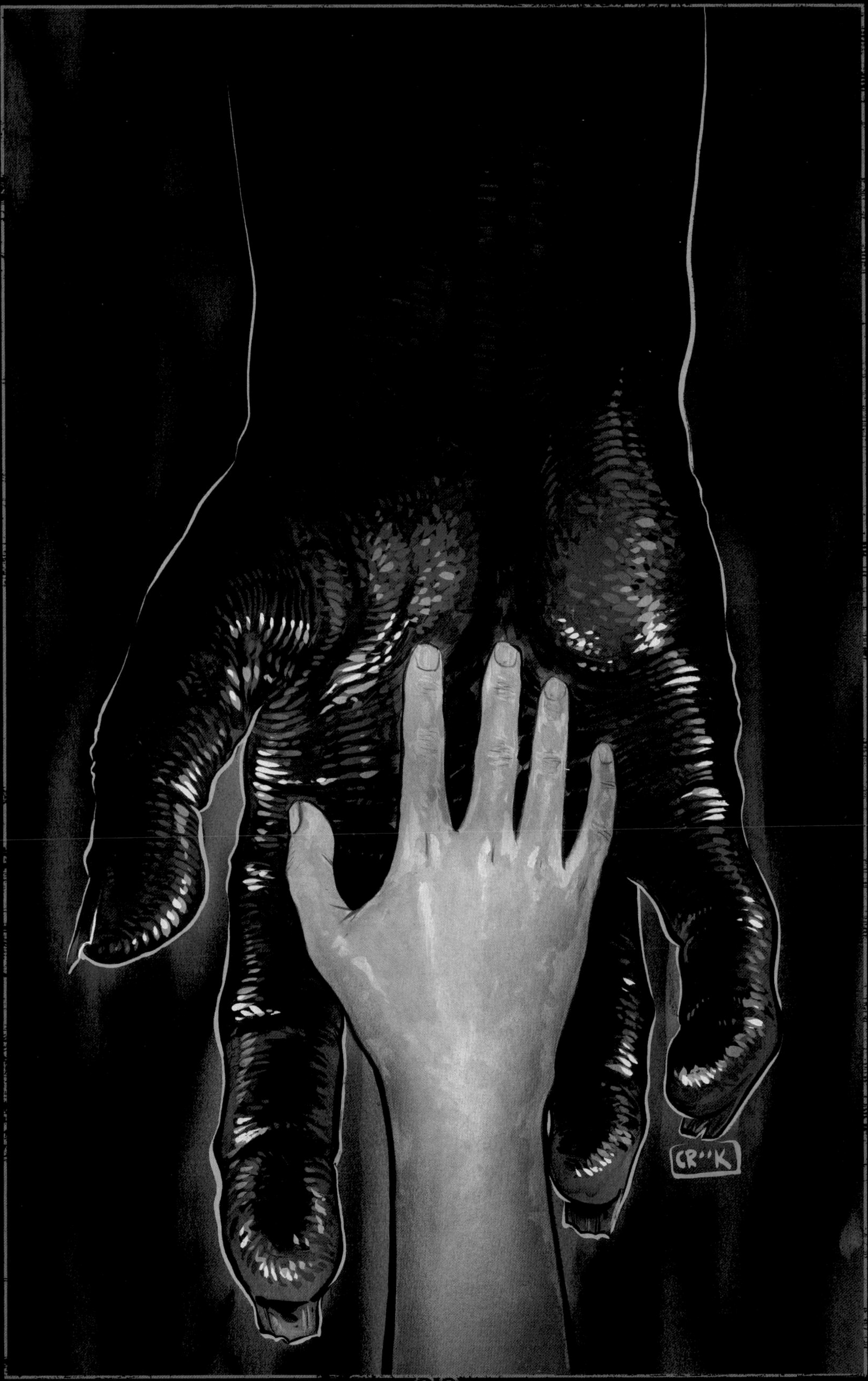
CR''K

TWO

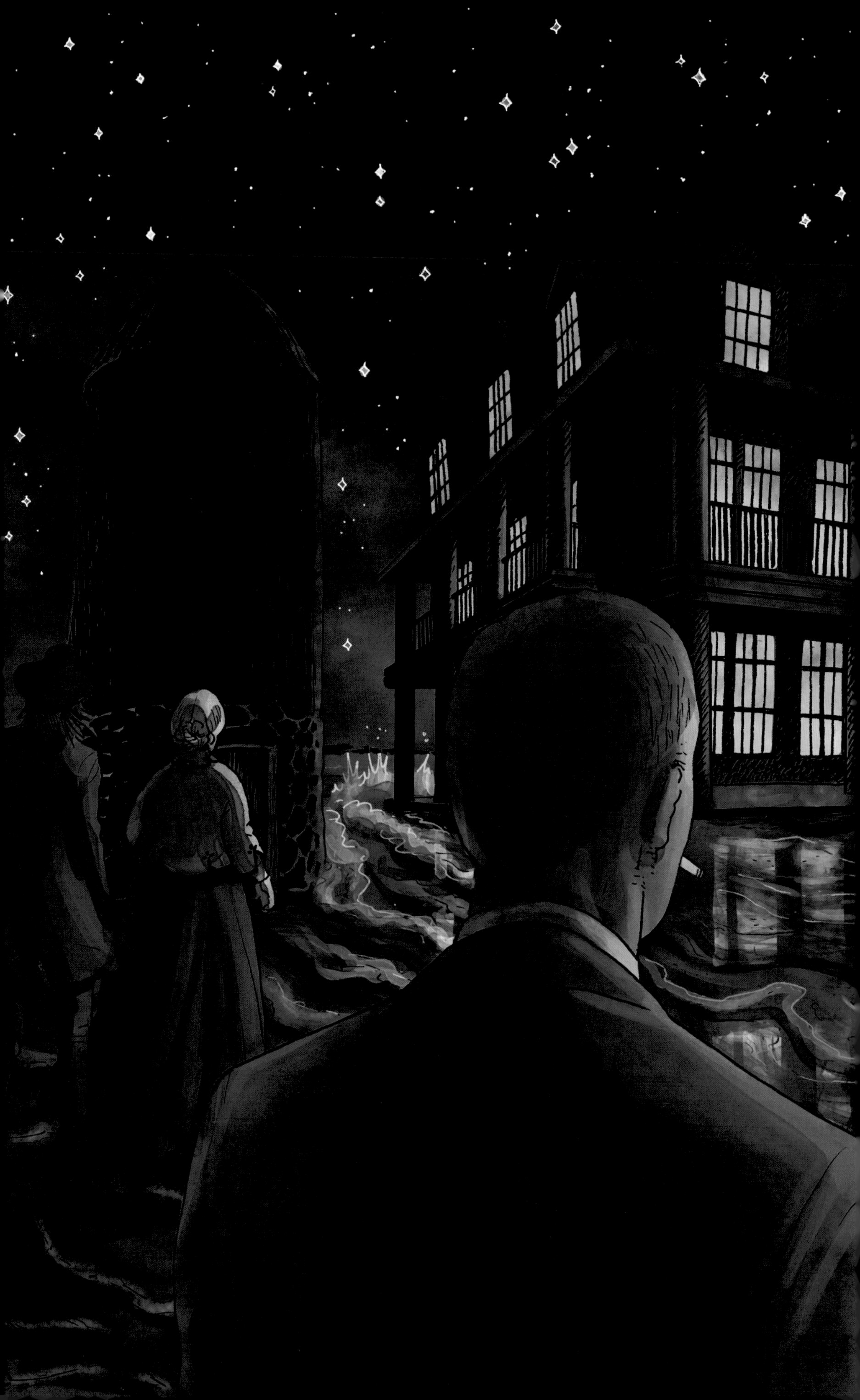

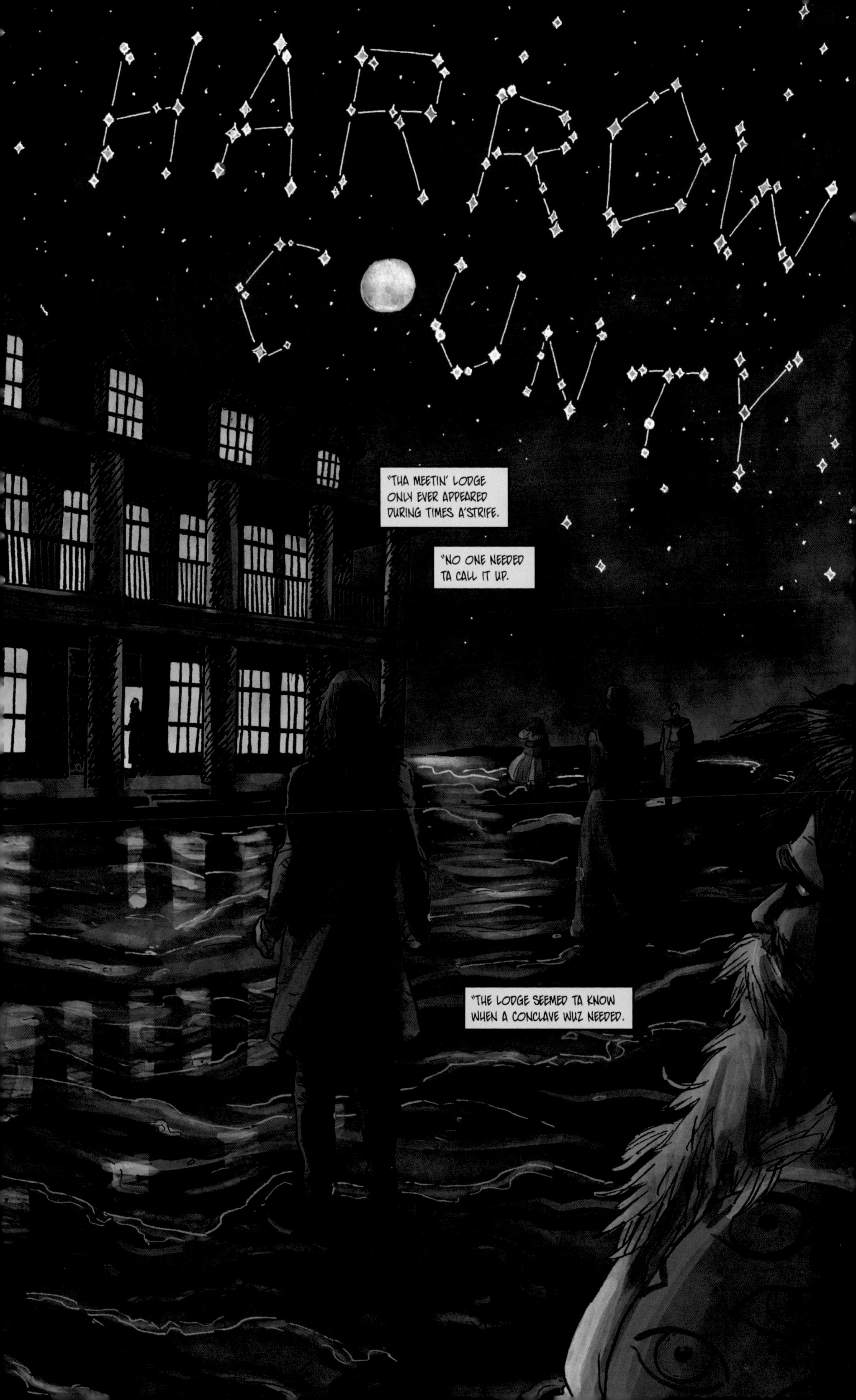
HARROW COUNTY
"THA MEETIN' LODGE ONLY EVER APPEARED DURING TIMES A'STRIFE.
"NO ONE NEEDED TA CALL IT UP.
"THE LODGE SEEMED TA KNOW WHEN A CONCLAVE WUZ NEEDED.

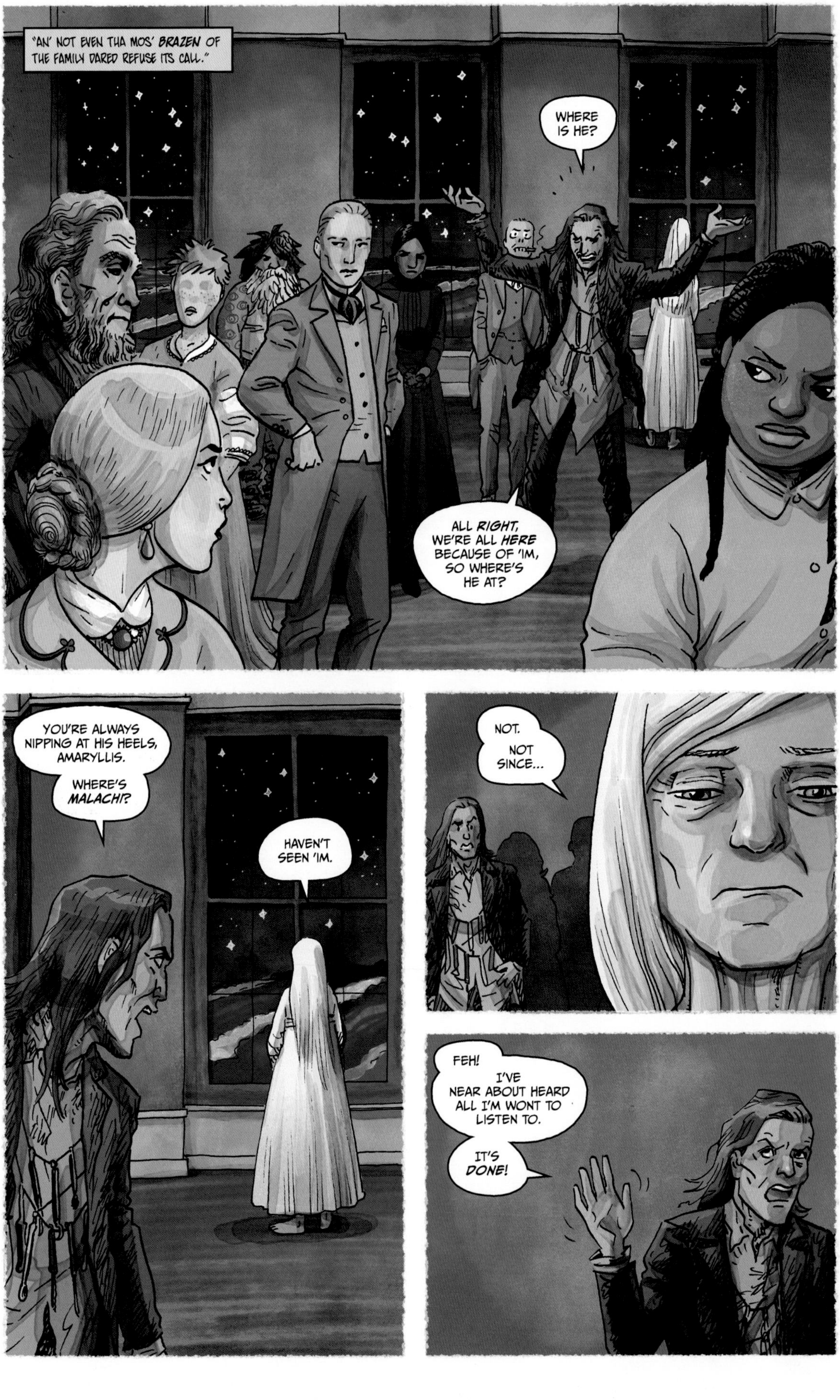
"AN' NOT EVEN THA MOS' BRAZEN OF THE FAMILY DARED REFUSE ITS CALL."
WHERE IS HE?
ALL RIGHT, WE'RE ALL HERE BECAUSE OF 'IM, SO WHERE'S HE AT?
YOU'RE ALWAYS NIPPING AT HIS HEELS, AMARYLLIS.
WHERE'S MALACHI?
HAVEN'T SEEN 'IM.
NOT.
NOT SINCE...
FEH!
I'VE NEAR ABOUT HEARD ALL I'M WONT TO LISTEN TO.
IT'S DONE!

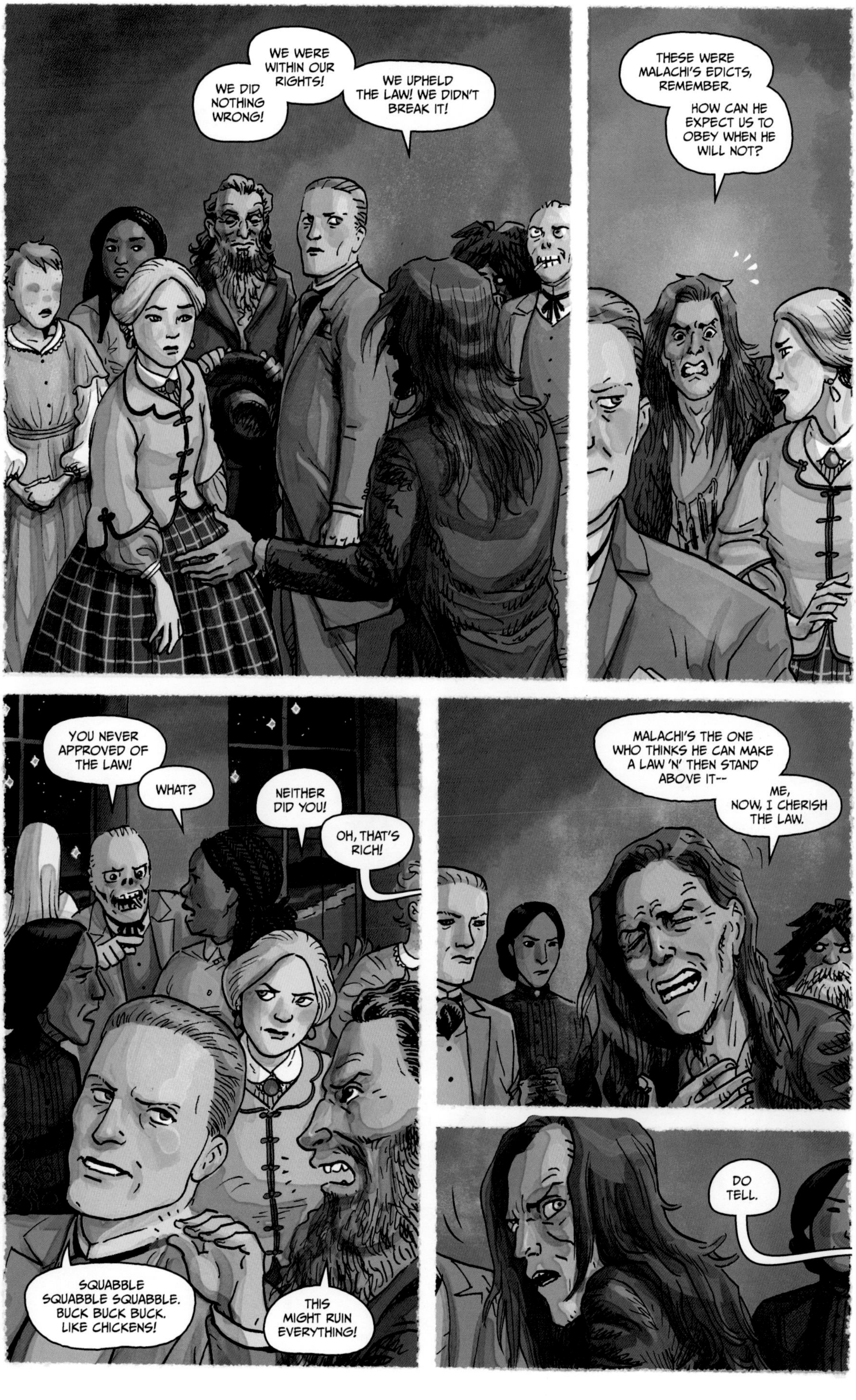
WE DID NOTHING WRONG!
WE WERE WITHIN OUR RIGHTS!
WE UPHELD THE LAW! WE DIDN'T BREAK IT!
THESE WERE MALACHI'S EDICTS, REMEMBER.
HOW CAN HE EXPECT US TO OBEY WHEN HE WILL NOT?
YOU NEVER APPROVED OF THE LAW!
WHAT?
NEITHER DID YOU!
OH, THAT'S RICH!
SQUABBLE SQUABBLE SQUABBLE. BUCK BUCK BUCK. LIKE CHICKENS!
THIS MIGHT RUIN EVERYTHING!
MALACHI'S THE ONE WHO THINKS HE CAN MAKE A LAW 'N' THEN STAND ABOVE IT--
ME, NOW, I CHERISH THE LAW.
DO TELL.

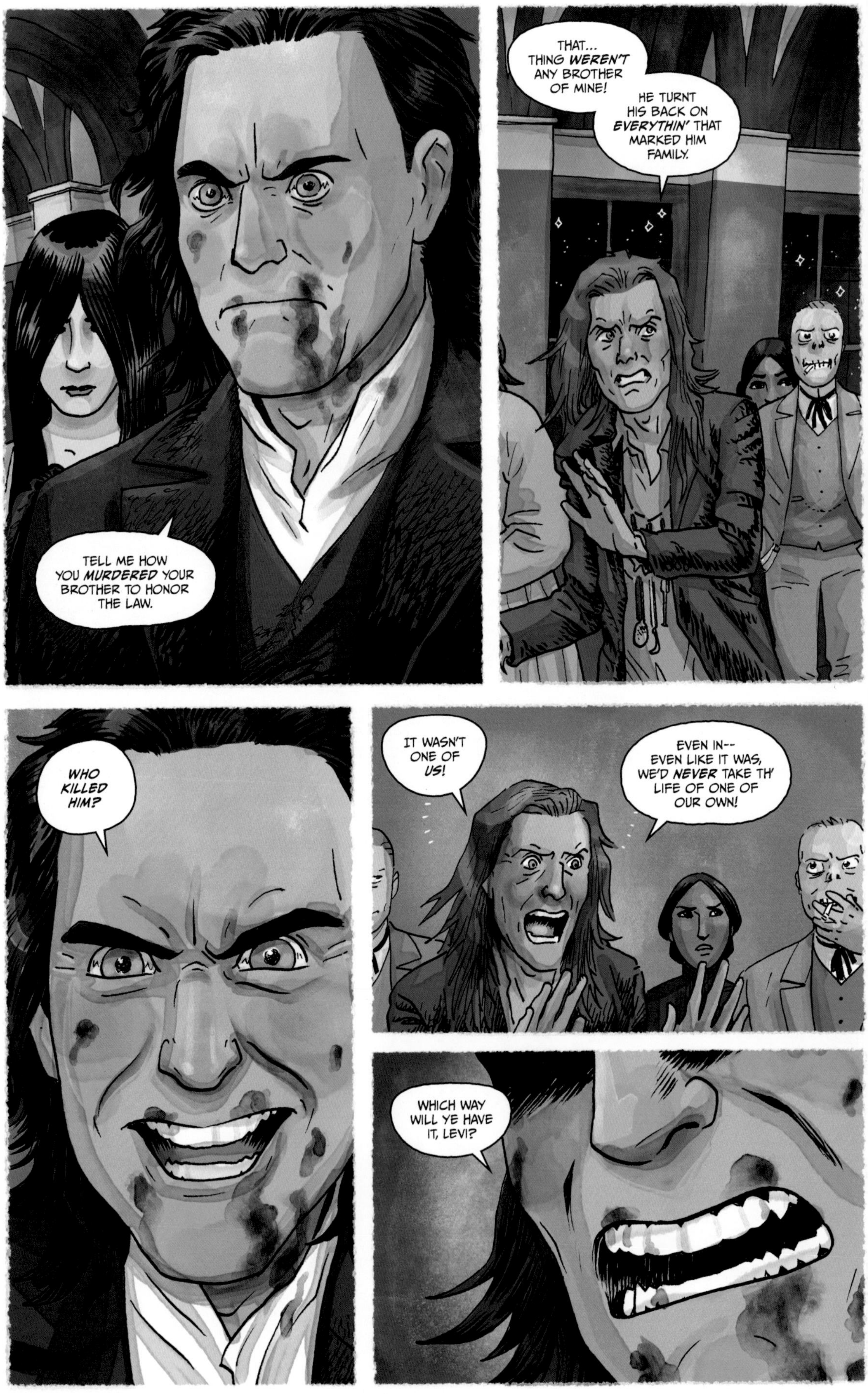

TELL ME HOW YOU MURDERED YOUR BROTHER TO HONOR THE LAW.
THAT... THING WEREN'T ANY BROTHER OF MINE!
HE TURNT HIS BACK ON EVERYTHIN' THAT MARKED HIM FAMILY.
WHO KILLED HIM?
IT WASN'T ONE OF US!
EVEN IN-- EVEN LIKE IT WAS, WE'D NEVER TAKE TH' LIFE OF ONE OF OUR OWN!
WHICH WAY WILL YE HAVE IT, LEVI?

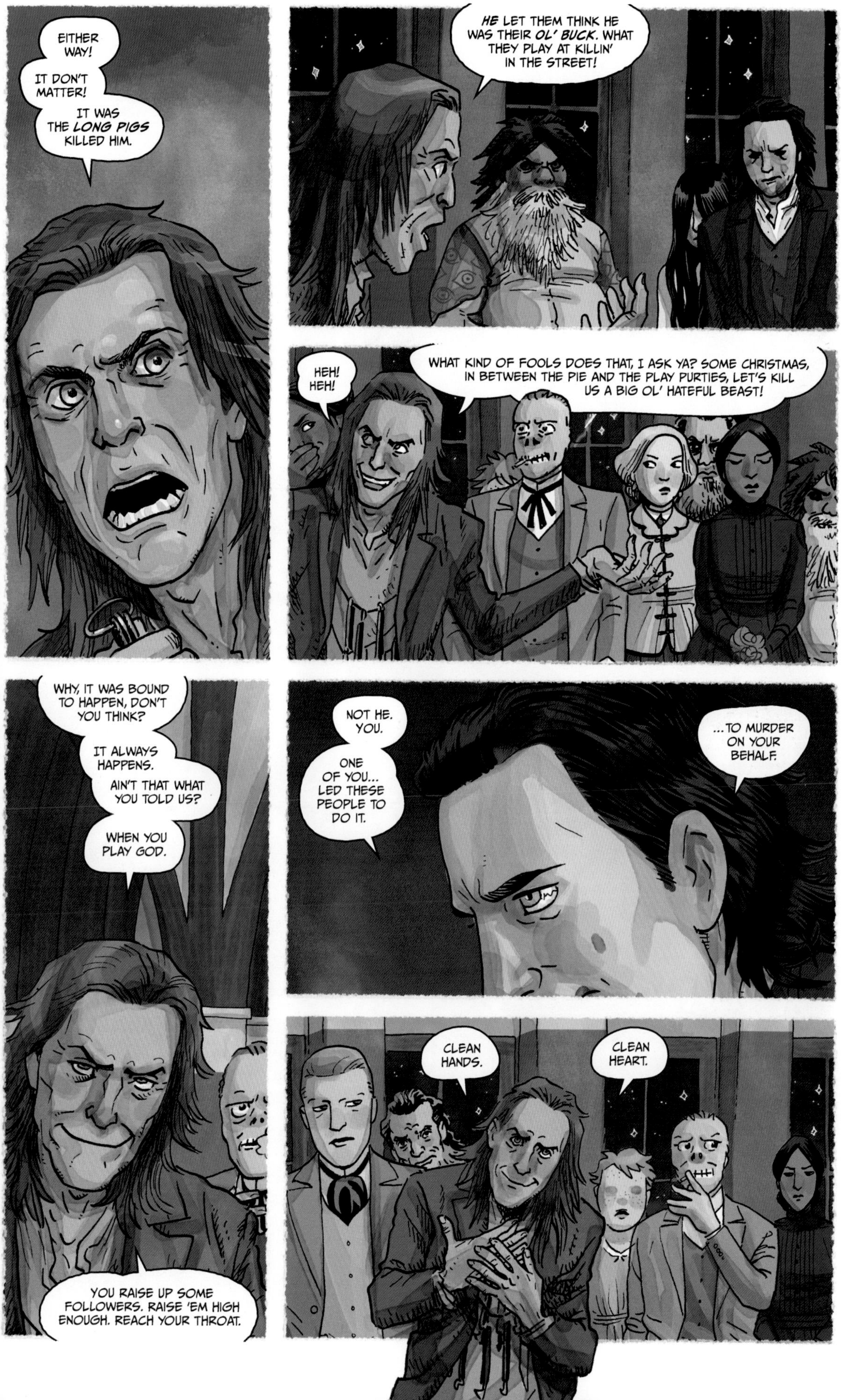
EITHER WAY!
IT DON'T MATTER!
IT WAS THE *LONG PIGS* KILLED HIM.
HE LET THEM THINK HE WAS THEIR *OL' BUCK*. WHAT THEY PLAY AT KILLIN' IN THE STREET!
HEH! HEH!
WHAT KIND OF FOOLS DOES THAT, I ASK YA? SOME CHRISTMAS, IN BETWEEN THE PIE AND THE PLAY PURTIES, LET'S KILL US A BIG OL' HATEFUL BEAST!
WHY, IT WAS BOUND TO HAPPEN, DON'T YOU THINK?
IT ALWAYS HAPPENS.
AIN'T THAT WHAT YOU TOLD US?
WHEN YOU PLAY GOD.
YOU RAISE UP SOME FOLLOWERS. RAISE 'EM HIGH ENOUGH. REACH YOUR THROAT.
NOT HE. YOU.
ONE OF YOU... LED THESE PEOPLE TO DO IT.
...TO MURDER ON YOUR BEHALF.
CLEAN HANDS.
CLEAN HEART.

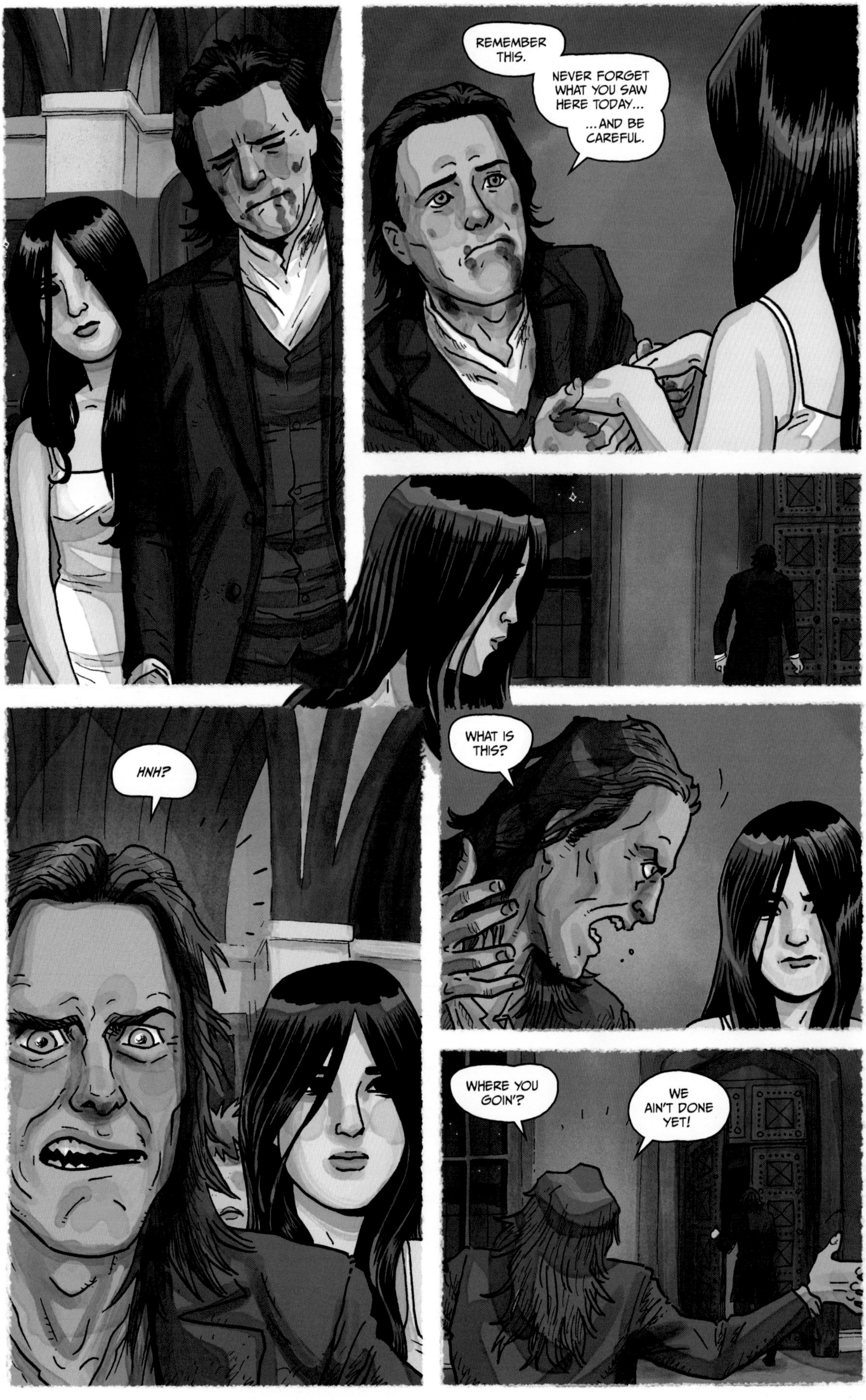
REMEMBER THIS.
NEVER FORGET WHAT YOU SAW HERE TODAY...
...AND BE CAREFUL.
HNH?
WHAT IS THIS?
WHERE YOU GOIN'?
WE AIN'T DONE YET!

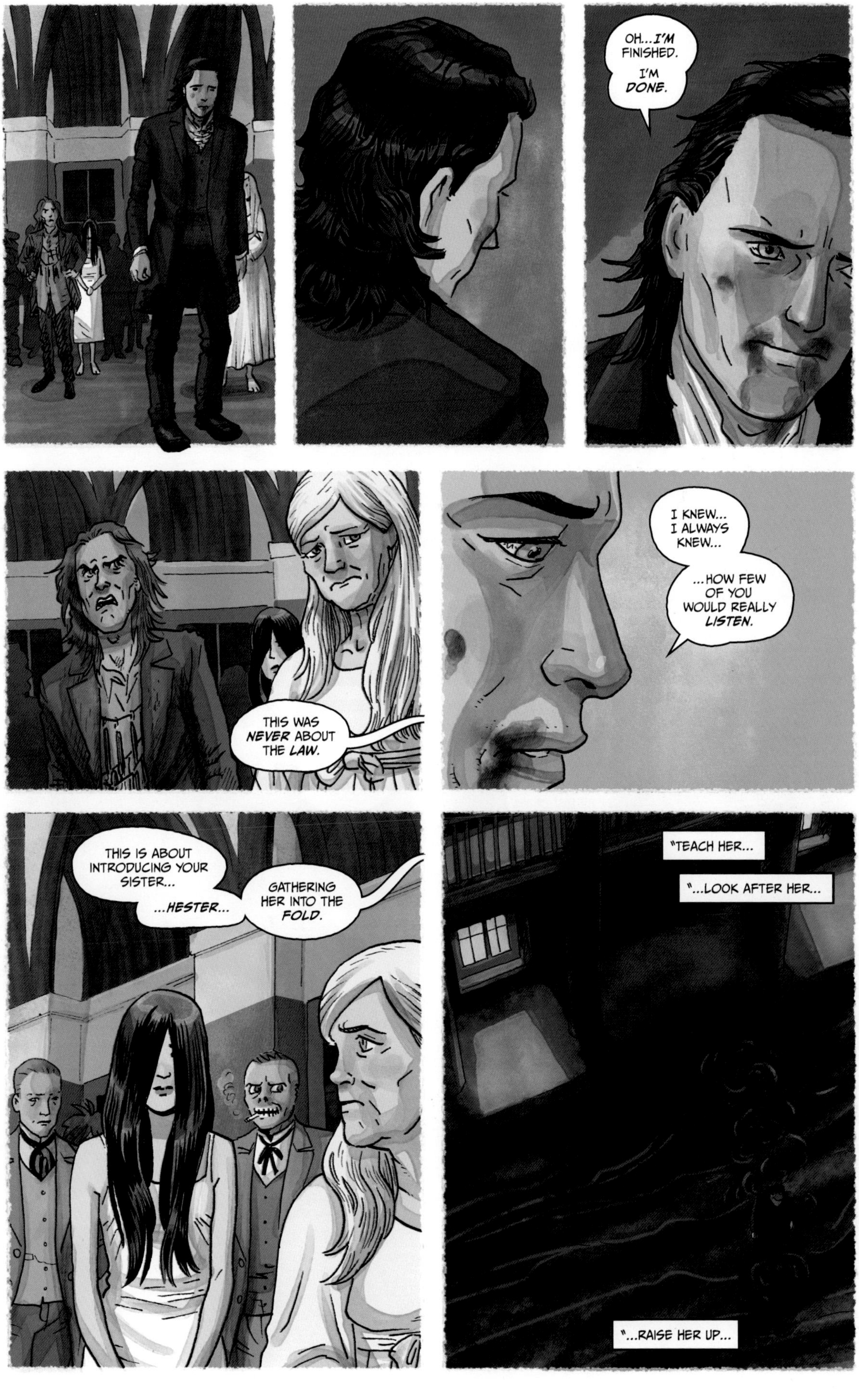

OH...I'M FINISHED.
I'M DONE.
THIS WAS NEVER ABOUT THE LAW.
I KNEW... I ALWAYS KNEW...
...HOW FEW OF YOU WOULD REALLY LISTEN.
THIS IS ABOUT INTRODUCING YOUR SISTER...
...HESTER...
GATHERING HER INTO THE FOLD.
"TEACH HER...
"...LOOK AFTER HER...
"...RAISE HER UP...

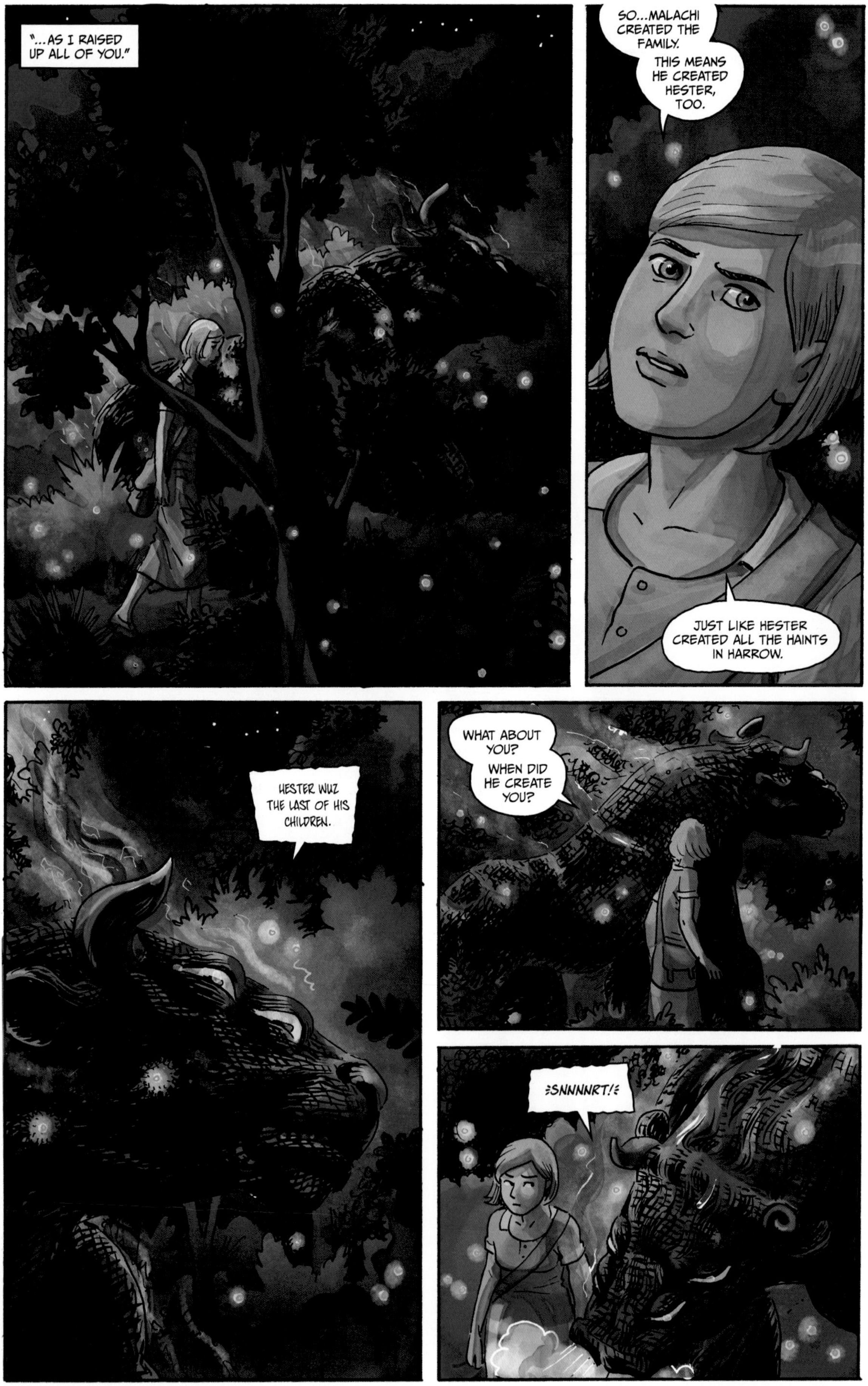
"...AS I RAISED UP ALL OF YOU."
SO...MALACHI CREATED THE FAMILY.
THIS MEANS HE CREATED HESTER, TOO.
JUST LIKE HESTER CREATED ALL THE HAINTS IN HARROW.
HESTER WUZ THE LAST OF HIS CHILDREN.
WHAT ABOUT YOU?
WHEN DID HE CREATE YOU?
SNNNNRT!

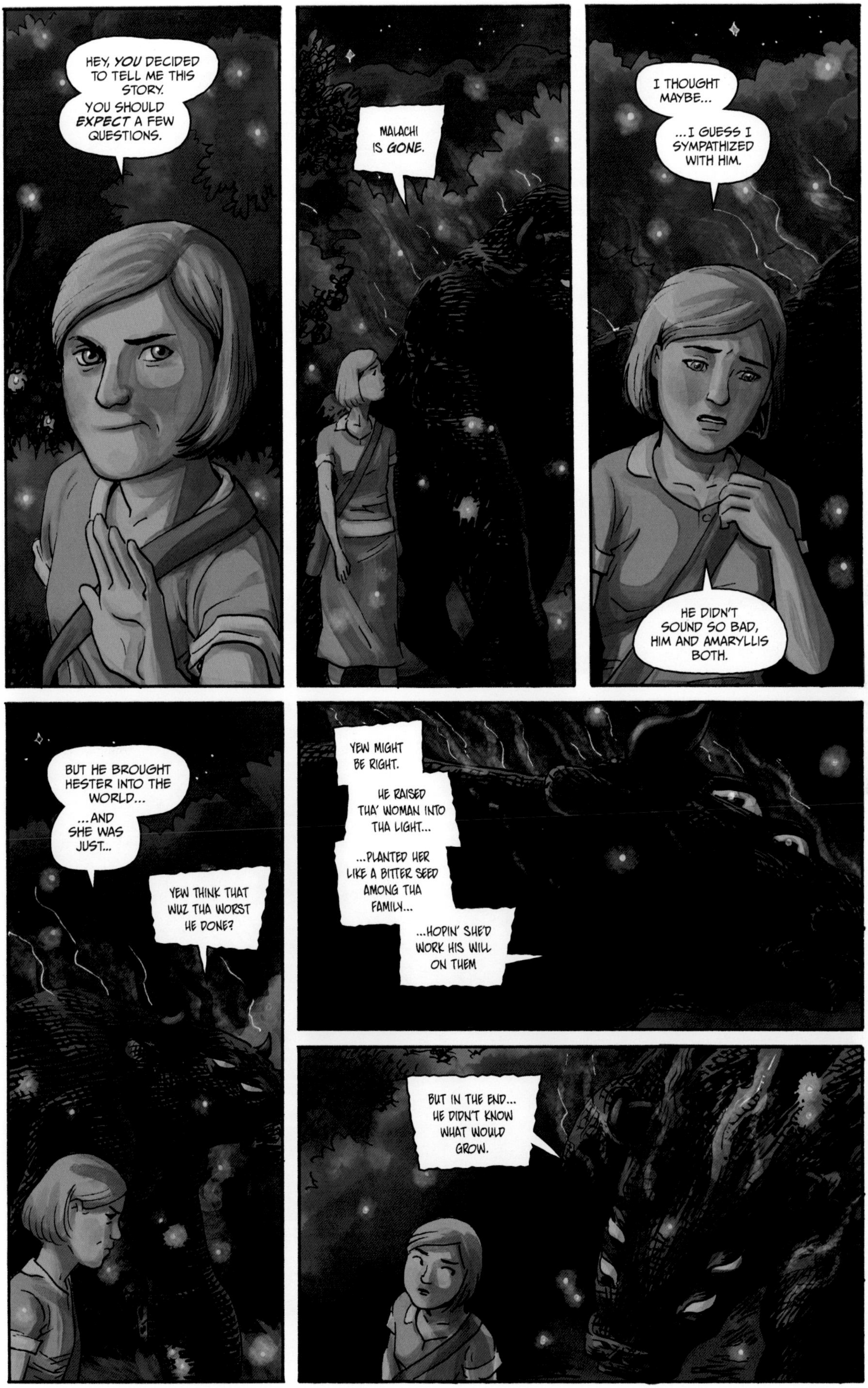
HEY, *YOU* DECIDED TO TELL ME THIS STORY.
YOU SHOULD *EXPECT* A FEW QUESTIONS.
MALACHI IS *GONE*.
I THOUGHT MAYBE...
...I GUESS I SYMPATHIZED WITH HIM.
HE DIDN'T SOUND SO BAD, HIM AND AMARYLLIS BOTH.
BUT HE BROUGHT HESTER INTO THE WORLD...
...AND SHE WAS JUST...
YEW THINK THAT WUZ THA WORST HE DONE?
YEW MIGHT BE RIGHT.
HE RAISED THA' WOMAN INTO THA LIGHT...
...PLANTED HER LIKE A BITTER SEED AMONG THA FAMILY...
...HOPIN' SHE'D WORK HIS WILL ON THEM
BUT IN THE END... HE DIDN'T KNOW WHAT WOULD GROW.

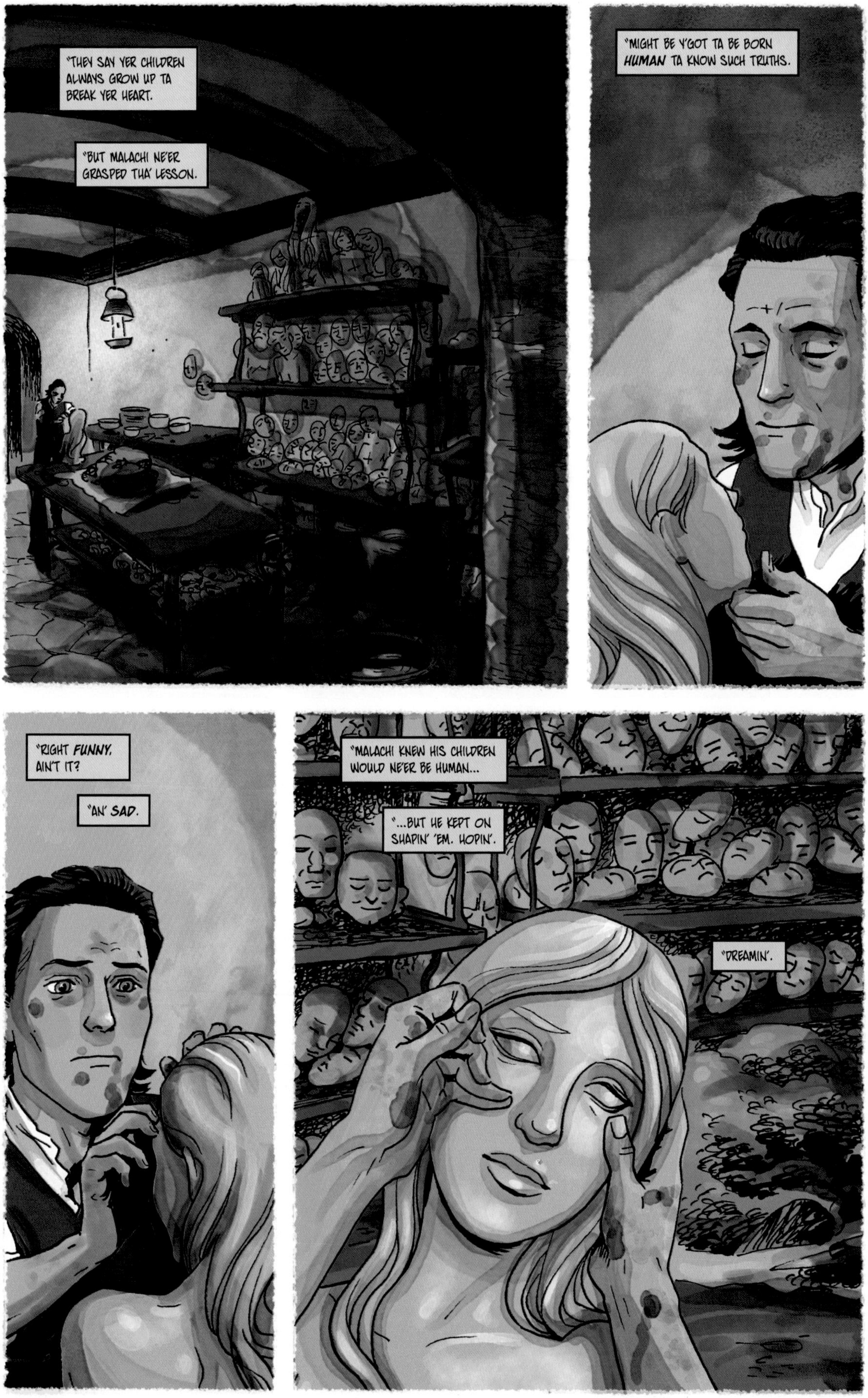
"THEY SAY YER CHILDREN ALWAYS GROW UP TA BREAK YER HEART.
"BUT MALACHI NE'ER GRASPED THA' LESSON.
"MIGHT BE Y'GOT TA BE BORN HUMAN TA KNOW SUCH TRUTHS.
"RIGHT FUNNY, AIN'T IT?
"AN' SAD.
"MALACHI KNEW HIS CHILDREN WOULD NE'ER BE HUMAN...
"...BUT HE KEPT ON SHAPIN' 'EM. HOPIN'.
"DREAMIN'.

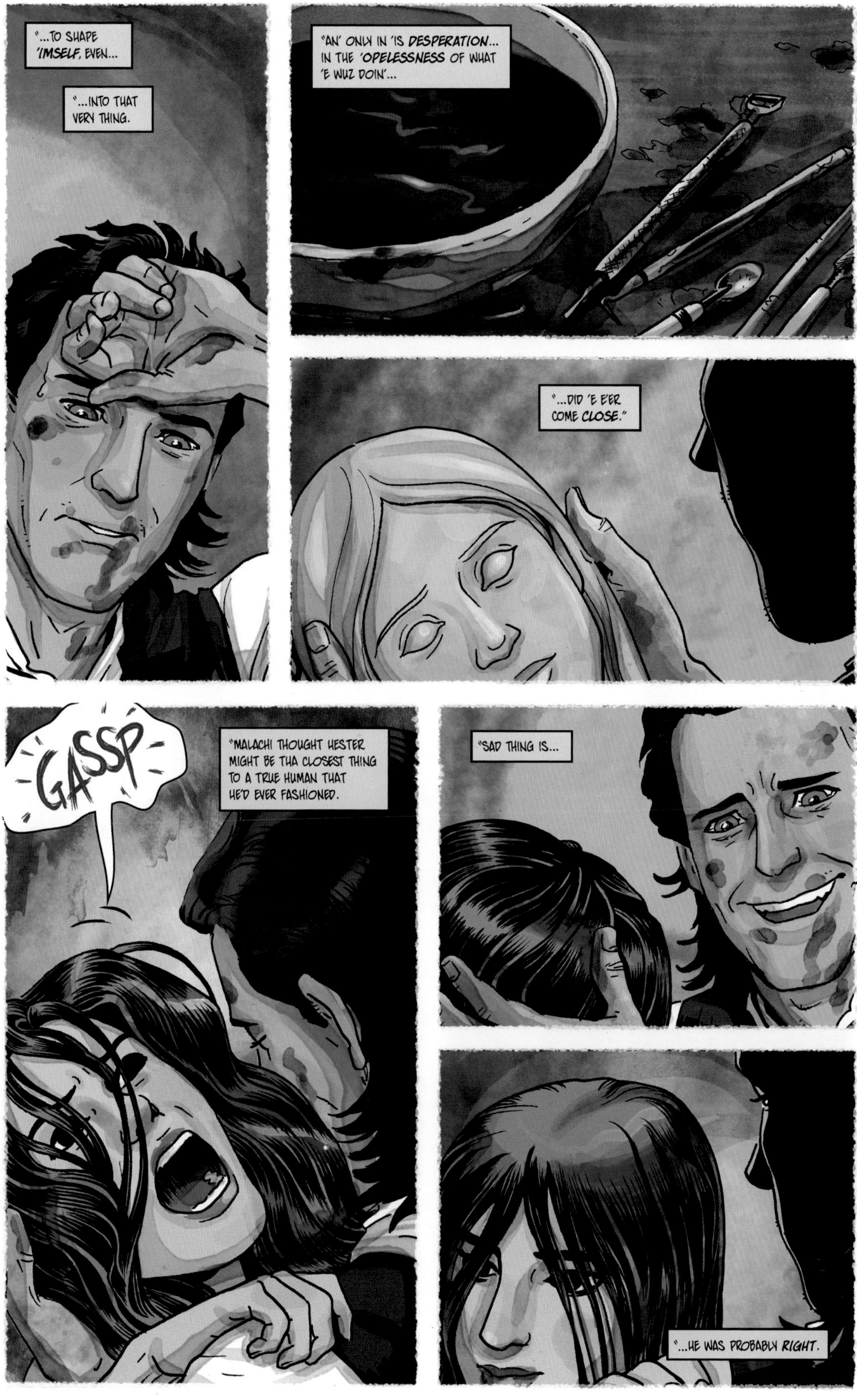
"...TO SHAPE 'IMSELF, EVEN...
"...INTO THAT VERY THING.
"AN' ONLY IN 'IS DESPERATION... IN THE 'OPELESSNESS OF WHAT 'E WUZ DOIN'...
"...DID 'E E'ER COME CLOSE."
GASSP
"MALACHI THOUGHT HESTER MIGHT BE THA CLOSEST THING TO A TRUE HUMAN THAT HE'D EVER FASHIONED.
"SAD THING IS...
"...HE WAS PROBABLY RIGHT.

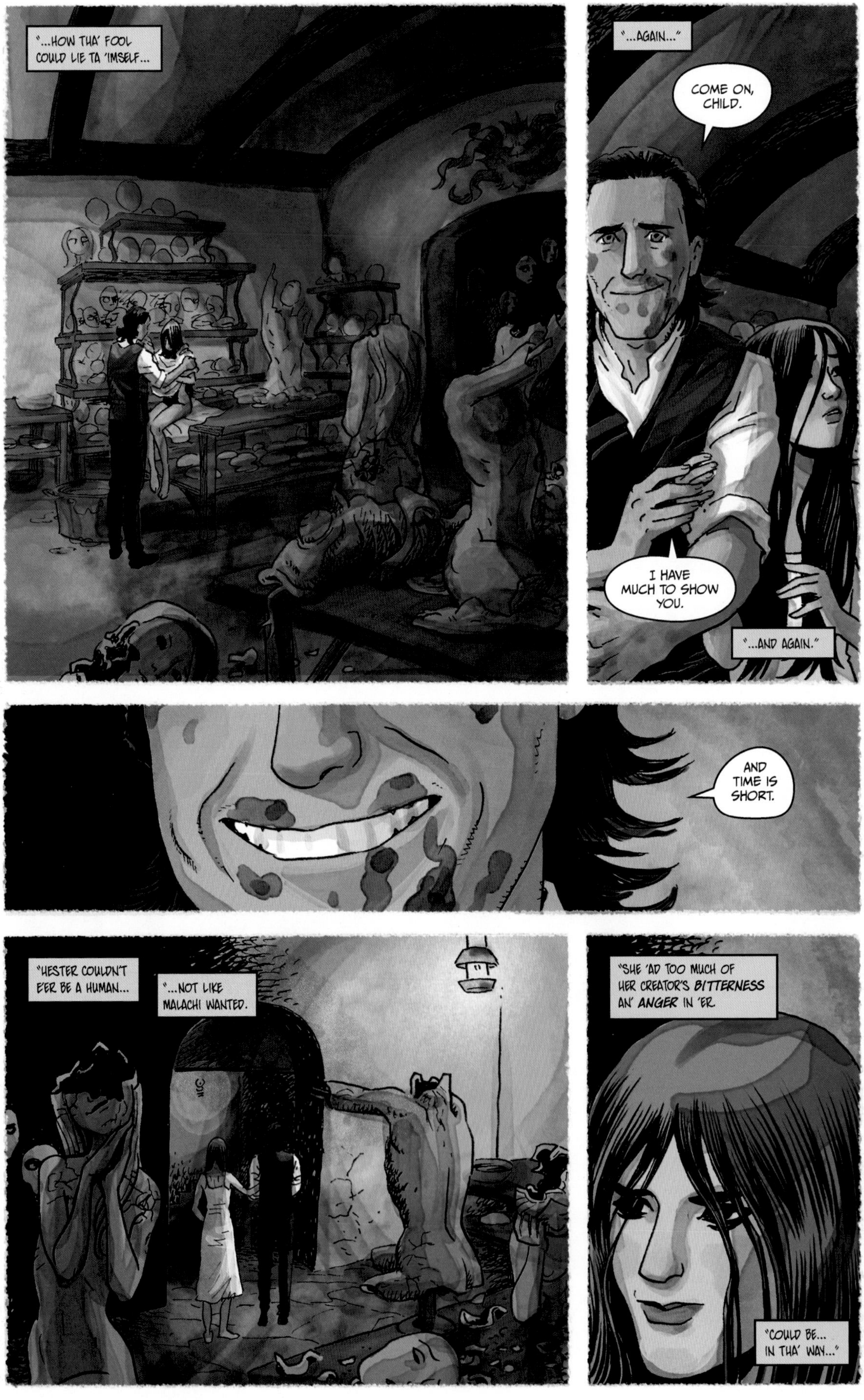
"...HOW THA' FOOL COULD LIE TA 'IMSELF...
"...AGAIN..."
COME ON, CHILD.
I HAVE MUCH TO SHOW YOU.
"...AND AGAIN."
AND TIME IS SHORT.
"HESTER COULDN'T E'ER BE A HUMAN...
"...NOT LIKE MALACHI WANTED.
"SHE 'AD TOO MUCH OF HER CREATOR'S BITTERNESS AN' ANGER IN 'ER.
"COULD BE... IN THA' WAY..."

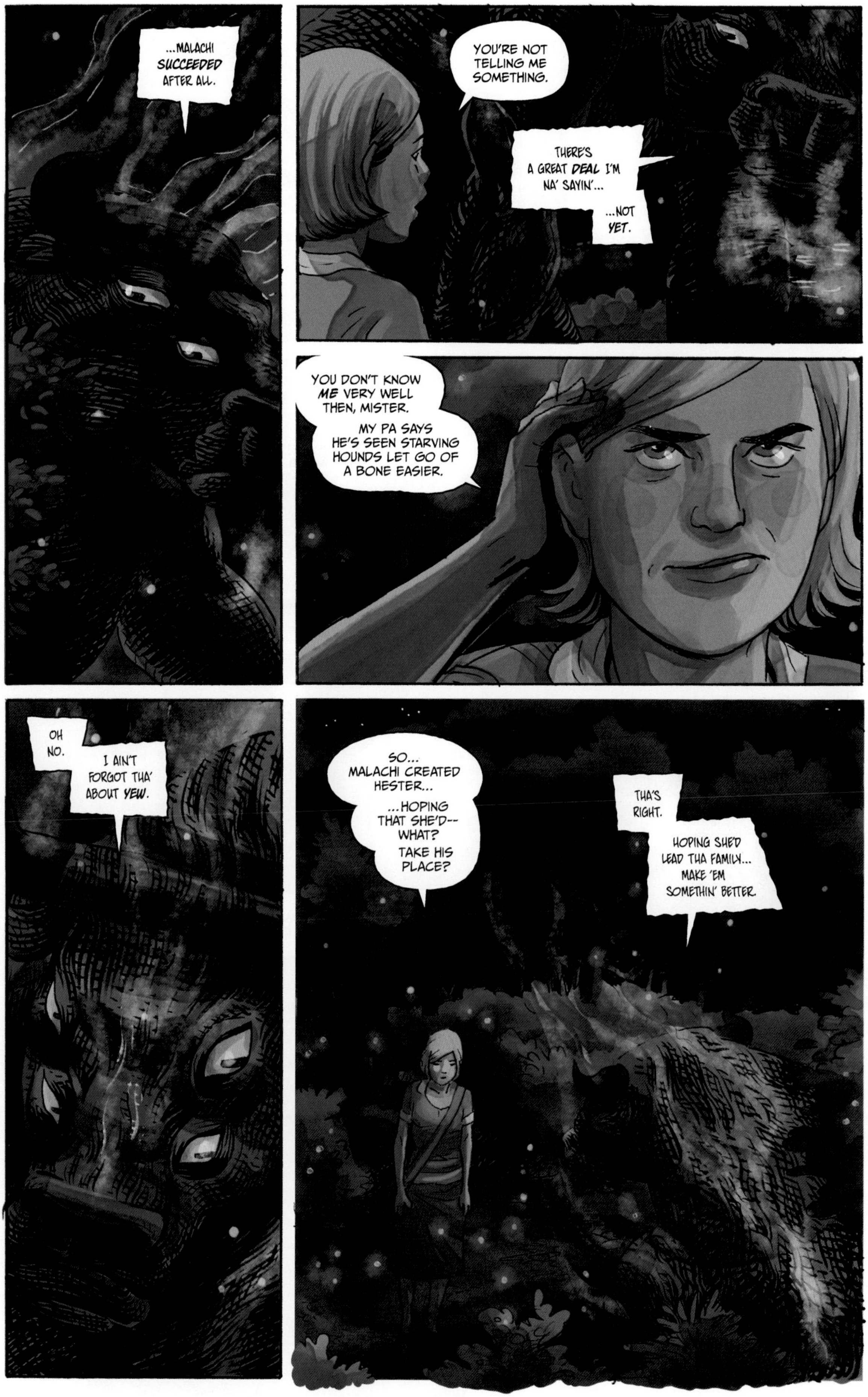
...MALACHI SUCCEEDED AFTER ALL.
YOU'RE NOT TELLING ME SOMETHING.
THERE'S A GREAT DEAL I'M NA' SAYIN'...
...NOT YET.
YOU DON'T KNOW ME VERY WELL THEN, MISTER.
MY PA SAYS HE'S SEEN STARVING HOUNDS LET GO OF A BONE EASIER.
OH NO.
I AIN'T FORGOT THA' ABOUT YEW.
SO... MALACHI CREATED HESTER...
...HOPING THAT SHE'D-- WHAT? TAKE HIS PLACE?
THA'S RIGHT.
HOPING SHE'D LEAD THA FAMILY... MAKE 'EM SOMETHIN' BETTER.

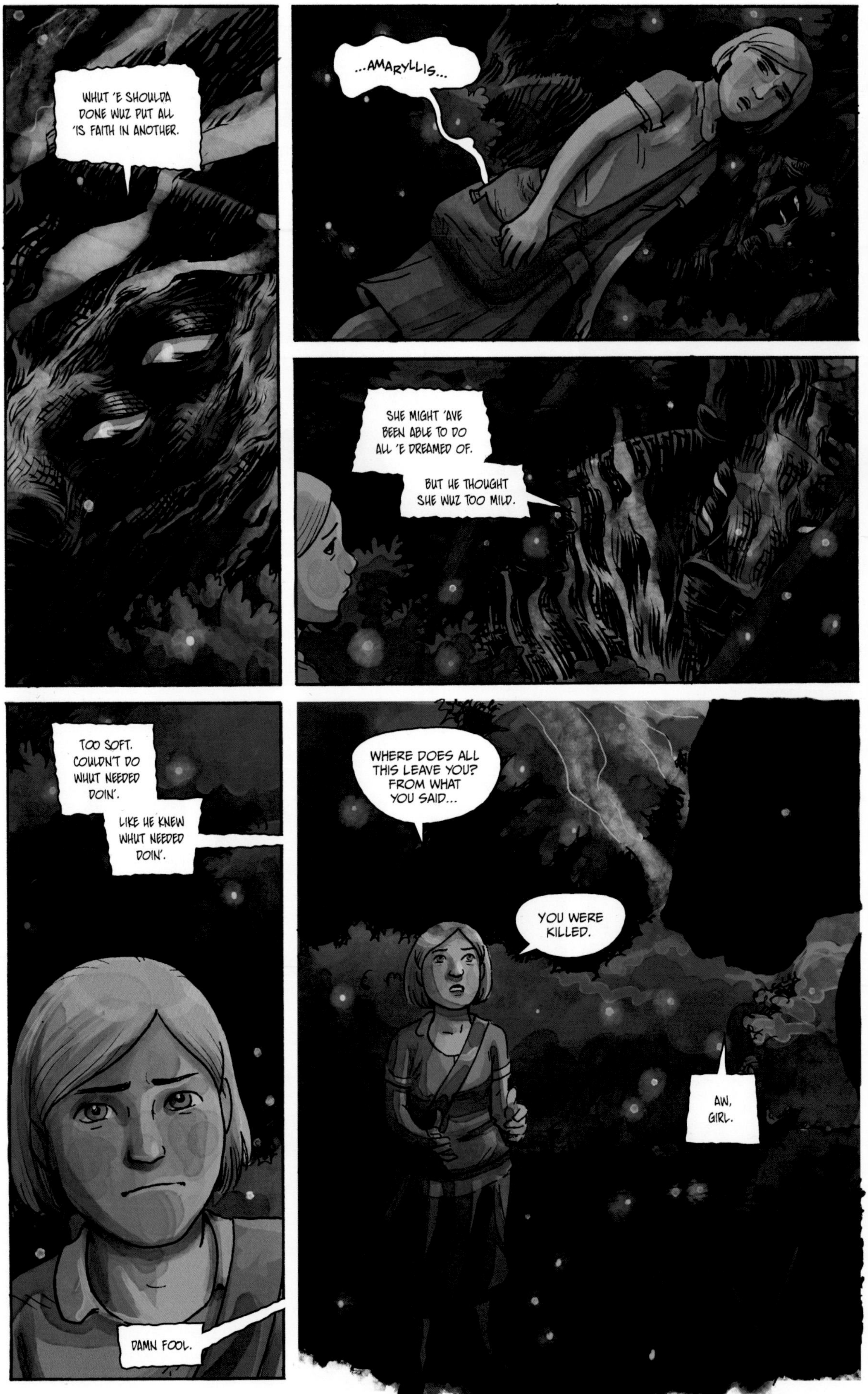
WHUT 'E SHOULDA DONE WUZ PUT ALL 'IS FAITH IN ANOTHER.
...AMARYLLIS...
SHE MIGHT 'AVE BEEN ABLE TO DO ALL 'E DREAMED OF.
BUT HE THOUGHT SHE WUZ TOO MILD.
TOO SOFT. COULDN'T DO WHUT NEEDED DOIN'.
LIKE HE KNEW WHUT NEEDED DOIN'.
DAMN FOOL.
WHERE DOES ALL THIS LEAVE YOU? FROM WHAT YOU SAID...
YOU WERE KILLED.
AW, GIRL.

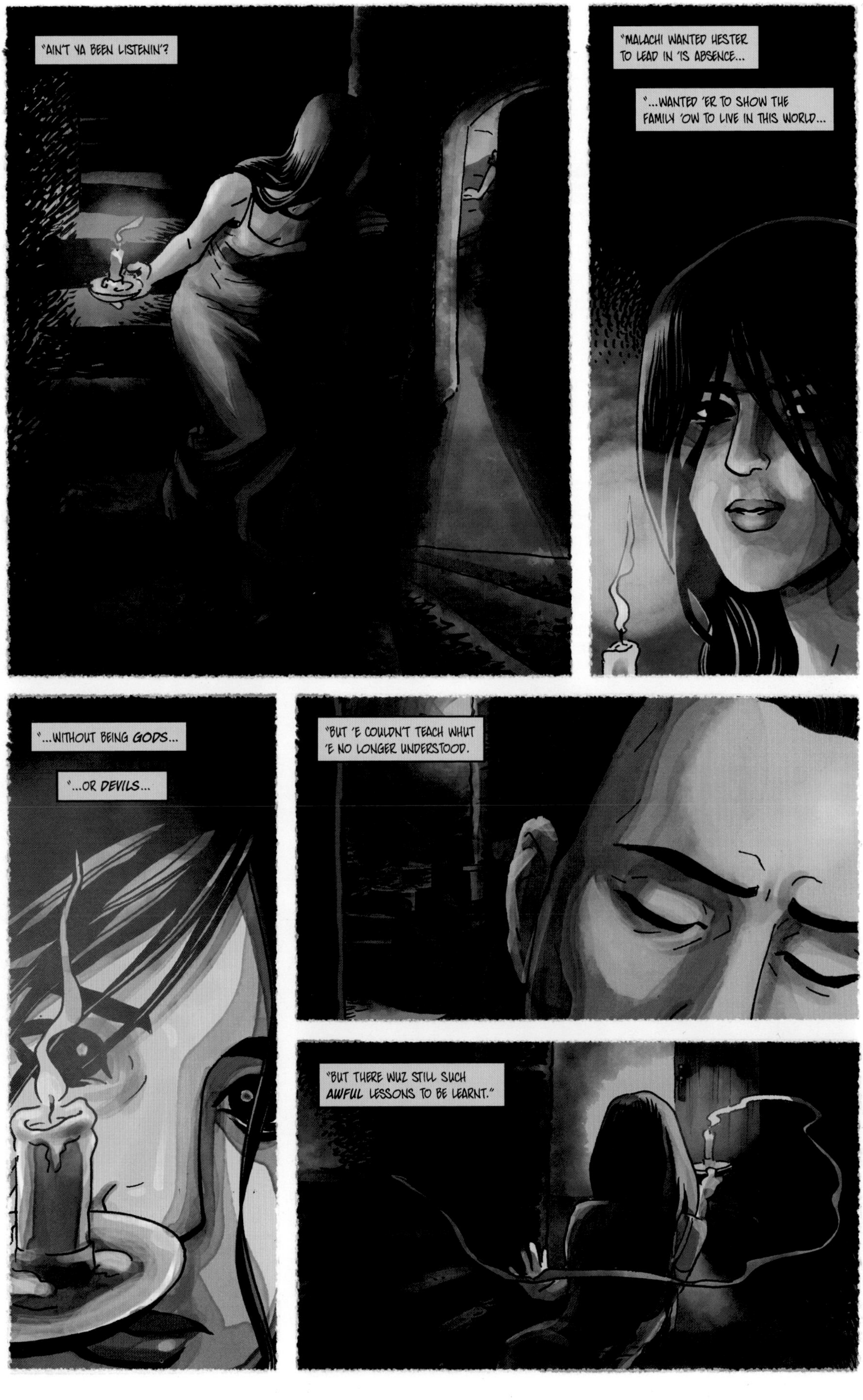
"AIN'T YA BEEN LISTENIN'?
"MALACHI WANTED HESTER TO LEAD IN 'IS ABSENCE...
"...WANTED 'ER TO SHOW THE FAMILY 'OW TO LIVE IN THIS WORLD...
"...WITHOUT BEING GODS...
"...OR DEVILS...
"BUT 'E COULDN'T TEACH WHUT 'E NO LONGER UNDERSTOOD.
"BUT THERE WUZ STILL SUCH AWFUL LESSONS TO BE LEARNT."

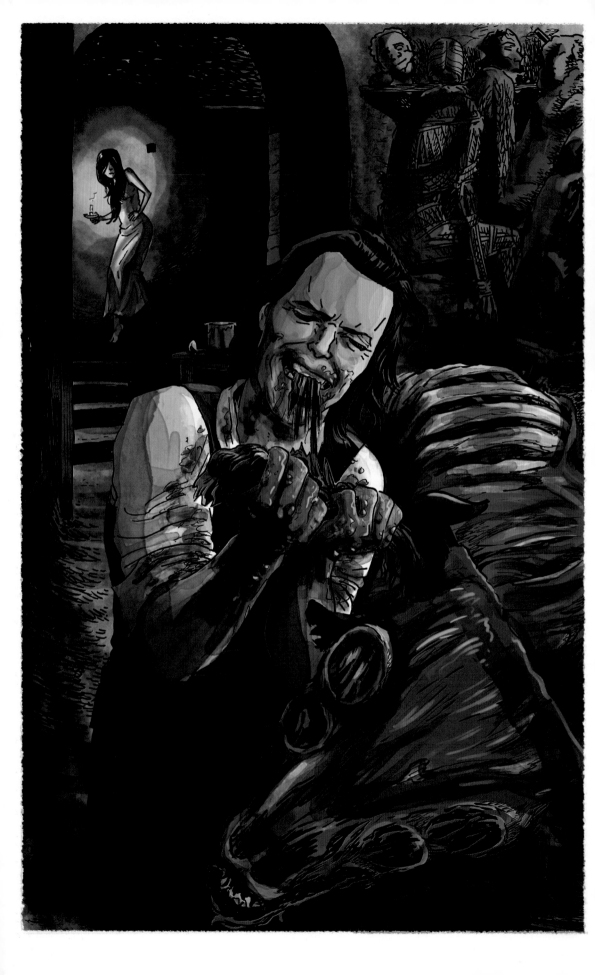

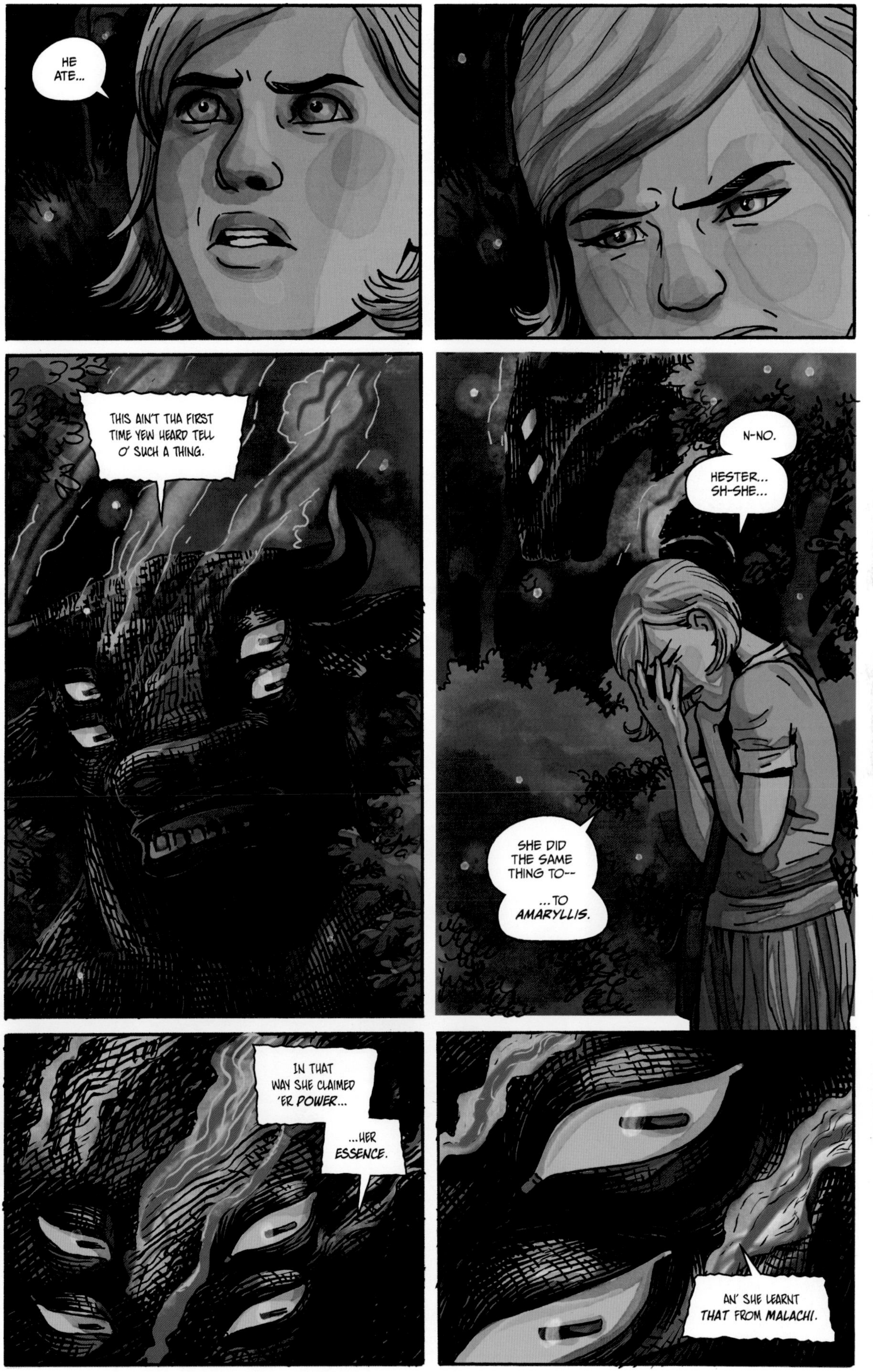
HE ATE...
THIS AIN'T THA FIRST TIME YEW HEARD TELL O' SUCH A THING.
N-NO.
HESTER... SH-SHE...
SHE DID THE SAME THING TO--
...TO AMARYLLIS.
IN THAT WAY SHE CLAIMED 'ER POWER...
...HER ESSENCE.
AN' SHE LEARNT THAT FROM MALACHI.

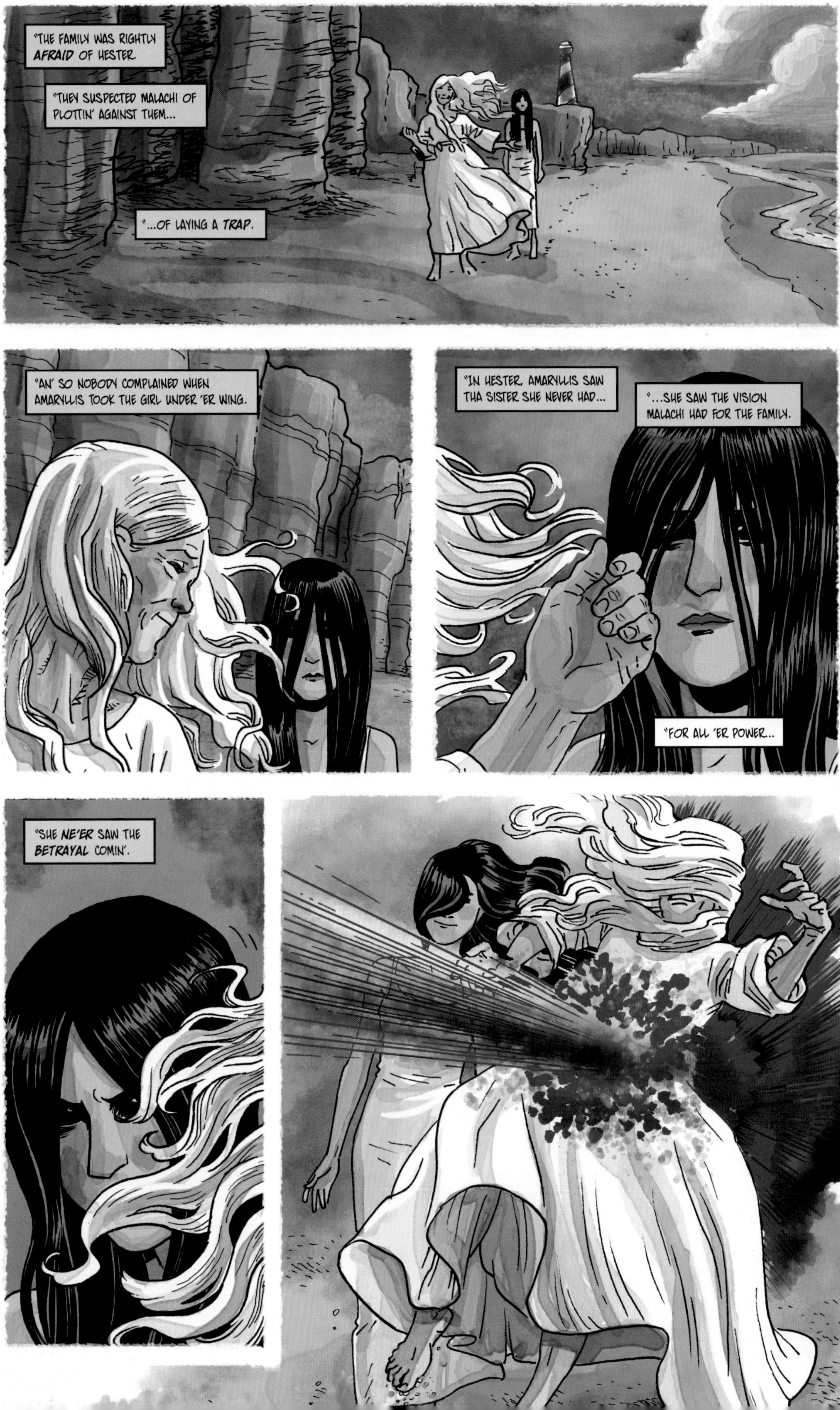
"THE FAMILY WAS RIGHTLY AFRAID OF HESTER.
"THEY SUSPECTED MALACHI OF PLOTTIN' AGAINST THEM...
"...OF LAYING A TRAP.
"AN' SO NOBODY COMPLAINED WHEN AMARYLLIS TOOK THE GIRL UNDER 'ER WING.
"IN HESTER, AMARYLLIS SAW THA SISTER SHE NEVER HAD...
"...SHE SAW THE VISION MALACHI HAD FOR THE FAMILY.
"FOR ALL 'ER POWER...
"SHE NE'ER SAW THE BETRAYAL COMIN'.

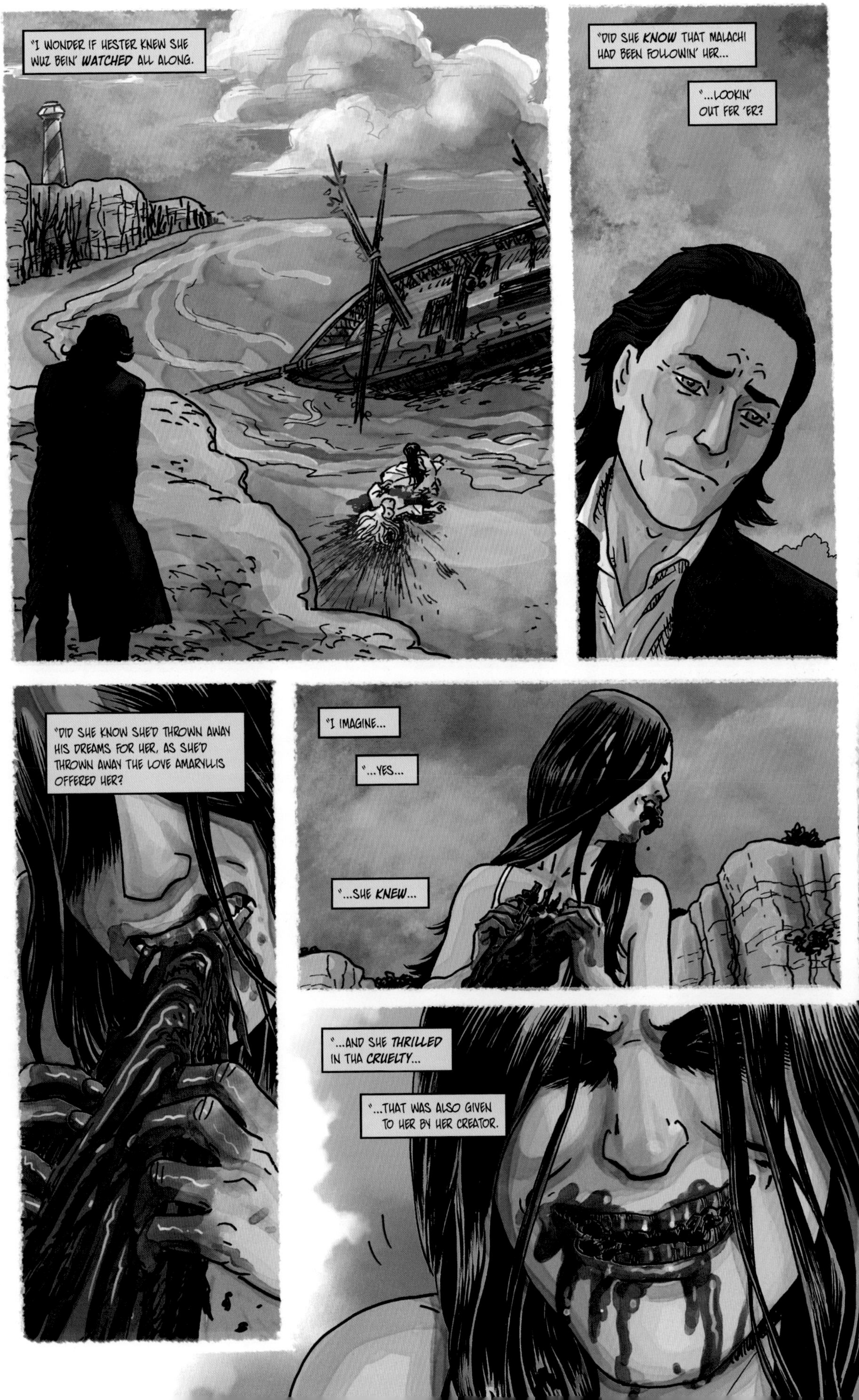
"I WONDER IF HESTER KNEW SHE WUZ BEIN' WATCHED ALL ALONG.
"DID SHE KNOW THAT MALACHI HAD BEEN FOLLOWIN' HER...
"...LOOKIN' OUT FER 'ER?
"DID SHE KNOW SHE'D THROWN AWAY HIS DREAMS FOR HER, AS SHE'D THROWN AWAY THE LOVE AMARYLLIS OFFERED HER?
"I IMAGINE...
"...YES...
"...SHE KNEW...
"...AND SHE THRILLED IN THA CRUELTY...
"...THAT WAS ALSO GIVEN TO HER BY HER CREATOR.

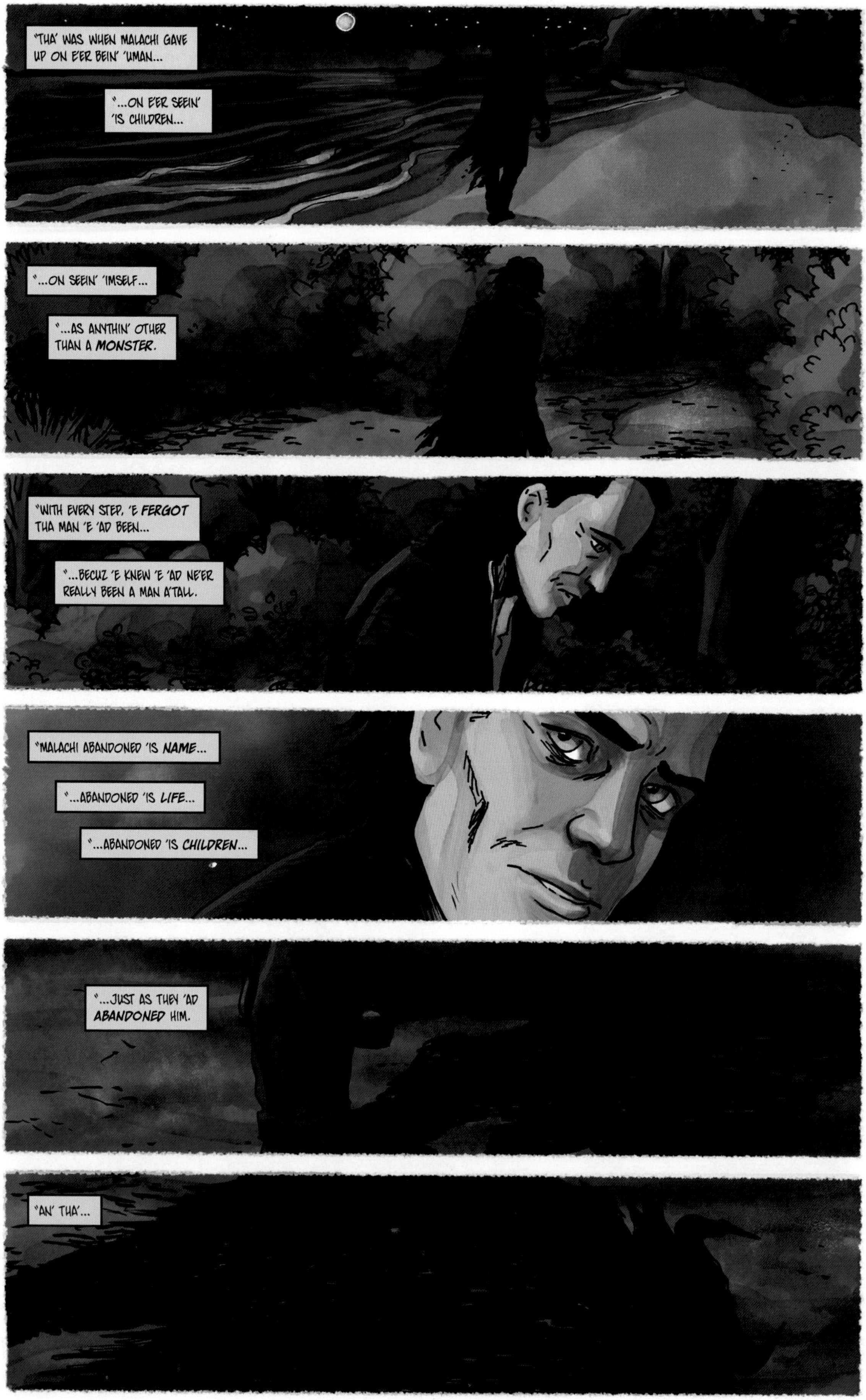
"THA' WAS WHEN MALACHI GAVE UP ON E'ER BEIN' 'UMAN...
"...ON E'ER SEEIN' 'IS CHILDREN...
"...ON SEEIN' 'IMSELF...
"...AS ANYTHIN' OTHER THAN A MONSTER.
"WITH EVERY STEP, 'E FERGOT THA MAN 'E 'AD BEEN...
"...BECUZ 'E KNEW 'E 'AD NE'ER REALLY BEEN A MAN A'TALL.
"MALACHI ABANDONED 'IS NAME...
"...ABANDONED 'IS LIFE...
"...ABANDONED 'IS CHILDREN...
"...JUST AS THEY 'AD ABANDONED HIM.
"AN' THA'...

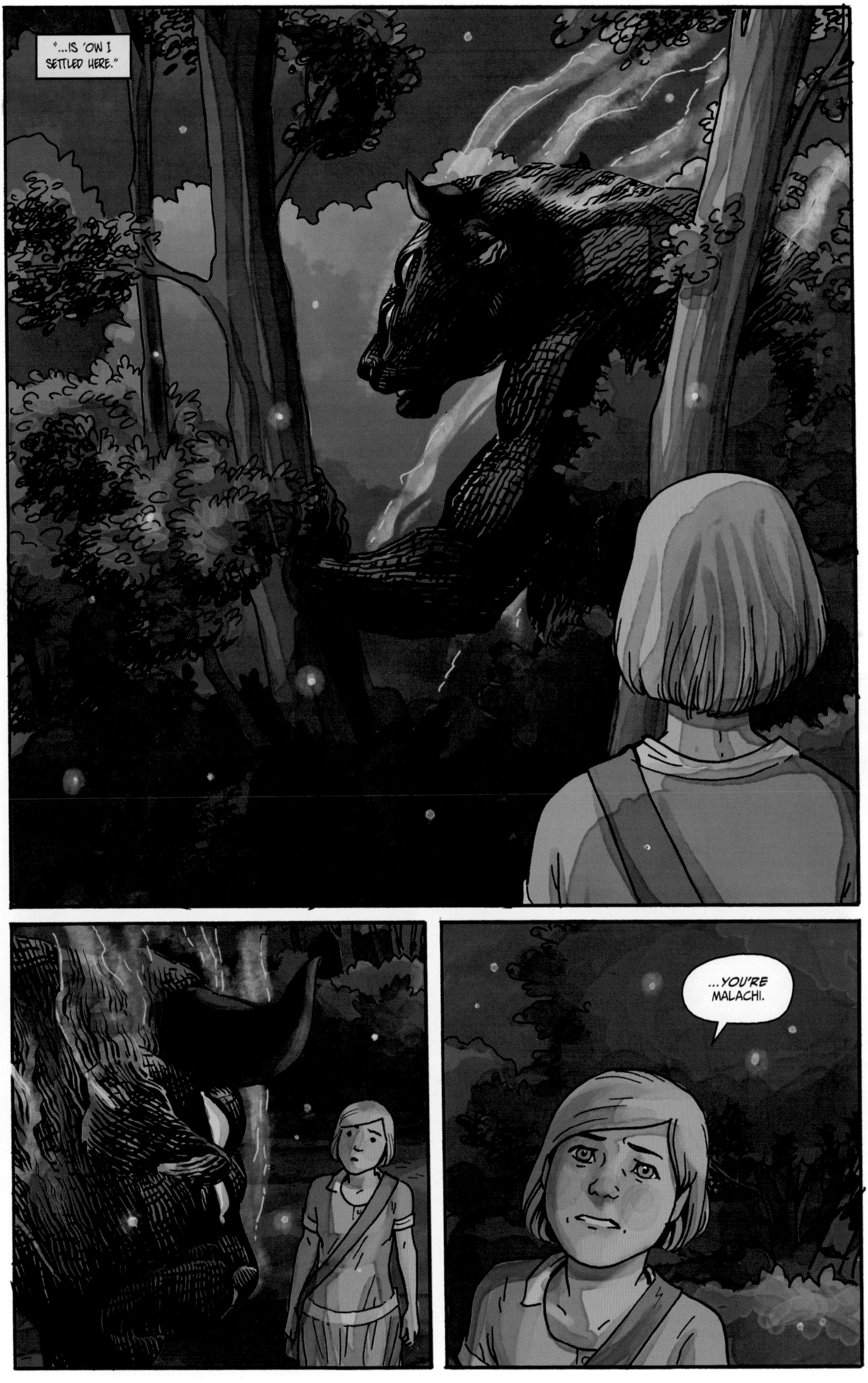
"...IS 'OW I SETTLED HERE."
...YOU'RE MALACHI.

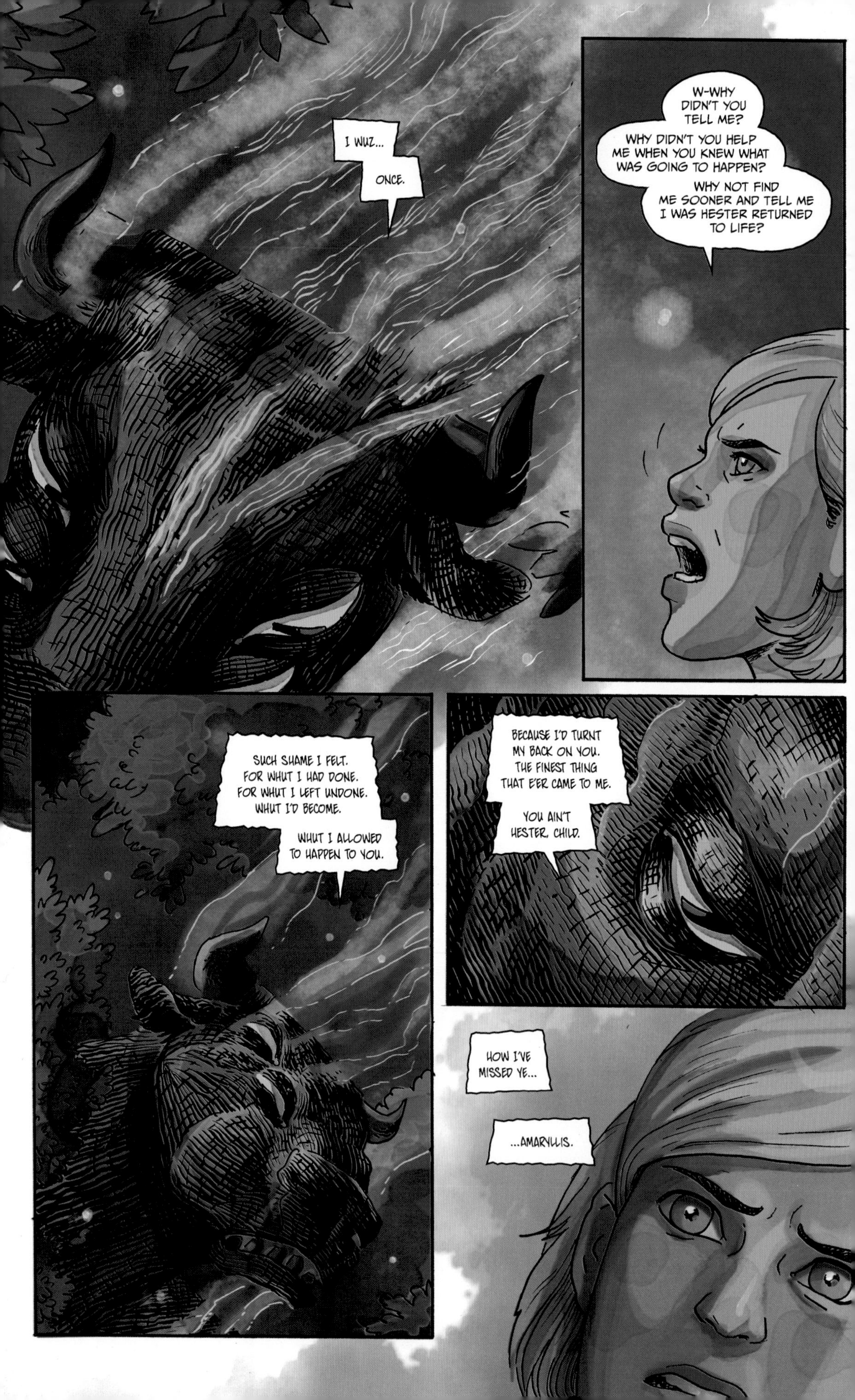
I WUZ...
ONCE.
W-WHY DIDN'T YOU TELL ME?
WHY DIDN'T YOU HELP ME WHEN YOU KNEW WHAT WAS GOING TO HAPPEN?
WHY NOT FIND ME SOONER AND TELL ME I WAS HESTER RETURNED TO LIFE?
SUCH SHAME I FELT. FOR WHUT I HAD DONE. FOR WHUT I LEFT UNDONE. WHUT I'D BECOME.
WHUT I ALLOWED TO HAPPEN TO YOU.
BECAUSE I'D TURNT MY BACK ON YOU. THE FINEST THING THAT E'ER CAME TO ME.
YOU AIN'T HESTER, CHILD.
HOW I'VE MISSED YE...
...AMARYLLIS.

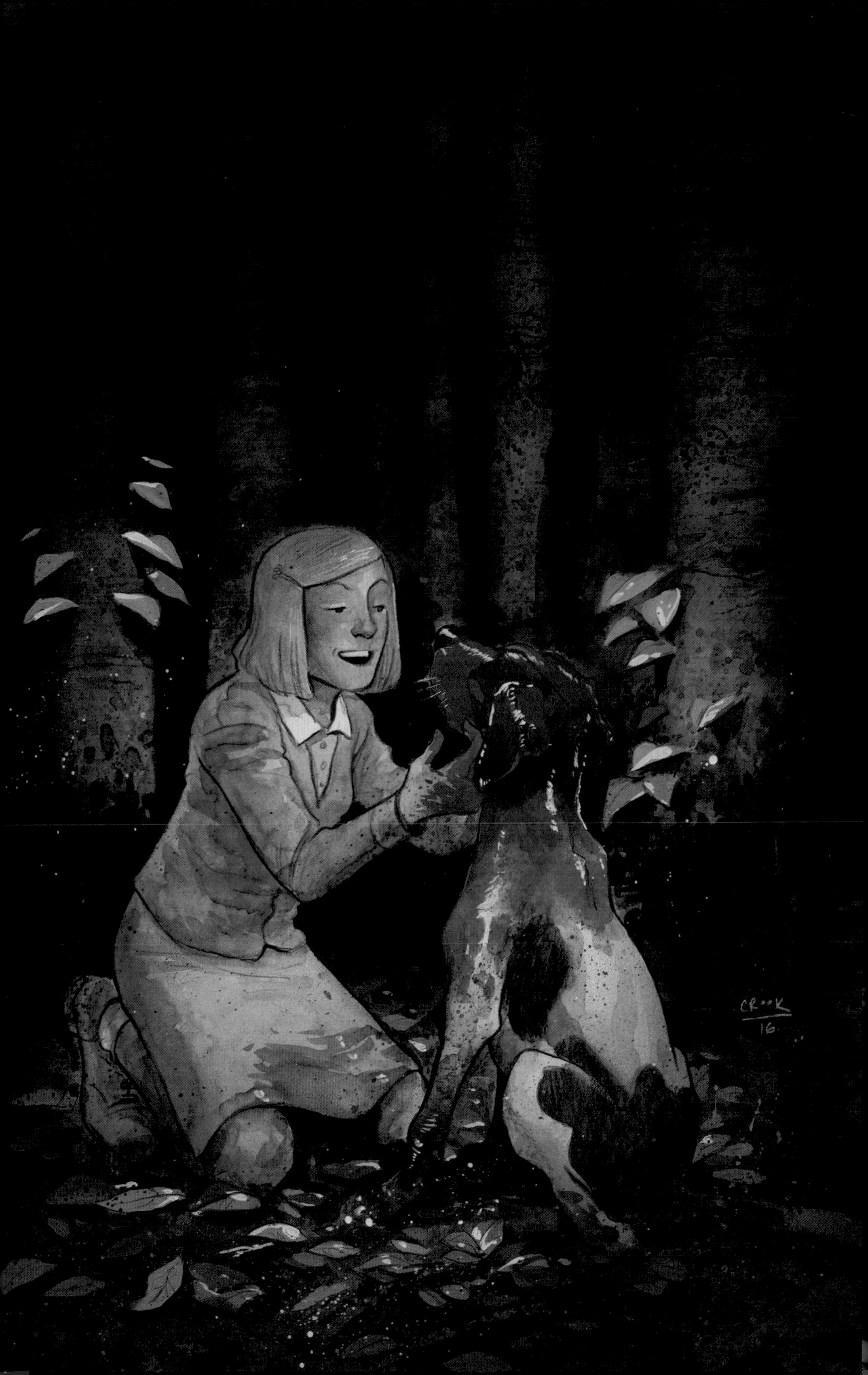
CROOK
16

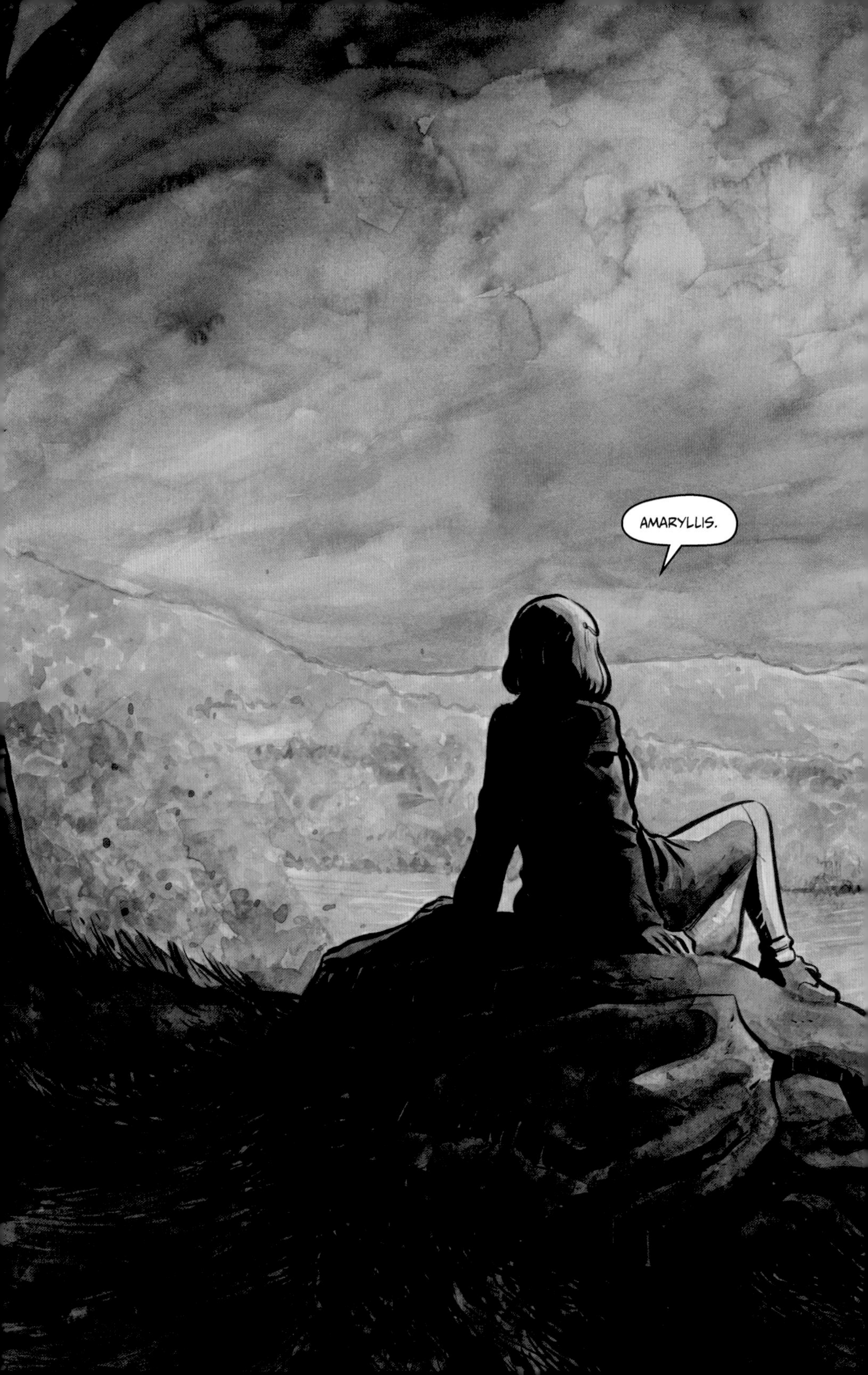
AMARYLLIS.

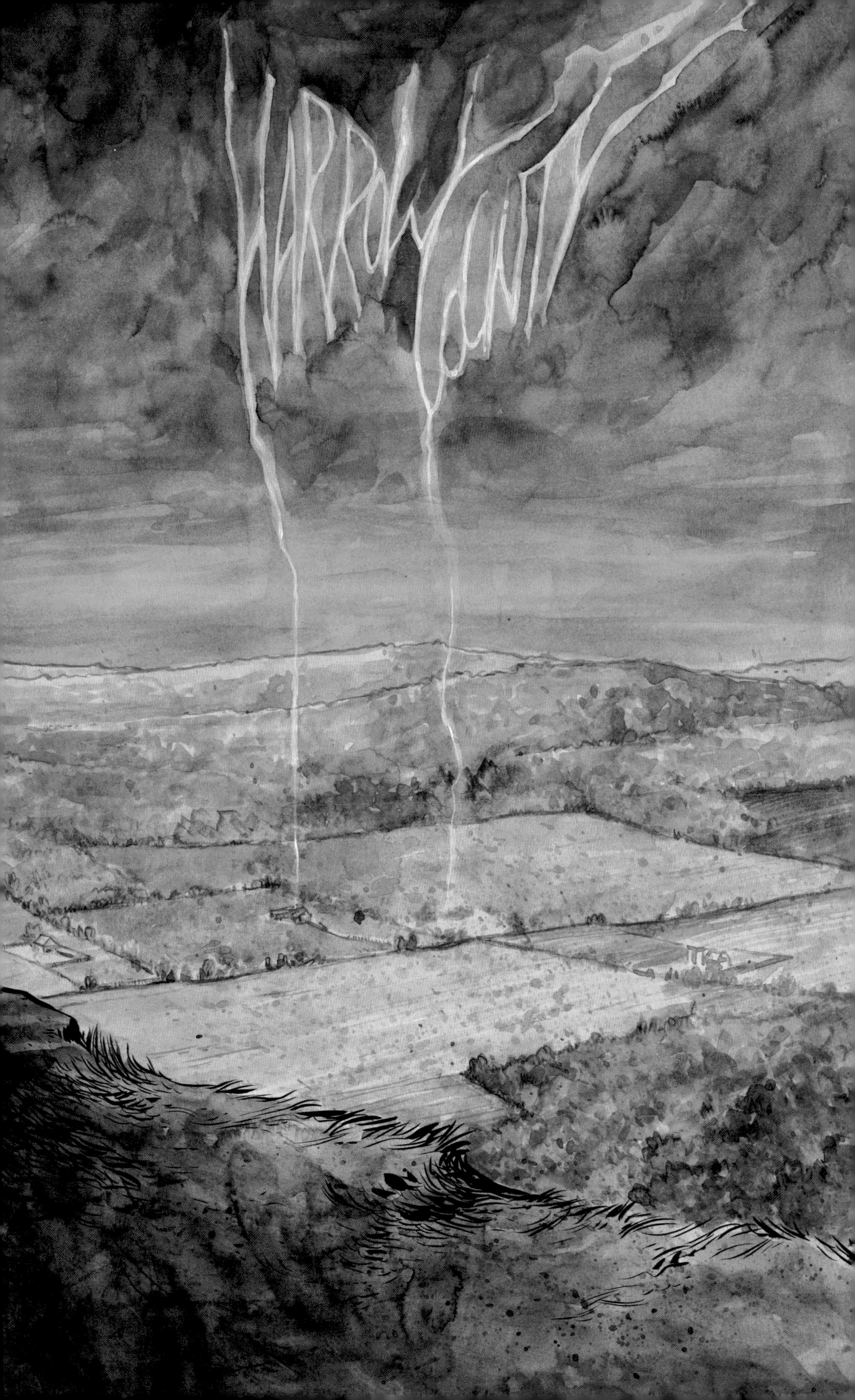
HARROW COUNTY

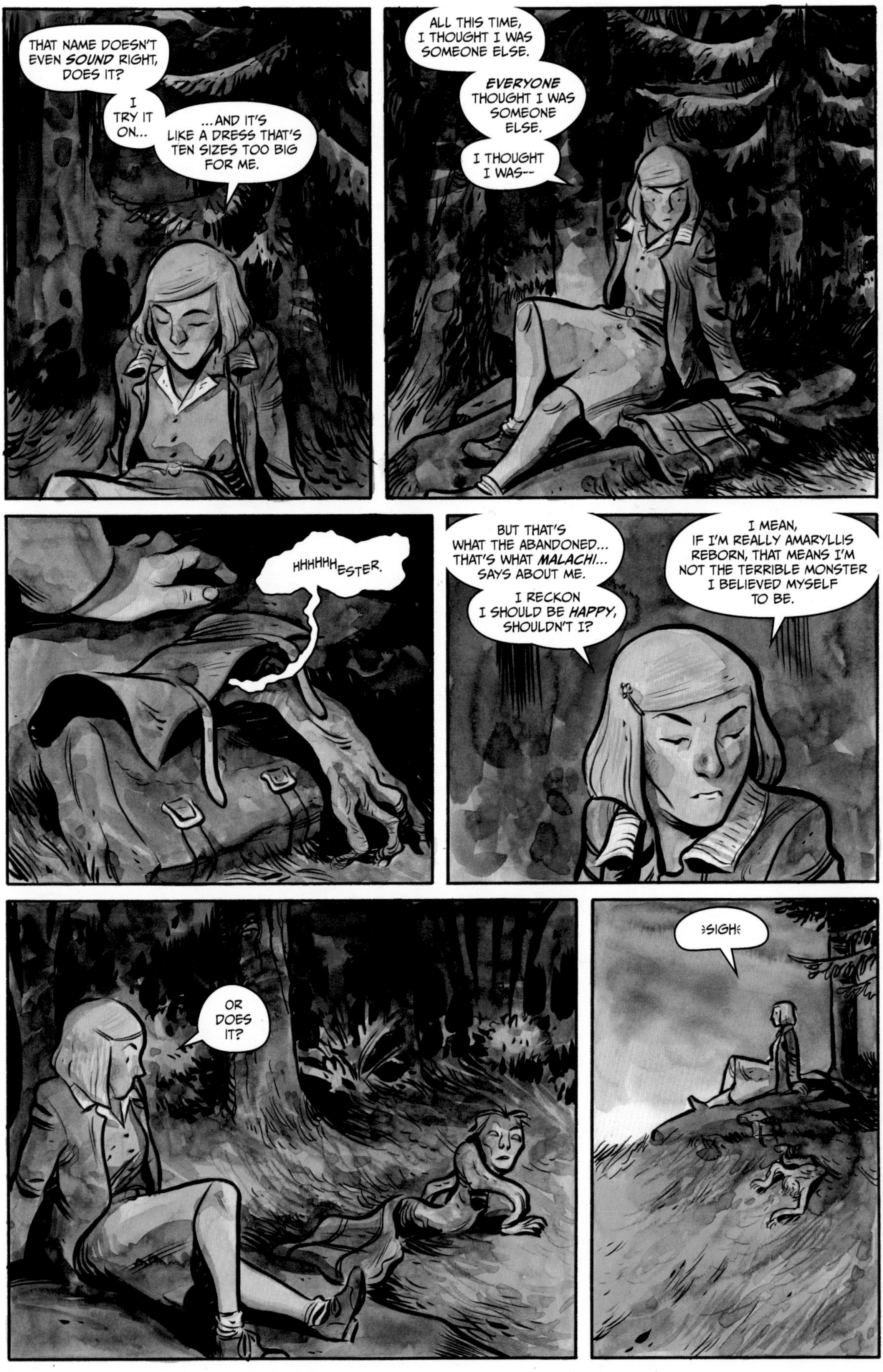
THAT NAME DOESN'T EVEN *SOUND* RIGHT, DOES IT?
I TRY IT ON...
...AND IT'S LIKE A DRESS THAT'S TEN SIZES TOO BIG FOR ME.
ALL THIS TIME, I THOUGHT I WAS SOMEONE ELSE.
EVERYONE THOUGHT I WAS SOMEONE ELSE.
I THOUGHT I WAS--
HHHHHHESTER.
BUT THAT'S WHAT THE ABANDONED... THAT'S WHAT *MALACHI*... SAYS ABOUT ME.
I RECKON I SHOULD BE *HAPPY*, SHOULDN'T I?
I MEAN, IF I'M REALLY AMARYLLIS REBORN, THAT MEANS I'M NOT THE TERRIBLE MONSTER I BELIEVED MYSELF TO BE.
OR DOES IT?
SIGH

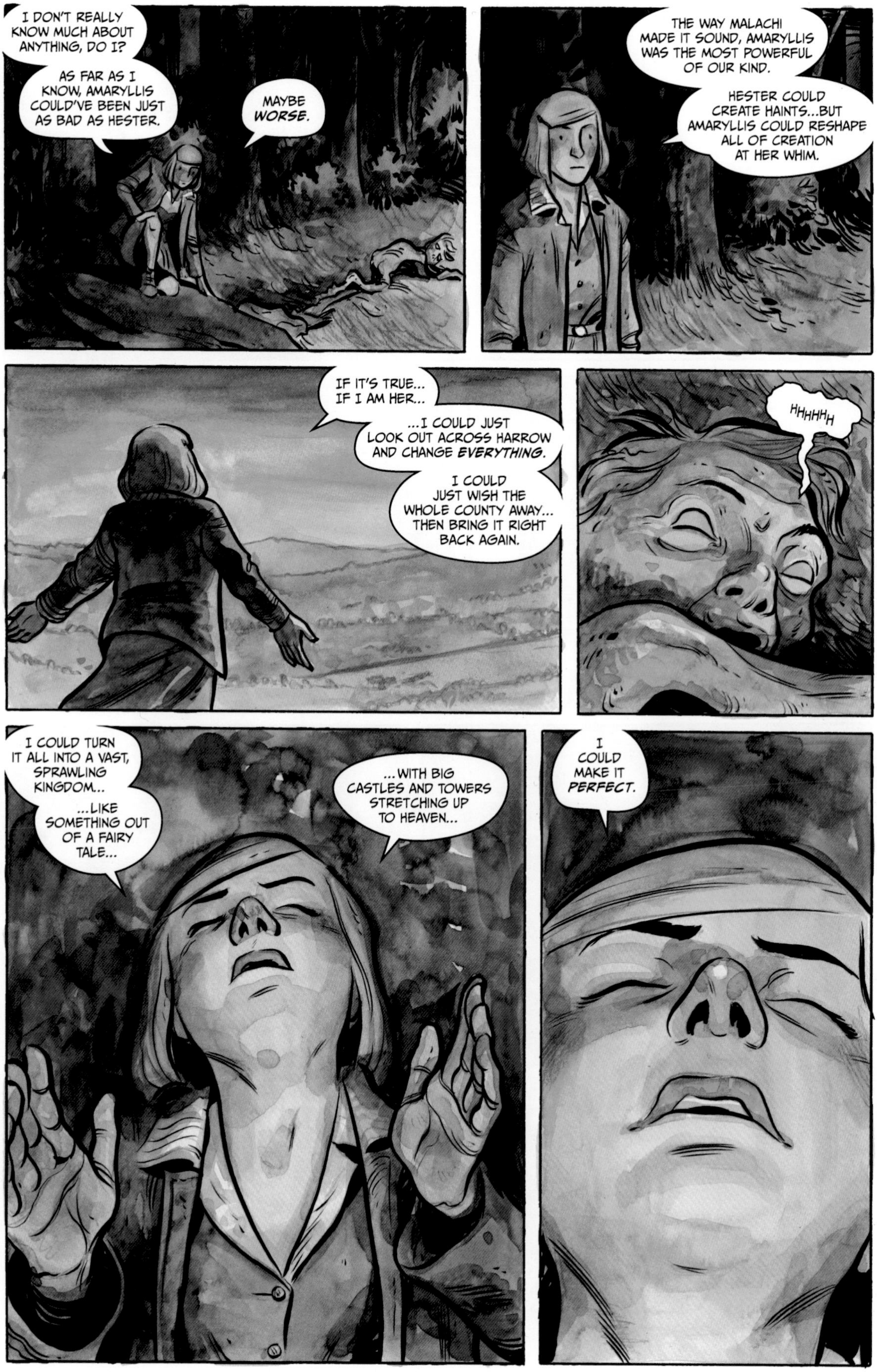

I DON'T REALLY KNOW MUCH ABOUT ANYTHING, DO I?
AS FAR AS I KNOW, AMARYLLIS COULD'VE BEEN JUST AS BAD AS HESTER.
MAYBE *WORSE*.
THE WAY MALACHI MADE IT SOUND, AMARYLLIS WAS THE MOST POWERFUL OF OUR KIND.
HESTER COULD CREATE HAINTS...BUT AMARYLLIS COULD RESHAPE ALL OF CREATION AT HER WHIM.
IF IT'S TRUE... IF I AM HER...
...I COULD JUST LOOK OUT ACROSS HARROW AND CHANGE *EVERYTHING*.
I COULD JUST WISH THE WHOLE COUNTY AWAY... THEN BRING IT RIGHT BACK AGAIN.
HHHHHH
I COULD TURN IT ALL INTO A VAST, SPRAWLING KINGDOM...
...LIKE SOMETHING OUT OF A FAIRY TALE...
...WITH BIG CASTLES AND TOWERS STRETCHING UP TO HEAVEN...
I COULD MAKE IT *PERFECT*.

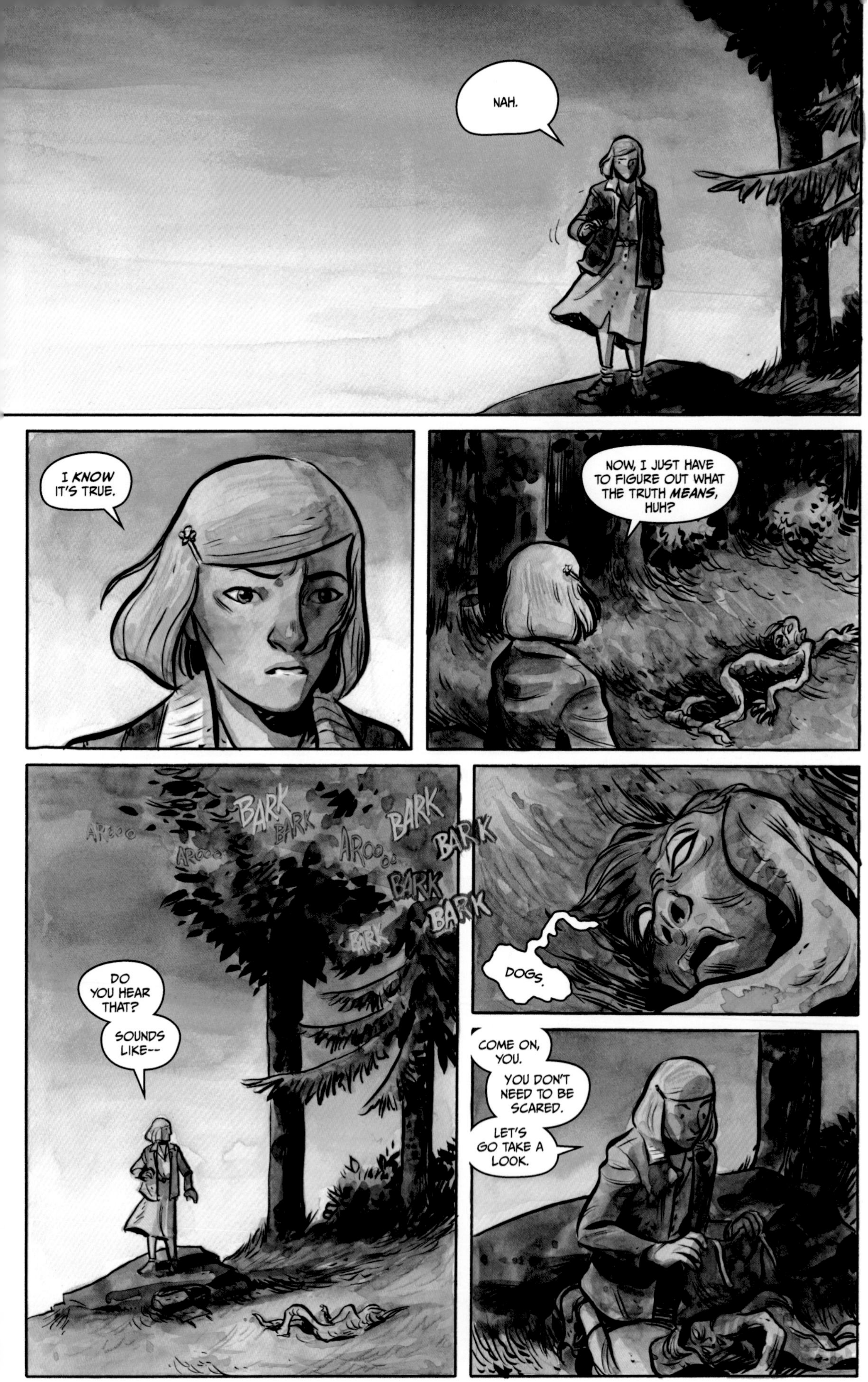
NAH.
I KNOW IT'S TRUE.
NOW, I JUST HAVE TO FIGURE OUT WHAT THE TRUTH MEANS, HUH?
AROOO
AROOO
BARK
BARK
AROOooo
BARK
BARK
BARK
BARK
BARK
DO YOU HEAR THAT?
SOUNDS LIKE--
DOGS.
COME ON, YOU.
YOU DON'T NEED TO BE SCARED.
LET'S GO TAKE A LOOK.

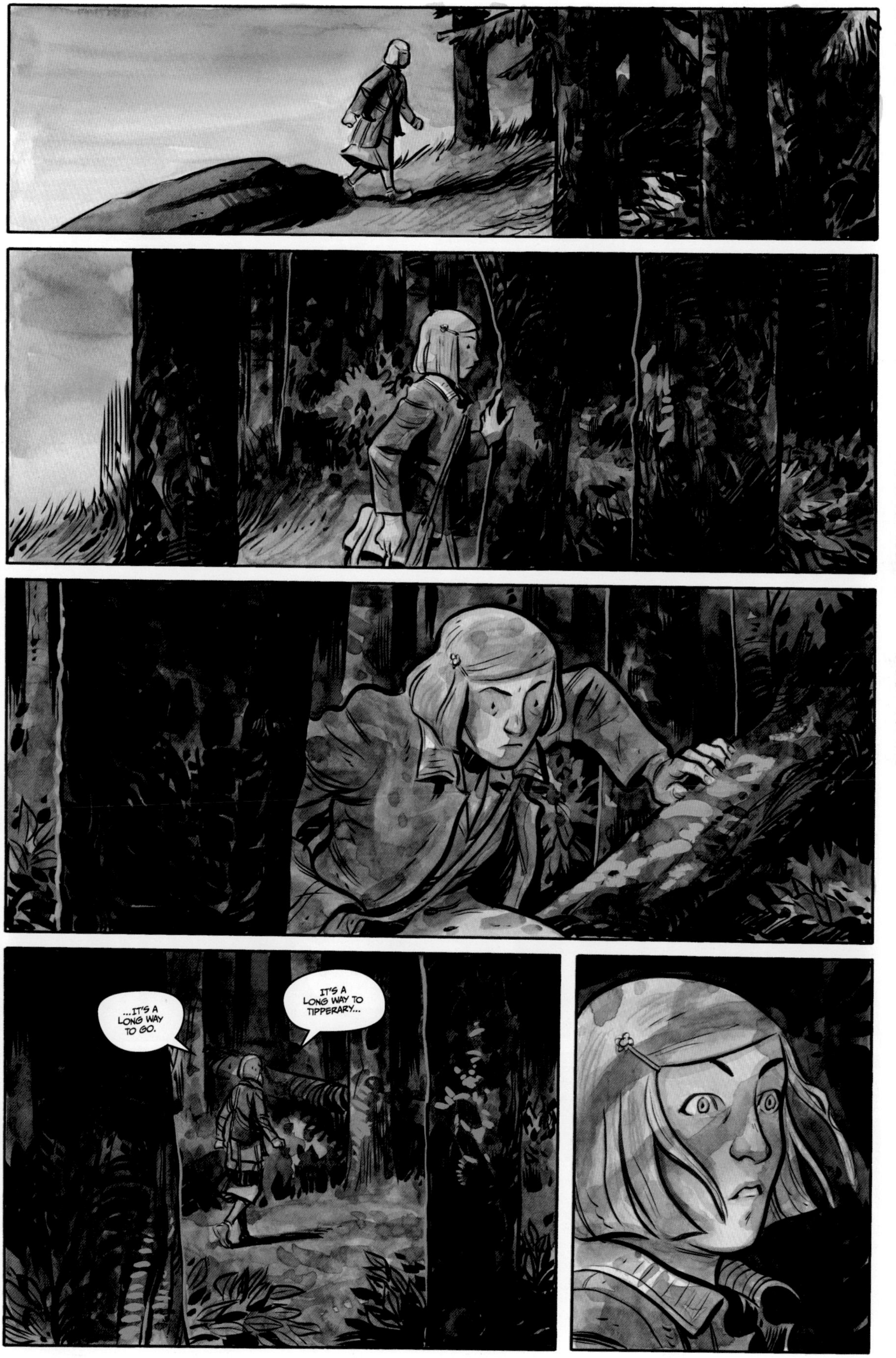
IT'S A
LONG WAY TO
TIPPERARY...
...IT'S A
LONG WAY
TO GO.

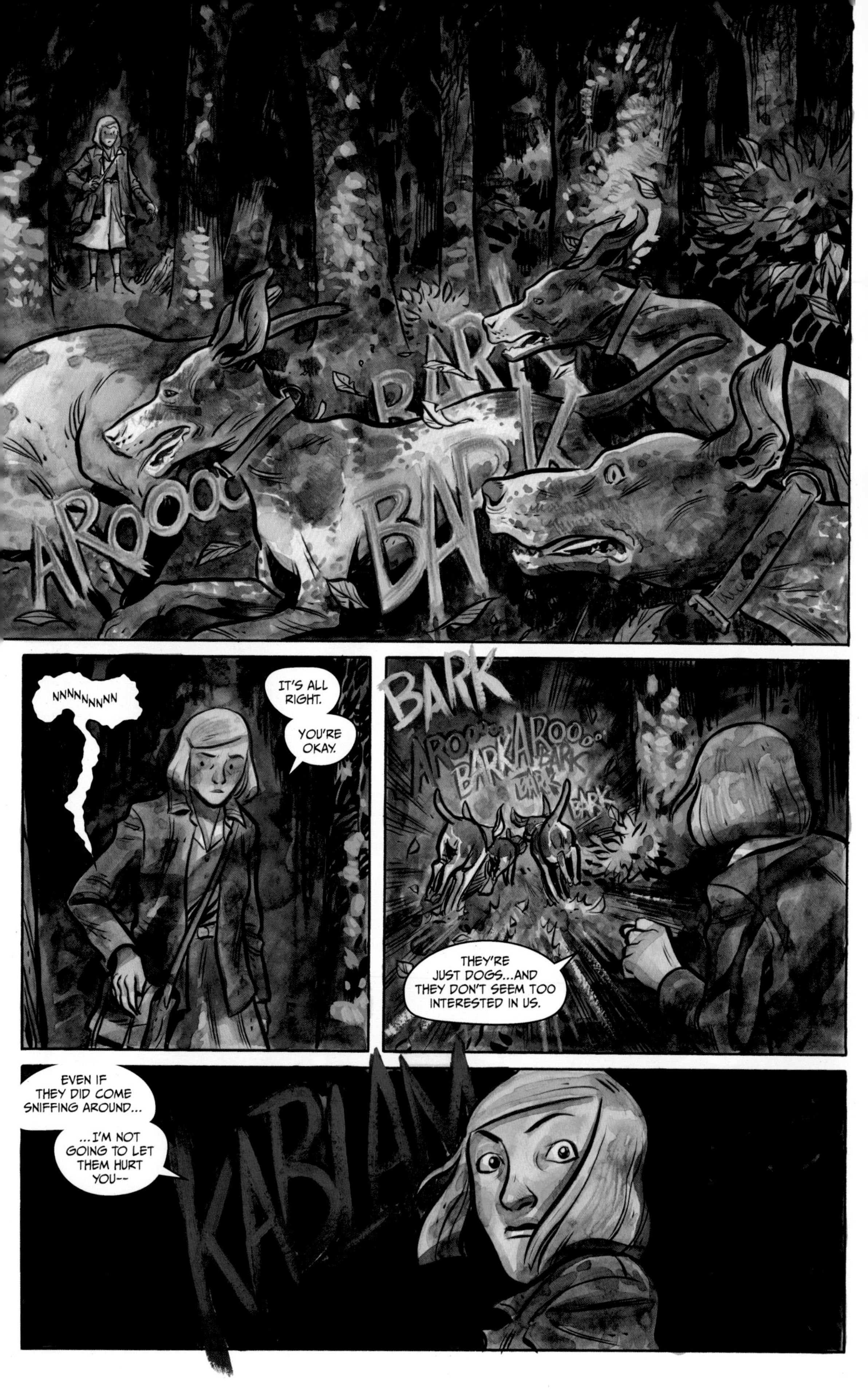
BARK
AROOOO
BARK
NNNNNNNNN
IT'S ALL RIGHT.
YOU'RE OKAY.
BARK
AROO...
BARK
AROO...
BARK
BARK
BARK
THEY'RE JUST DOGS...AND THEY DON'T SEEM TOO INTERESTED IN US.
EVEN IF THEY DID COME SNIFFING AROUND...
...I'M NOT GOING TO LET THEM HURT YOU--
KABLAM

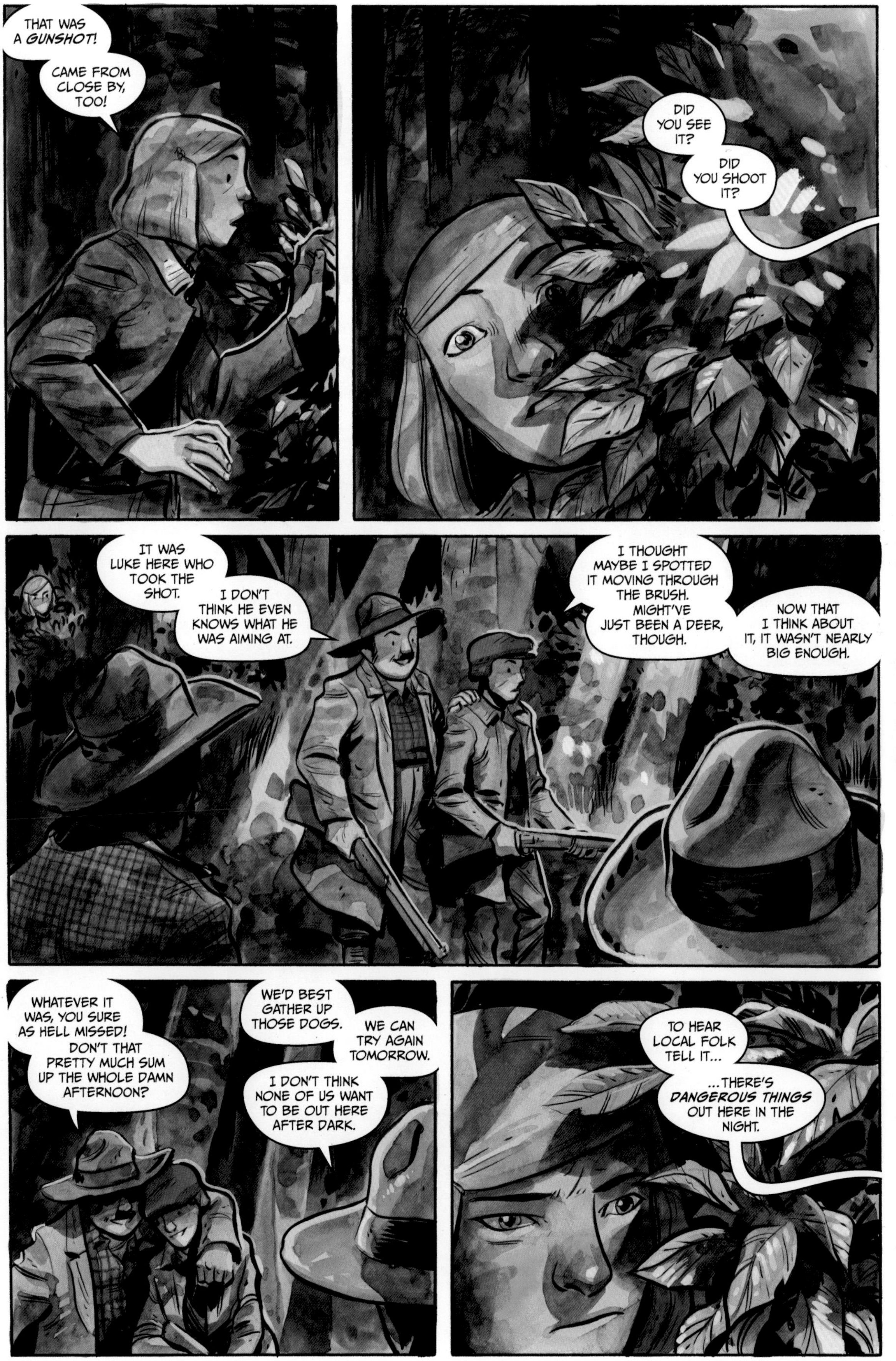
THAT WAS A *GUNSHOT*!
CAME FROM CLOSE BY, TOO!
DID YOU SEE IT?
DID YOU SHOOT IT?
IT WAS LUKE HERE WHO TOOK THE SHOT.
I DON'T THINK HE EVEN KNOWS WHAT HE WAS AIMING AT.
I THOUGHT MAYBE I SPOTTED IT MOVING THROUGH THE BRUSH. MIGHT'VE JUST BEEN A DEER, THOUGH.
NOW THAT I THINK ABOUT IT, IT WASN'T NEARLY BIG ENOUGH.
WHATEVER IT WAS, YOU SURE AS HELL MISSED!
DON'T THAT PRETTY MUCH SUM UP THE WHOLE DAMN AFTERNOON?
WE'D BEST GATHER UP THOSE DOGS.
WE CAN TRY AGAIN TOMORROW.
I DON'T THINK NONE OF US WANT TO BE OUT HERE AFTER DARK.
TO HEAR LOCAL FOLK TELL IT...
...THERE'S *DANGEROUS THINGS* OUT HERE IN THE NIGHT.

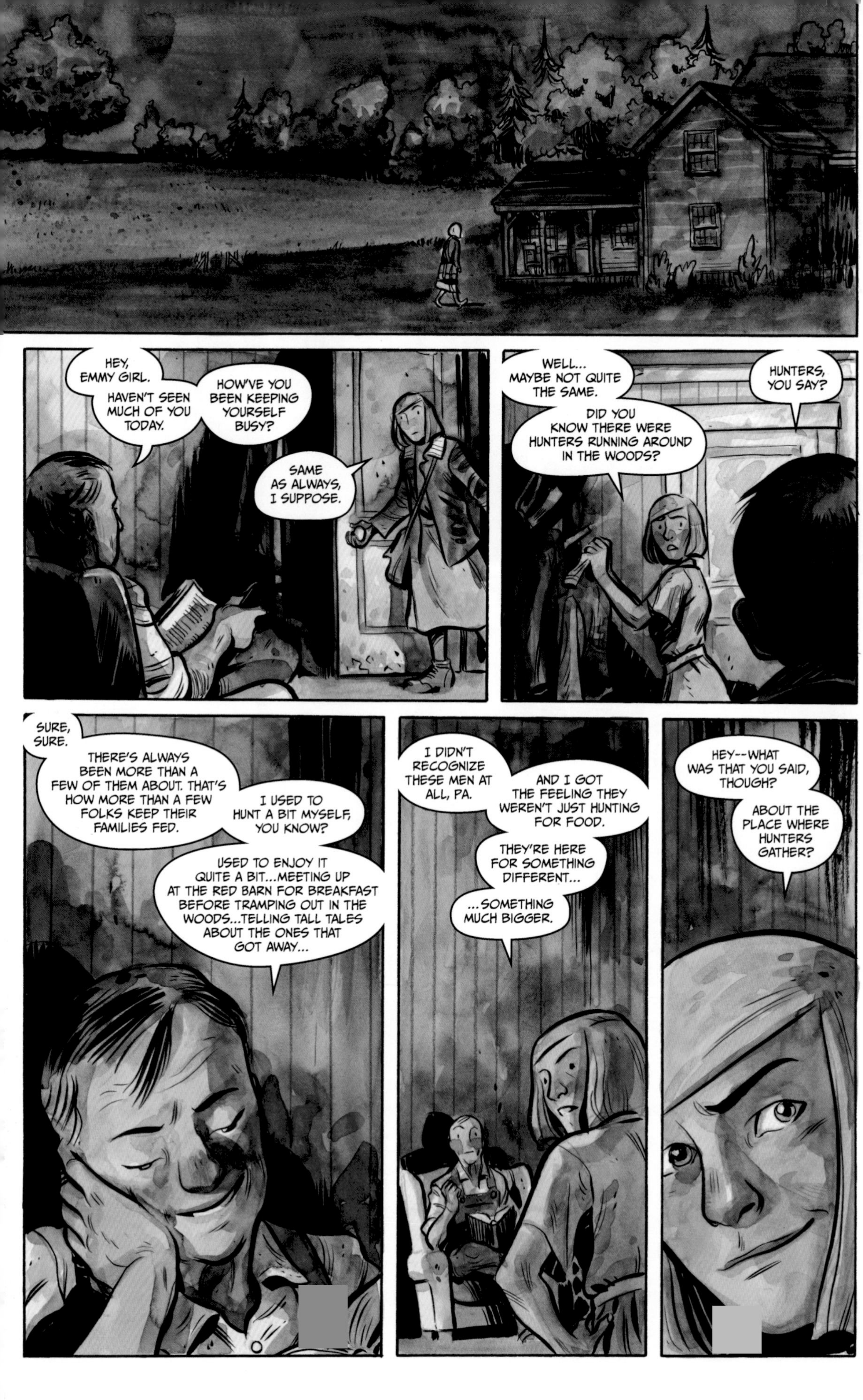
HEY, EMMY GIRL.
HAVEN'T SEEN MUCH OF YOU TODAY.
HOW'VE YOU BEEN KEEPING YOURSELF BUSY?
SAME AS ALWAYS, I SUPPOSE.
WELL... MAYBE NOT QUITE THE SAME.
DID YOU KNOW THERE WERE HUNTERS RUNNING AROUND IN THE WOODS?
HUNTERS, YOU SAY?
SURE, SURE.
THERE'S ALWAYS BEEN MORE THAN A FEW OF THEM ABOUT. THAT'S HOW MORE THAN A FEW FOLKS KEEP THEIR FAMILIES FED.
I USED TO HUNT A BIT MYSELF, YOU KNOW?
USED TO ENJOY IT QUITE A BIT...MEETING UP AT THE RED BARN FOR BREAKFAST BEFORE TRAMPING OUT IN THE WOODS...TELLING TALL TALES ABOUT THE ONES THAT GOT AWAY...
I DIDN'T RECOGNIZE THESE MEN AT ALL, PA.
AND I GOT THE FEELING THEY WEREN'T JUST HUNTING FOR FOOD.
THEY'RE HERE FOR SOMETHING DIFFERENT...
...SOMETHING MUCH BIGGER.
HEY--WHAT WAS THAT YOU SAID, THOUGH?
ABOUT THE PLACE WHERE HUNTERS GATHER?

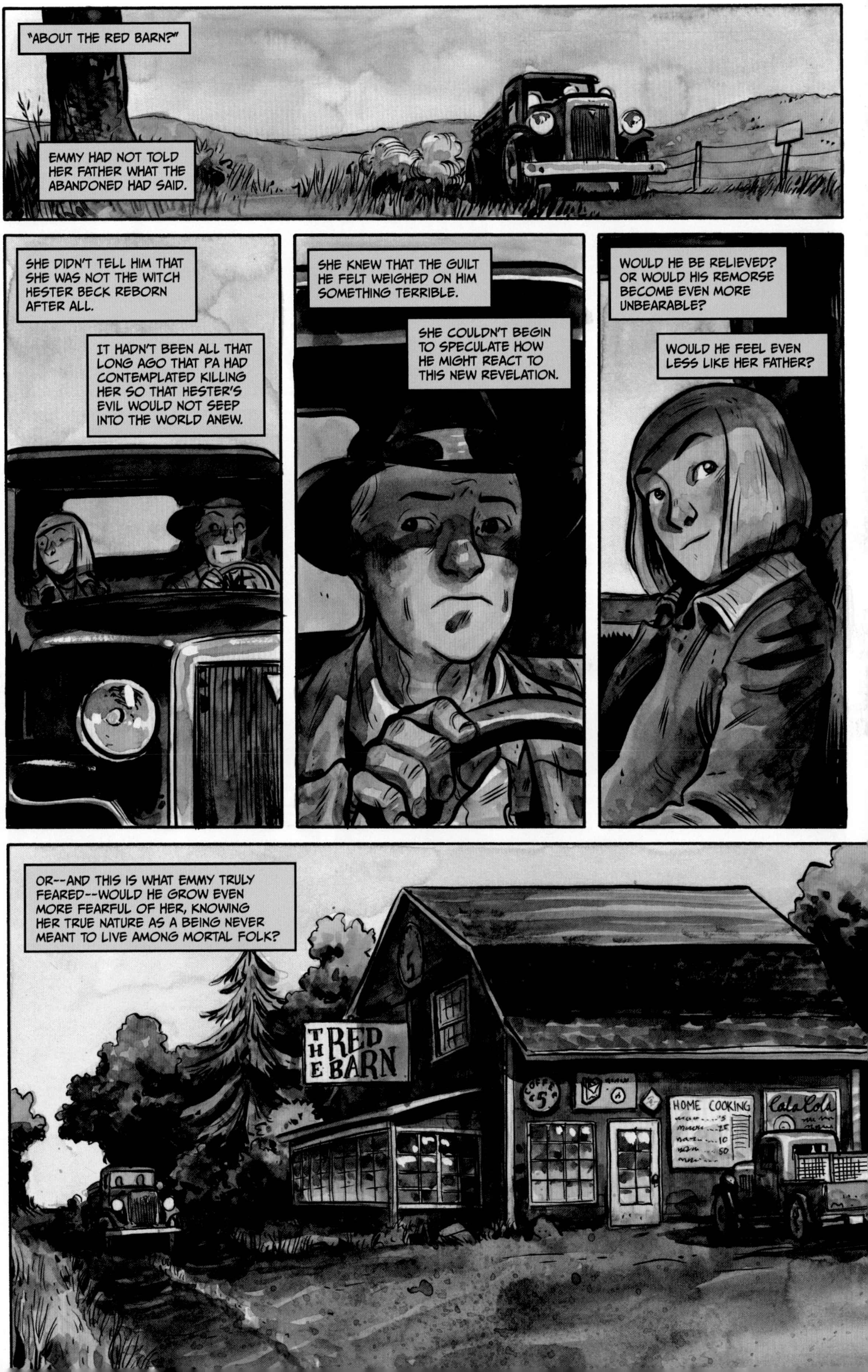
"ABOUT THE RED BARN?"
EMMY HAD NOT TOLD HER FATHER WHAT THE ABANDONED HAD SAID.
SHE DIDN'T TELL HIM THAT SHE WAS NOT THE WITCH HESTER BECK REBORN AFTER ALL.
IT HADN'T BEEN ALL THAT LONG AGO THAT PA HAD CONTEMPLATED KILLING HER SO THAT HESTER'S EVIL WOULD NOT SEEP INTO THE WORLD ANEW.
SHE KNEW THAT THE GUILT HE FELT WEIGHED ON HIM SOMETHING TERRIBLE.
SHE COULDN'T BEGIN TO SPECULATE HOW HE MIGHT REACT TO THIS NEW REVELATION.
WOULD HE BE RELIEVED? OR WOULD HIS REMORSE BECOME EVEN MORE UNBEARABLE?
WOULD HE FEEL EVEN LESS LIKE HER FATHER?
OR--AND THIS IS WHAT EMMY TRULY FEARED--WOULD HE GROW EVEN MORE FEARFUL OF HER, KNOWING HER TRUE NATURE AS A BEING NEVER MEANT TO LIVE AMONG MORTAL FOLK?
THE RED BARN
HOME COOKING

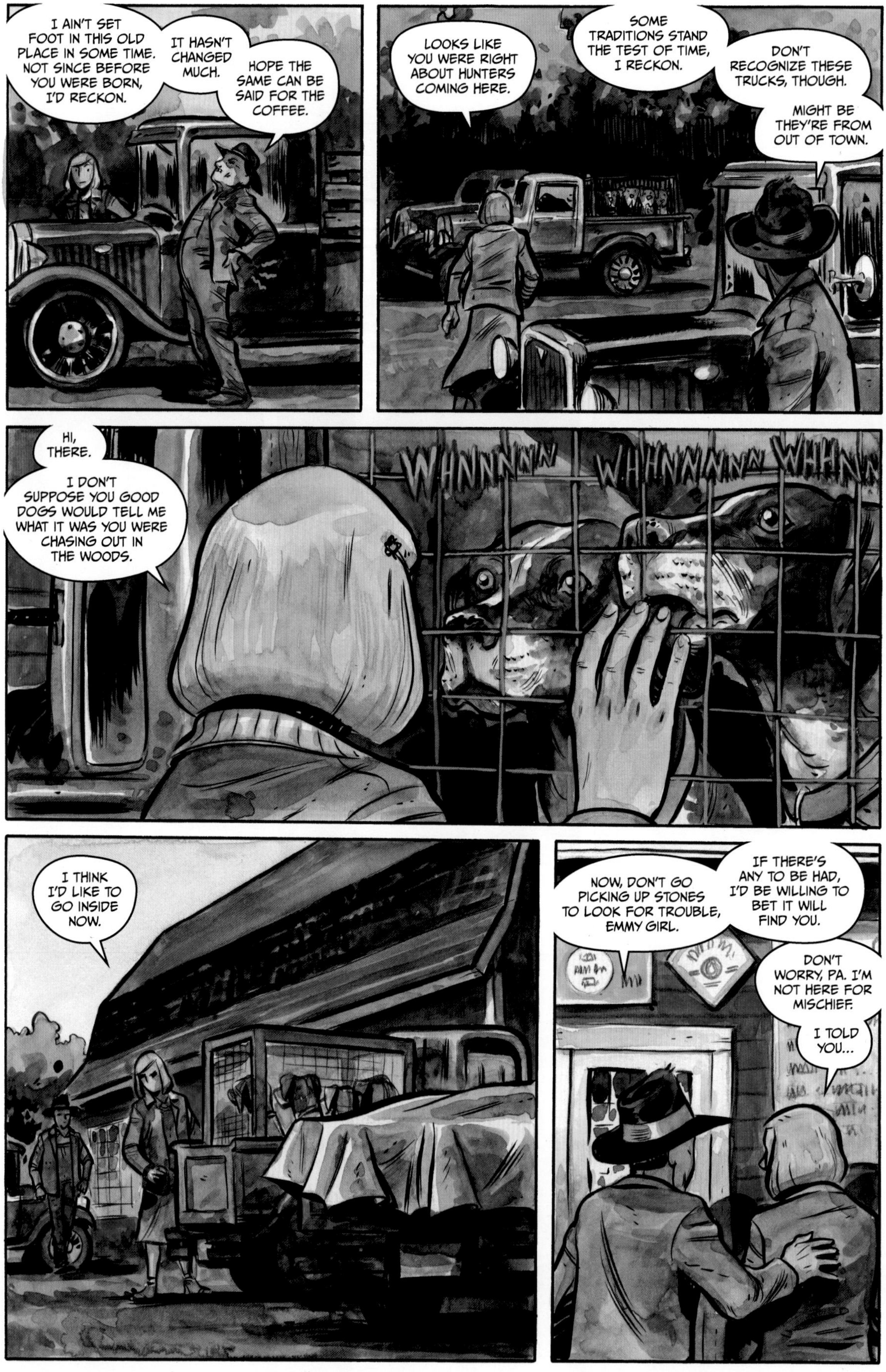
I AIN'T SET FOOT IN THIS OLD PLACE IN SOME TIME. NOT SINCE BEFORE YOU WERE BORN, I'D RECKON.
IT HASN'T CHANGED MUCH.
HOPE THE SAME CAN BE SAID FOR THE COFFEE.
LOOKS LIKE YOU WERE RIGHT ABOUT HUNTERS COMING HERE.
SOME TRADITIONS STAND THE TEST OF TIME, I RECKON.
DON'T RECOGNIZE THESE TRUCKS, THOUGH.
MIGHT BE THEY'RE FROM OUT OF TOWN.
HI, THERE.
I DON'T SUPPOSE YOU GOOD DOGS WOULD TELL ME WHAT IT WAS YOU WERE CHASING OUT IN THE WOODS.
WHNNNNN WHNNNNNN WHHN
I THINK I'D LIKE TO GO INSIDE NOW.
NOW, DON'T GO PICKING UP STONES TO LOOK FOR TROUBLE, EMMY GIRL.
IF THERE'S ANY TO BE HAD, I'D BE WILLING TO BET IT WILL FIND YOU.
DON'T WORRY, PA. I'M NOT HERE FOR MISCHIEF.
I TOLD YOU...

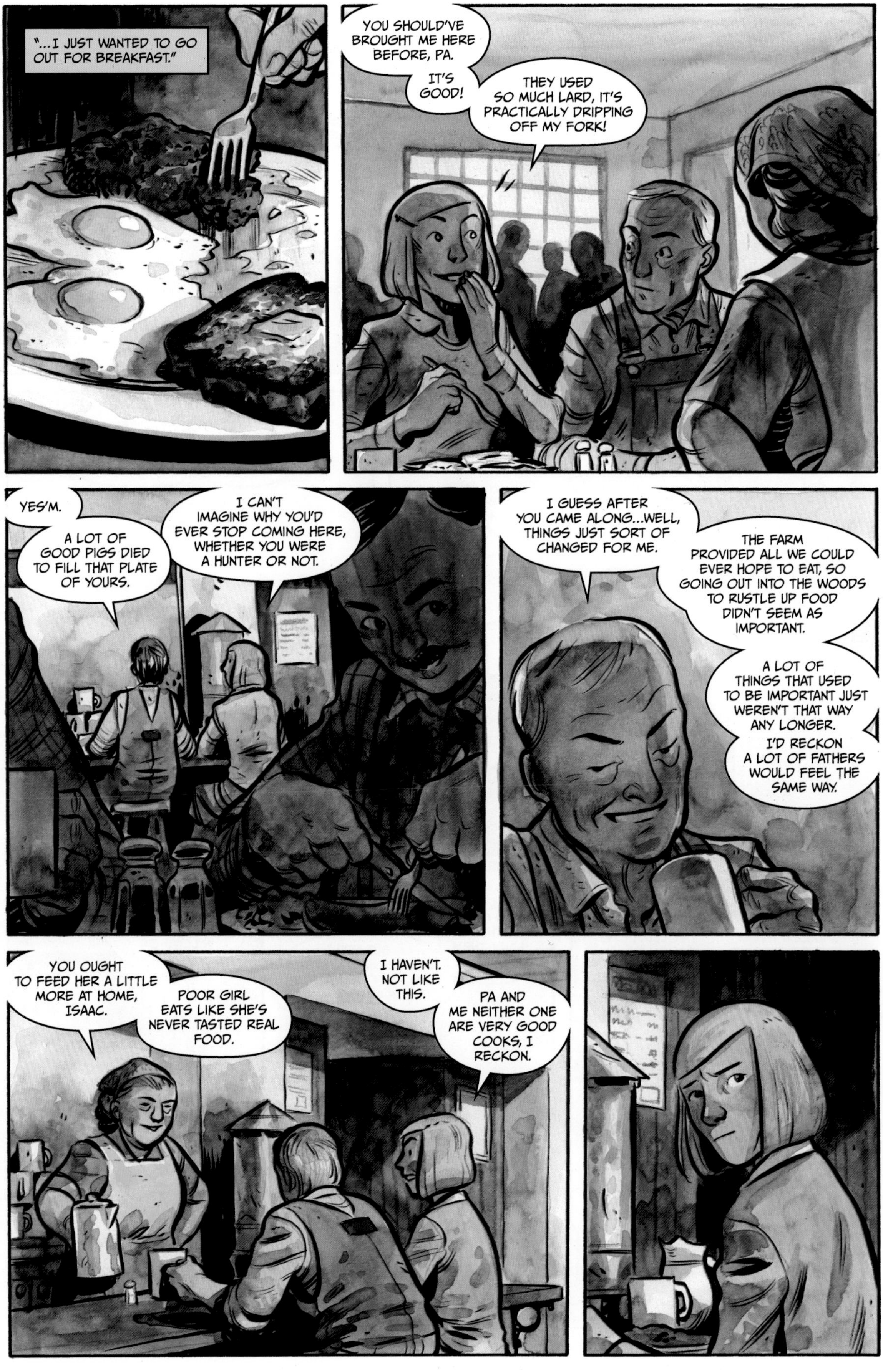
"...I JUST WANTED TO GO OUT FOR BREAKFAST."
YOU SHOULD'VE BROUGHT ME HERE BEFORE, PA.
IT'S GOOD!
THEY USED SO MUCH LARD, IT'S PRACTICALLY DRIPPING OFF MY FORK!
YES'M.
A LOT OF GOOD PIGS DIED TO FILL THAT PLATE OF YOURS.
I CAN'T IMAGINE WHY YOU'D EVER STOP COMING HERE, WHETHER YOU WERE A HUNTER OR NOT.
I GUESS AFTER YOU CAME ALONG...WELL, THINGS JUST SORT OF CHANGED FOR ME.
THE FARM PROVIDED ALL WE COULD EVER HOPE TO EAT, SO GOING OUT INTO THE WOODS TO RUSTLE UP FOOD DIDN'T SEEM AS IMPORTANT.
A LOT OF THINGS THAT USED TO BE IMPORTANT JUST WEREN'T THAT WAY ANY LONGER.
I'D RECKON A LOT OF FATHERS WOULD FEEL THE SAME WAY.
YOU OUGHT TO FEED HER A LITTLE MORE AT HOME, ISAAC.
POOR GIRL EATS LIKE SHE'S NEVER TASTED REAL FOOD.
I HAVEN'T. NOT LIKE THIS.
PA AND ME NEITHER ONE ARE VERY GOOD COOKS, I RECKON.

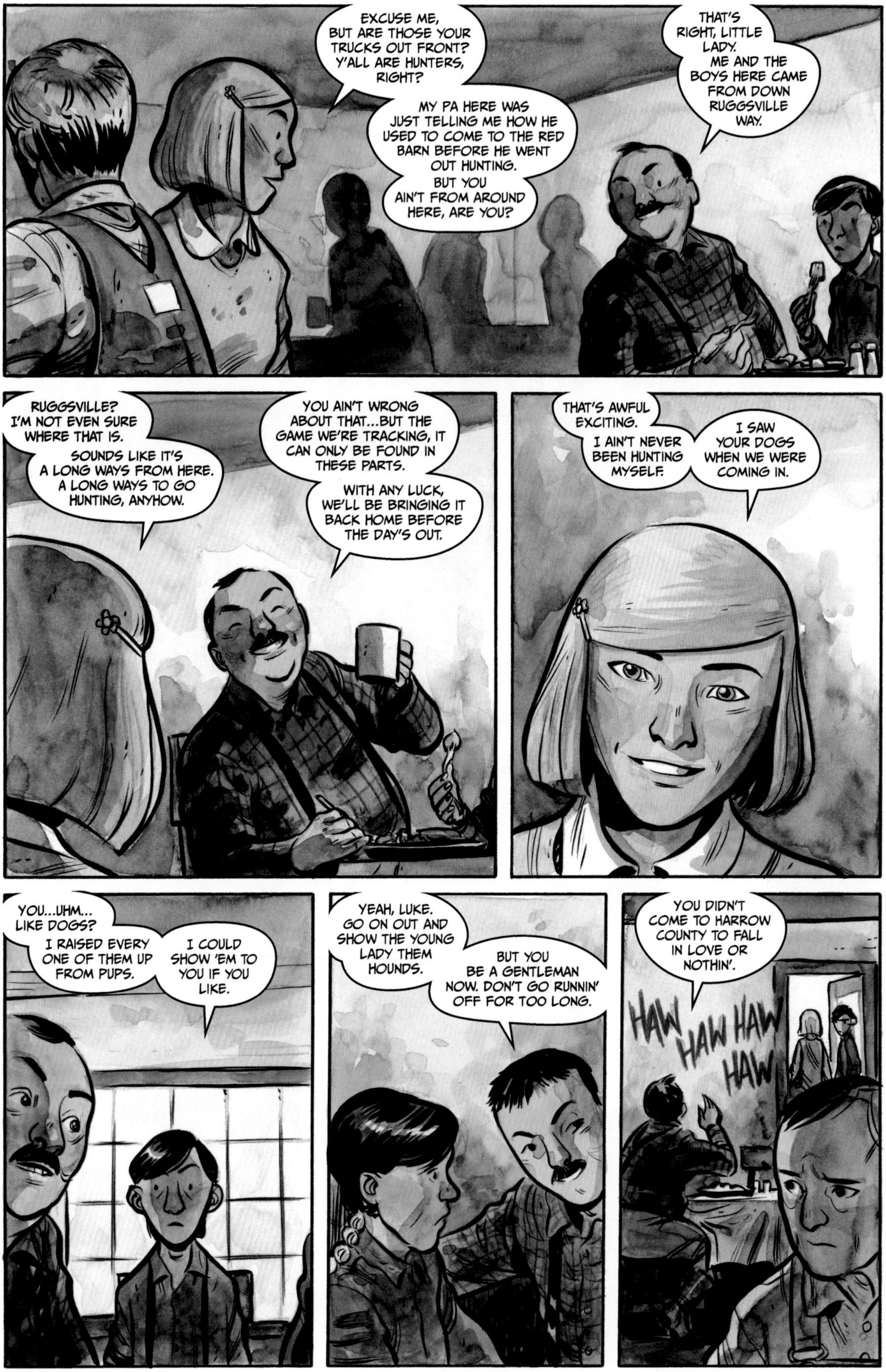
EXCUSE ME, BUT ARE THOSE YOUR TRUCKS OUT FRONT? Y'ALL ARE HUNTERS, RIGHT?
MY PA HERE WAS JUST TELLING ME HOW HE USED TO COME TO THE RED BARN BEFORE HE WENT OUT HUNTING.
BUT YOU AIN'T FROM AROUND HERE, ARE YOU?
THAT'S RIGHT, LITTLE LADY.
ME AND THE BOYS HERE CAME FROM DOWN RUGGSVILLE WAY.
RUGGSVILLE? I'M NOT EVEN SURE WHERE THAT IS.
SOUNDS LIKE IT'S A LONG WAYS FROM HERE. A LONG WAYS TO GO HUNTING, ANYHOW.
YOU AIN'T WRONG ABOUT THAT...BUT THE GAME WE'RE TRACKING, IT CAN ONLY BE FOUND IN THESE PARTS.
WITH ANY LUCK, WE'LL BE BRINGING IT BACK HOME BEFORE THE DAY'S OUT.
THAT'S AWFUL EXCITING.
I AIN'T NEVER BEEN HUNTING MYSELF.
I SAW YOUR DOGS WHEN WE WERE COMING IN.
YOU...UHM... LIKE DOGS?
I RAISED EVERY ONE OF THEM UP FROM PUPS.
I COULD SHOW 'EM TO YOU IF YOU LIKE.
YEAH, LUKE. GO ON OUT AND SHOW THE YOUNG LADY THEM HOUNDS.
BUT YOU BE A GENTLEMAN NOW. DON'T GO RUNNIN' OFF FOR TOO LONG.
YOU DIDN'T COME TO HARROW COUNTY TO FALL IN LOVE OR NOTHIN'.
HAW HAW HAW HAW

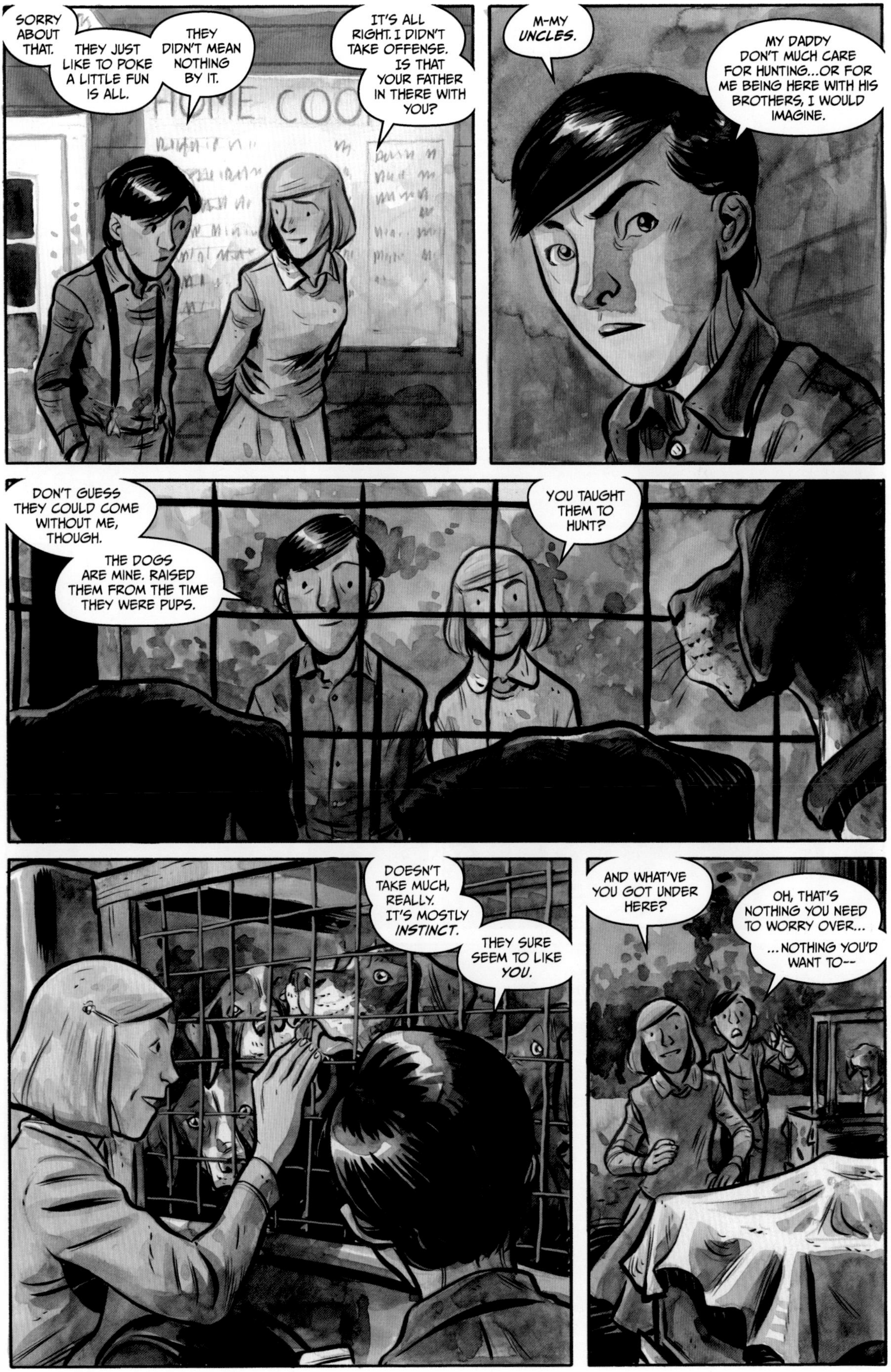
SORRY ABOUT THAT.
THEY JUST LIKE TO POKE A LITTLE FUN IS ALL.
THEY DIDN'T MEAN NOTHING BY IT.
HOME COO
IT'S ALL RIGHT. I DIDN'T TAKE OFFENSE.
IS THAT YOUR FATHER IN THERE WITH YOU?
M-MY *UNCLES*.
MY DADDY DON'T MUCH CARE FOR HUNTING...OR FOR ME BEING HERE WITH HIS BROTHERS, I WOULD IMAGINE.
DON'T GUESS THEY COULD COME WITHOUT ME, THOUGH.
THE DOGS ARE MINE. RAISED THEM FROM THE TIME THEY WERE PUPS.
YOU TAUGHT THEM TO HUNT?
DOESN'T TAKE MUCH, REALLY.
IT'S MOSTLY *INSTINCT*.
THEY SURE SEEM TO LIKE *YOU*.
AND WHAT'VE YOU GOT UNDER HERE?
OH, THAT'S NOTHING YOU NEED TO WORRY OVER...
...NOTHING YOU'D WANT TO--

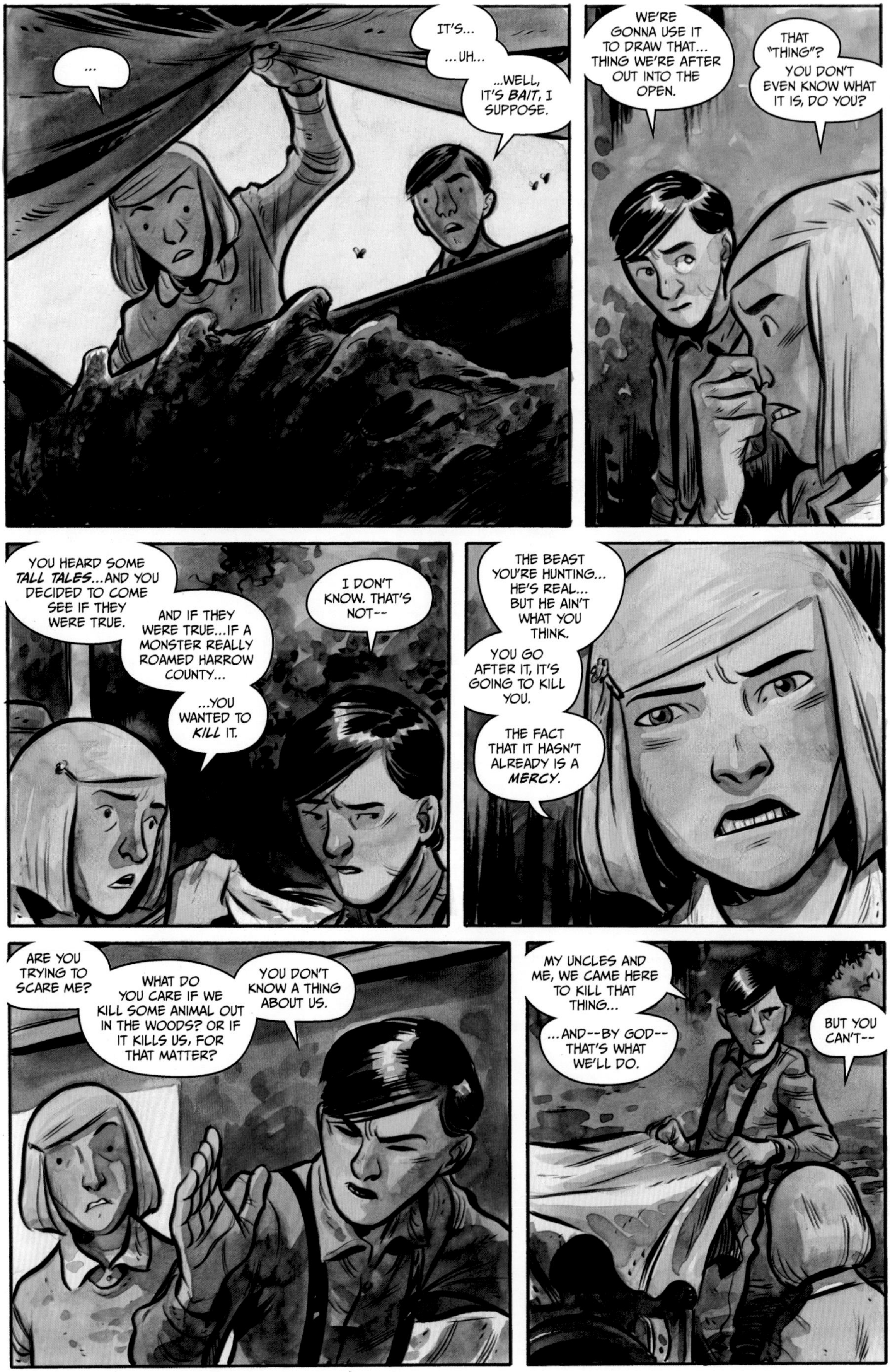
...
IT'S...
...UH...
...WELL, IT'S BAIT, I SUPPOSE.
WE'RE GONNA USE IT TO DRAW THAT... THING WE'RE AFTER OUT INTO THE OPEN.
THAT "THING"? YOU DON'T EVEN KNOW WHAT IT IS, DO YOU?
YOU HEARD SOME TALL TALES...AND YOU DECIDED TO COME SEE IF THEY WERE TRUE.
AND IF THEY WERE TRUE...IF A MONSTER REALLY ROAMED HARROW COUNTY...
...YOU WANTED TO KILL IT.
I DON'T KNOW. THAT'S NOT--
THE BEAST YOU'RE HUNTING... HE'S REAL... BUT HE AIN'T WHAT YOU THINK.
YOU GO AFTER IT, IT'S GOING TO KILL YOU.
THE FACT THAT IT HASN'T ALREADY IS A MERCY.
ARE YOU TRYING TO SCARE ME?
WHAT DO YOU CARE IF WE KILL SOME ANIMAL OUT IN THE WOODS? OR IF IT KILLS US, FOR THAT MATTER?
YOU DON'T KNOW A THING ABOUT US.
MY UNCLES AND ME, WE CAME HERE TO KILL THAT THING...
...AND--BY GOD--THAT'S WHAT WE'LL DO.
BUT YOU CAN'T--

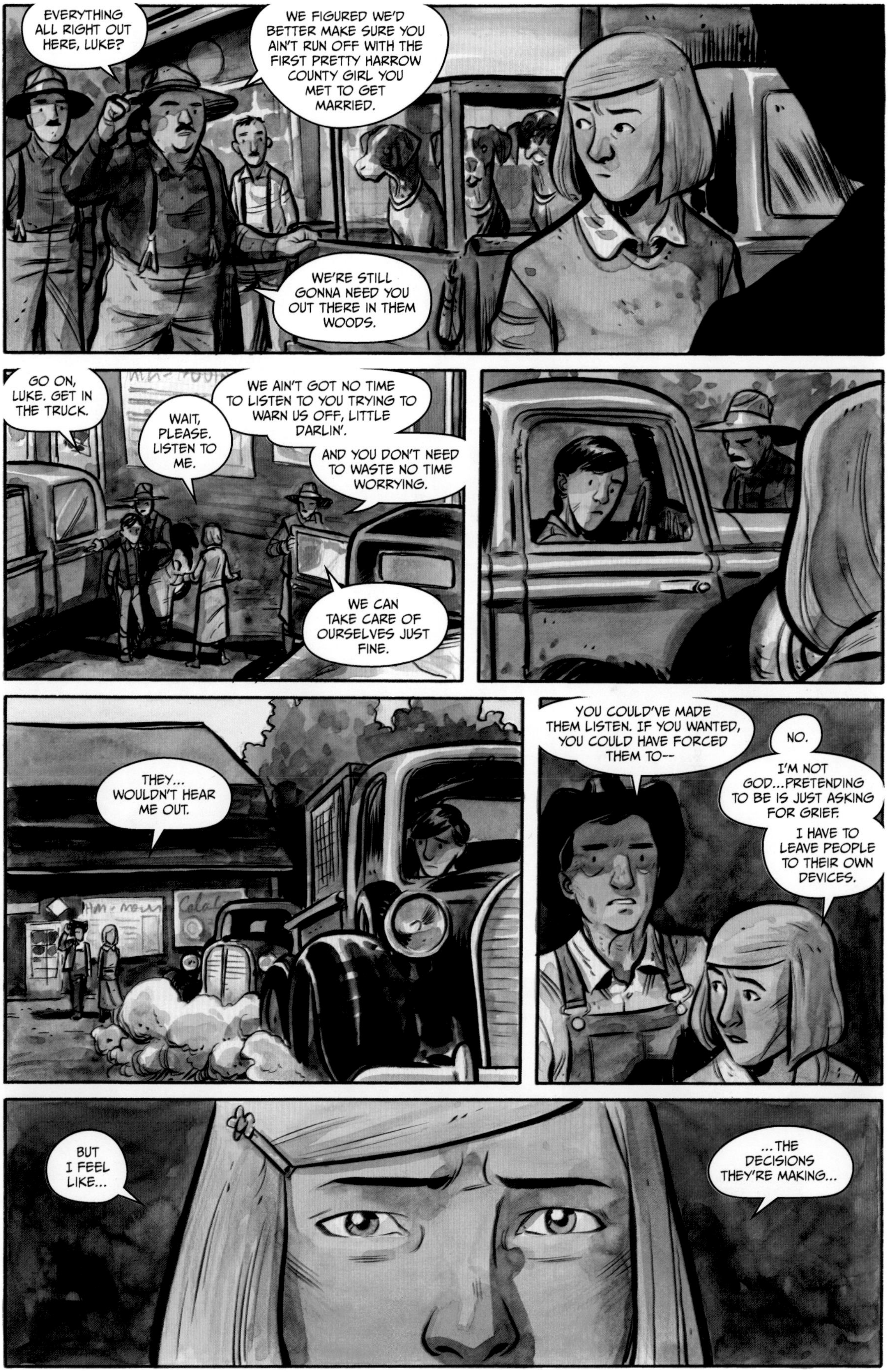
EVERYTHING ALL RIGHT OUT HERE, LUKE?
WE FIGURED WE'D BETTER MAKE SURE YOU AIN'T RUN OFF WITH THE FIRST PRETTY HARROW COUNTY GIRL YOU MET TO GET MARRIED.
WE'RE STILL GONNA NEED YOU OUT THERE IN THEM WOODS.
GO ON, LUKE. GET IN THE TRUCK.
WAIT, PLEASE. LISTEN TO ME.
WE AIN'T GOT NO TIME TO LISTEN TO YOU TRYING TO WARN US OFF, LITTLE DARLIN'.
AND YOU DON'T NEED TO WASTE NO TIME WORRYING.
WE CAN TAKE CARE OF OURSELVES JUST FINE.
THEY... WOULDN'T HEAR ME OUT.
YOU COULD'VE MADE THEM LISTEN. IF YOU WANTED, YOU COULD HAVE FORCED THEM TO--
NO.
I'M NOT GOD...PRETENDING TO BE IS JUST ASKING FOR GRIEF.
I HAVE TO LEAVE PEOPLE TO THEIR OWN DEVICES.
BUT I FEEL LIKE...
...THE DECISIONS THEY'RE MAKING...

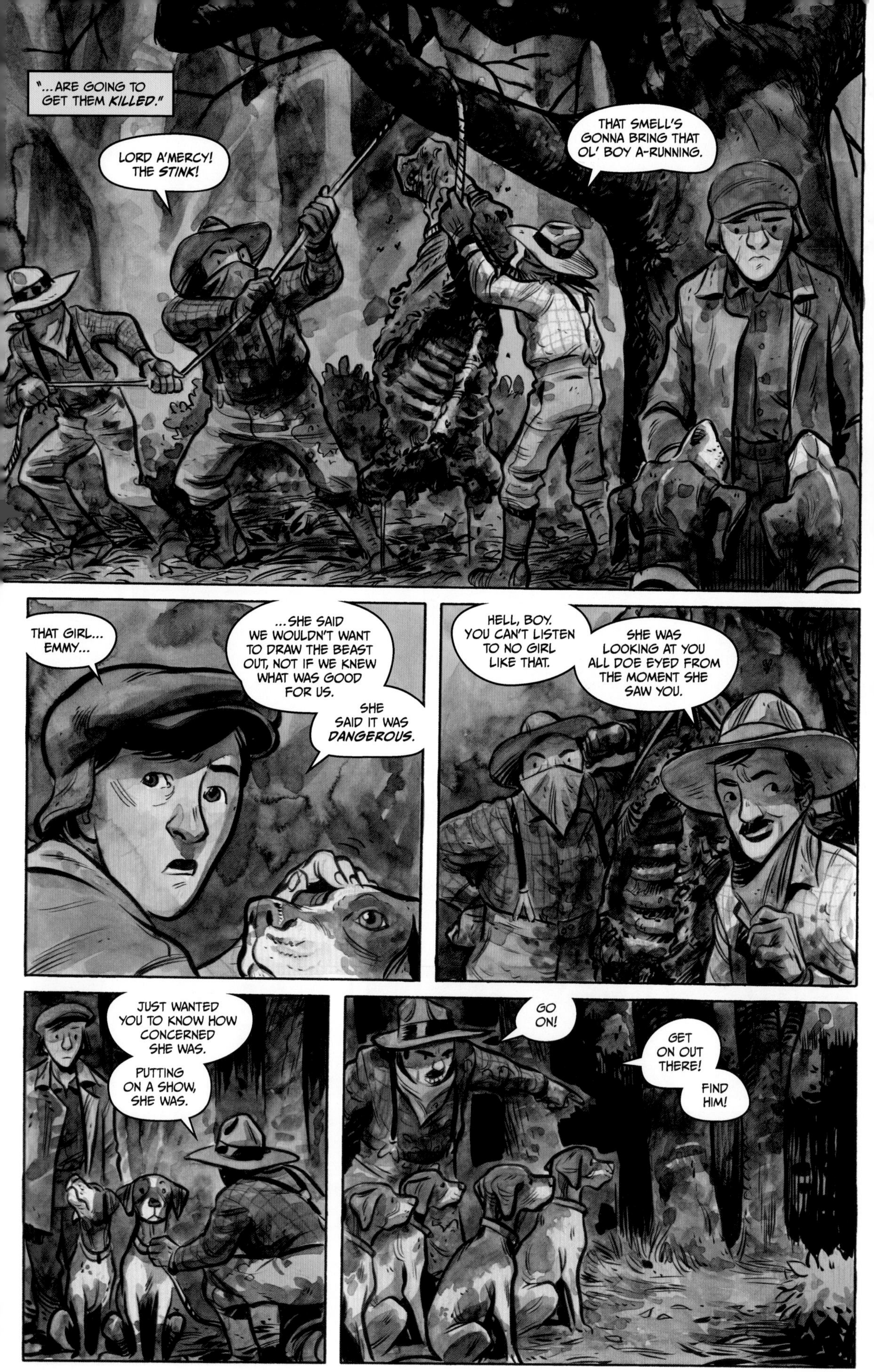
"...ARE GOING TO GET THEM *KILLED*."
LORD A'MERCY! THE *STINK*!
THAT SMELL'S GONNA BRING THAT OL' BOY A-RUNNING.
THAT GIRL... EMMY...
...SHE SAID WE WOULDN'T WANT TO DRAW THE BEAST OUT, NOT IF WE KNEW WHAT WAS GOOD FOR US.
SHE SAID IT WAS *DANGEROUS*.
HELL, BOY. YOU CAN'T LISTEN TO NO GIRL LIKE THAT.
SHE WAS LOOKING AT YOU ALL DOE EYED FROM THE MOMENT SHE SAW YOU.
JUST WANTED YOU TO KNOW HOW CONCERNED SHE WAS.
PUTTING ON A SHOW, SHE WAS.
GO ON!
GET ON OUT THERE!
FIND HIM!

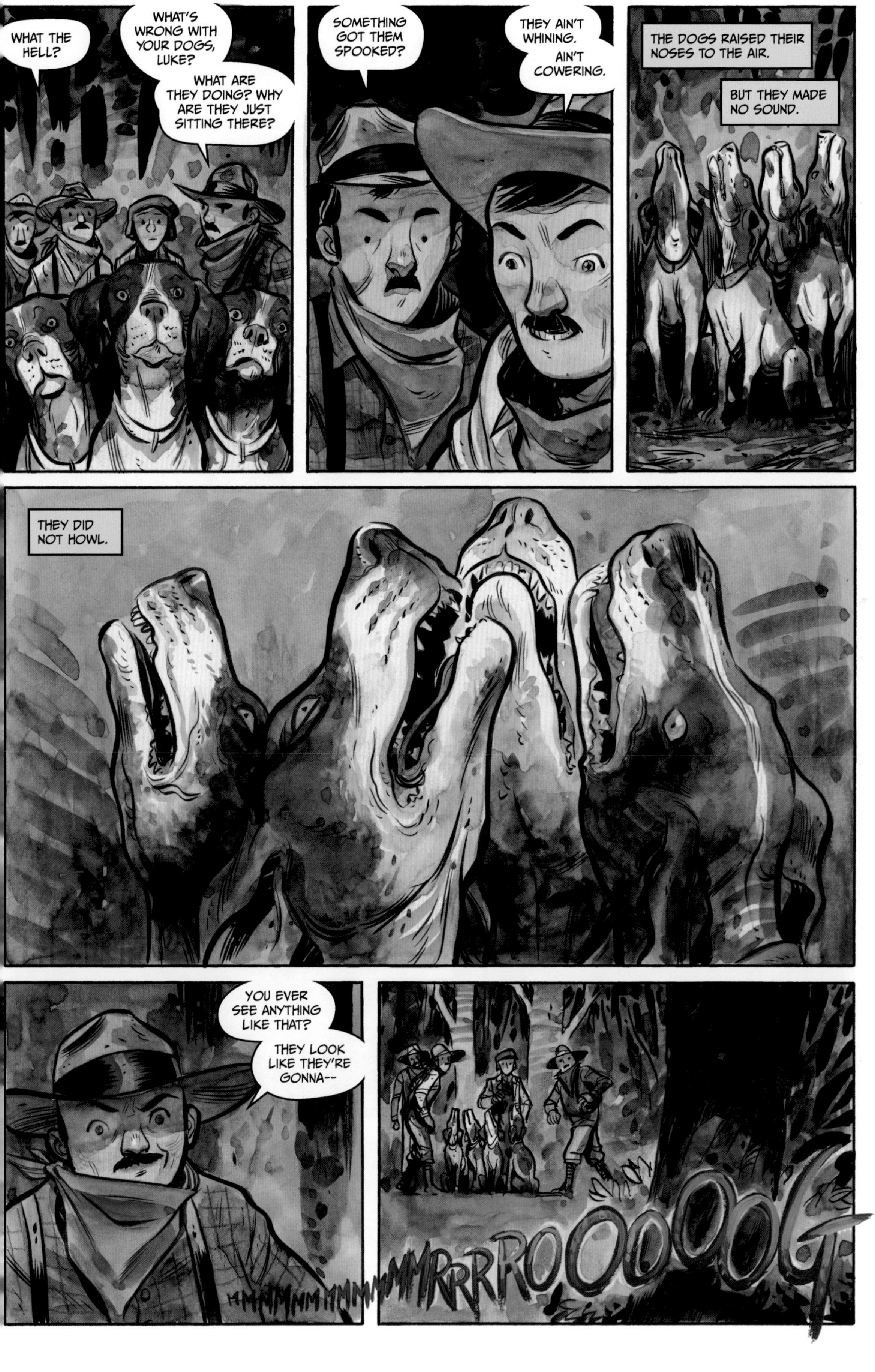
WHAT THE HELL?
WHAT'S WRONG WITH YOUR DOGS, LUKE?
WHAT ARE THEY DOING? WHY ARE THEY JUST SITTING THERE?
SOMETHING GOT THEM SPOOKED?
THEY AIN'T WHINING.
AIN'T COWERING.
THE DOGS RAISED THEIR NOSES TO THE AIR.
BUT THEY MADE NO SOUND.
THEY DID NOT HOWL.
YOU EVER SEE ANYTHING LIKE THAT?
THEY LOOK LIKE THEY'RE GONNA--
MMMMMMMMMMMMMMRRRROOOOOOG

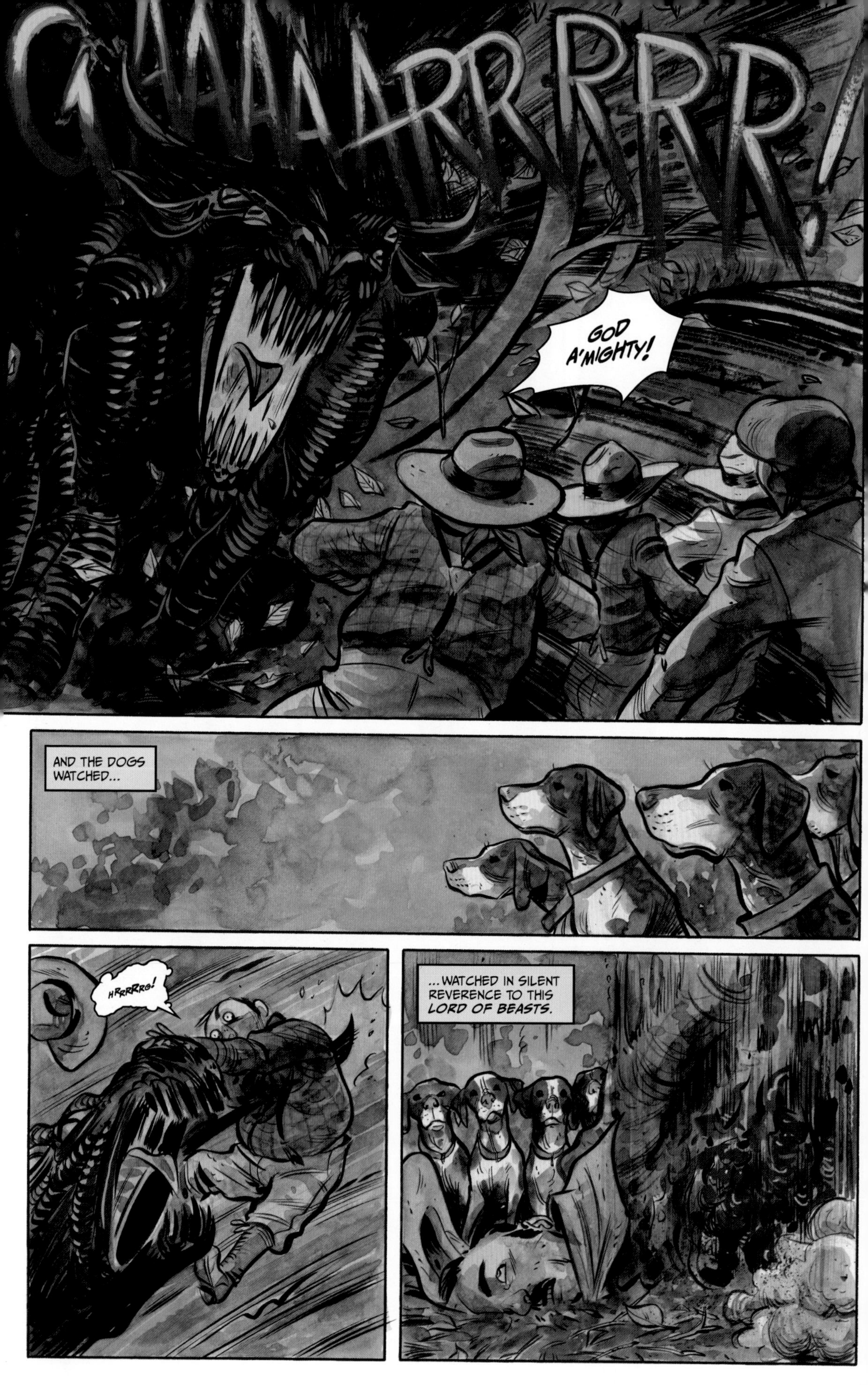
GAAAARRRRRRR!
GOD A'MIGHTY!
AND THE DOGS WATCHED...
HRRRRRG!
...WATCHED IN SILENT REVERENCE TO THIS LORD OF BEASTS.

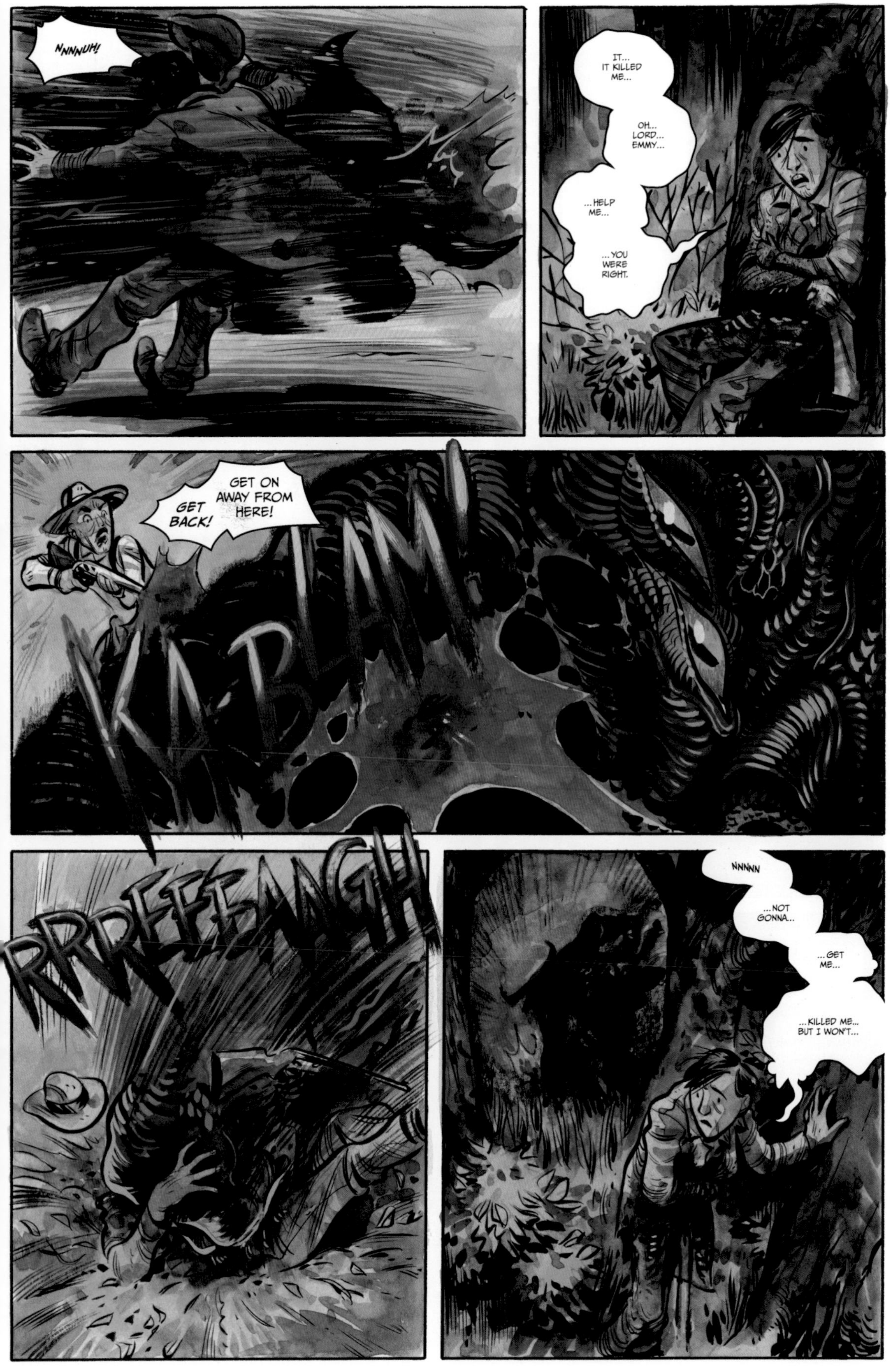
NNNNUH!
IT... IT KILLED ME...
OH... LORD... EMMY...
...HELP ME...
...YOU WERE RIGHT.
GET BACK!
GET ON AWAY FROM HERE!
KA-BLAM!
RRREEEAAAGH
NNNNN
...NOT GONNA...
...GET ME...
...KILLED ME... BUT I WON'T...

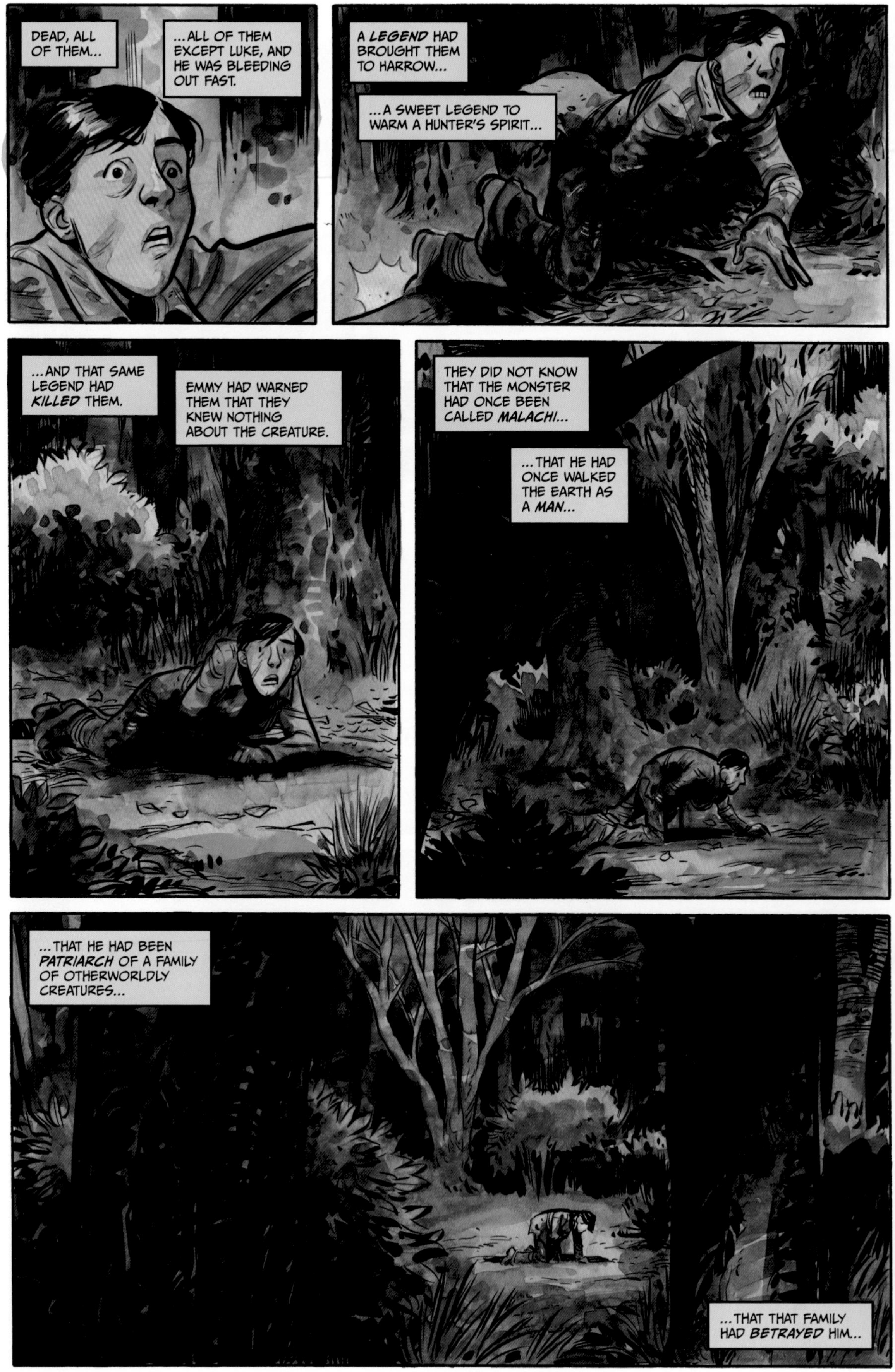
DEAD, ALL OF THEM...
...ALL OF THEM EXCEPT LUKE, AND HE WAS BLEEDING OUT FAST.
A LEGEND HAD BROUGHT THEM TO HARROW...
...A SWEET LEGEND TO WARM A HUNTER'S SPIRIT...
...AND THAT SAME LEGEND HAD KILLED THEM.
EMMY HAD WARNED THEM THAT THEY KNEW NOTHING ABOUT THE CREATURE.
THEY DID NOT KNOW THAT THE MONSTER HAD ONCE BEEN CALLED MALACHI...
...THAT HE HAD ONCE WALKED THE EARTH AS A MAN...
...THAT HE HAD BEEN PATRIARCH OF A FAMILY OF OTHERWORLDLY CREATURES...
...THAT THAT FAMILY HAD BETRAYED HIM...

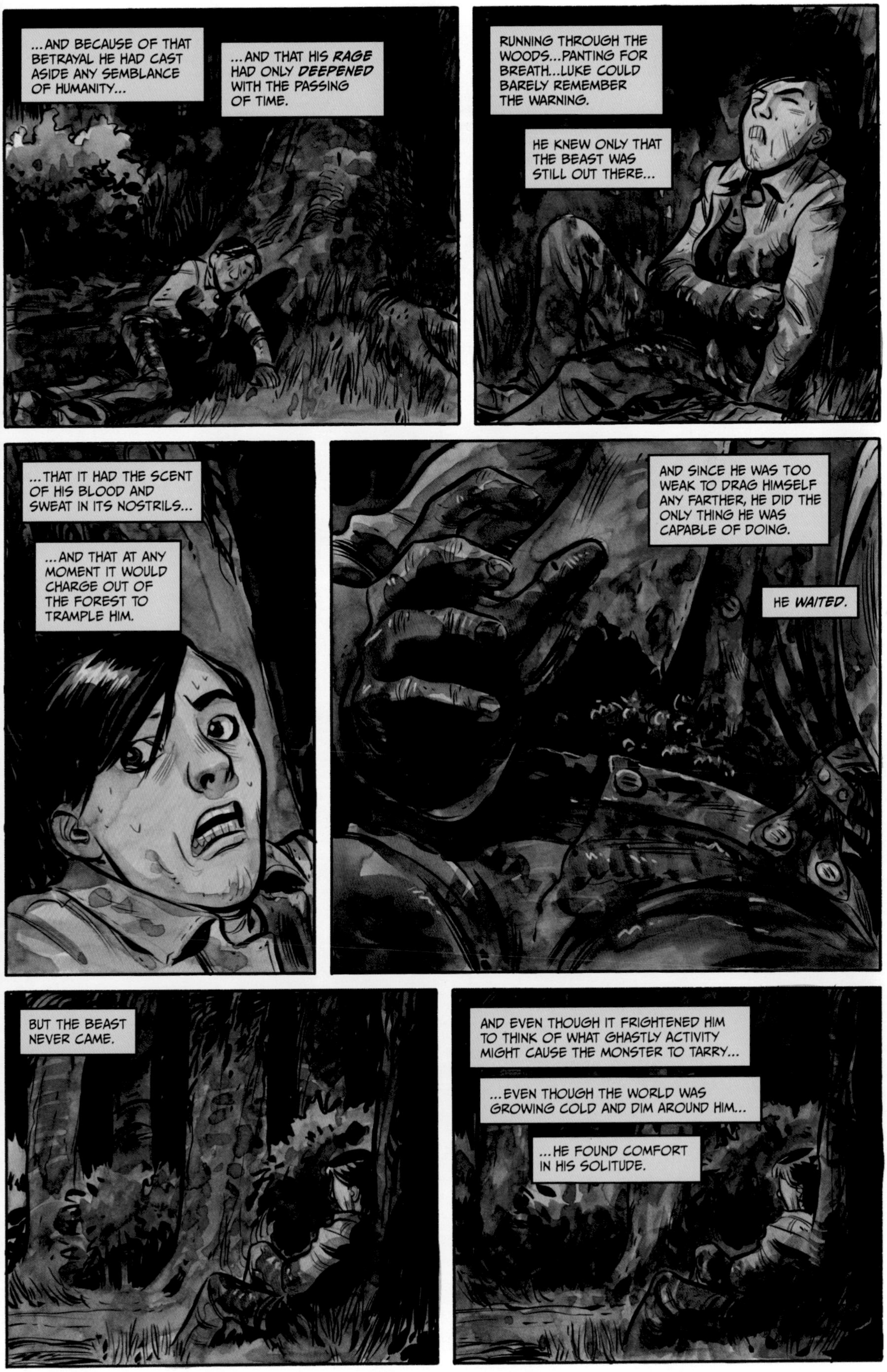
...AND BECAUSE OF THAT BETRAYAL HE HAD CAST ASIDE ANY SEMBLANCE OF HUMANITY...
...AND THAT HIS *RAGE* HAD ONLY *DEEPENED* WITH THE PASSING OF TIME.
RUNNING THROUGH THE WOODS...PANTING FOR BREATH...LUKE COULD BARELY REMEMBER THE WARNING.
HE KNEW ONLY THAT THE BEAST WAS STILL OUT THERE...
...THAT IT HAD THE SCENT OF HIS BLOOD AND SWEAT IN ITS NOSTRILS...
...AND THAT AT ANY MOMENT IT WOULD CHARGE OUT OF THE FOREST TO TRAMPLE HIM.
AND SINCE HE WAS TOO WEAK TO DRAG HIMSELF ANY FARTHER, HE DID THE ONLY THING HE WAS CAPABLE OF DOING.
HE *WAITED.*
BUT THE BEAST NEVER CAME.
AND EVEN THOUGH IT FRIGHTENED HIM TO THINK OF WHAT GHASTLY ACTIVITY MIGHT CAUSE THE MONSTER TO TARRY...
...EVEN THOUGH THE WORLD WAS GROWING COLD AND DIM AROUND HIM...
...HE FOUND COMFORT IN HIS SOLITUDE.

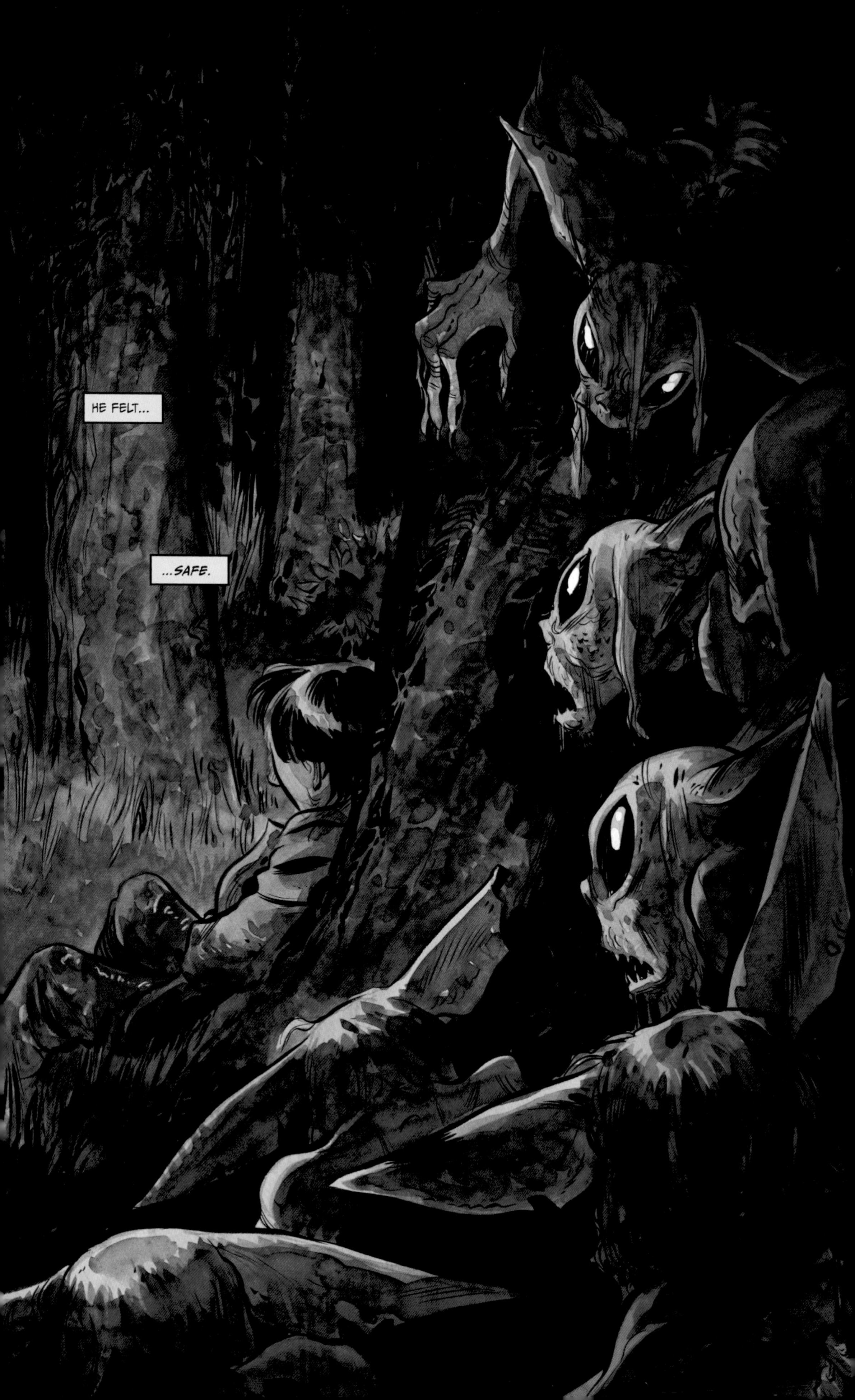
HE FELT...
...SAFE.

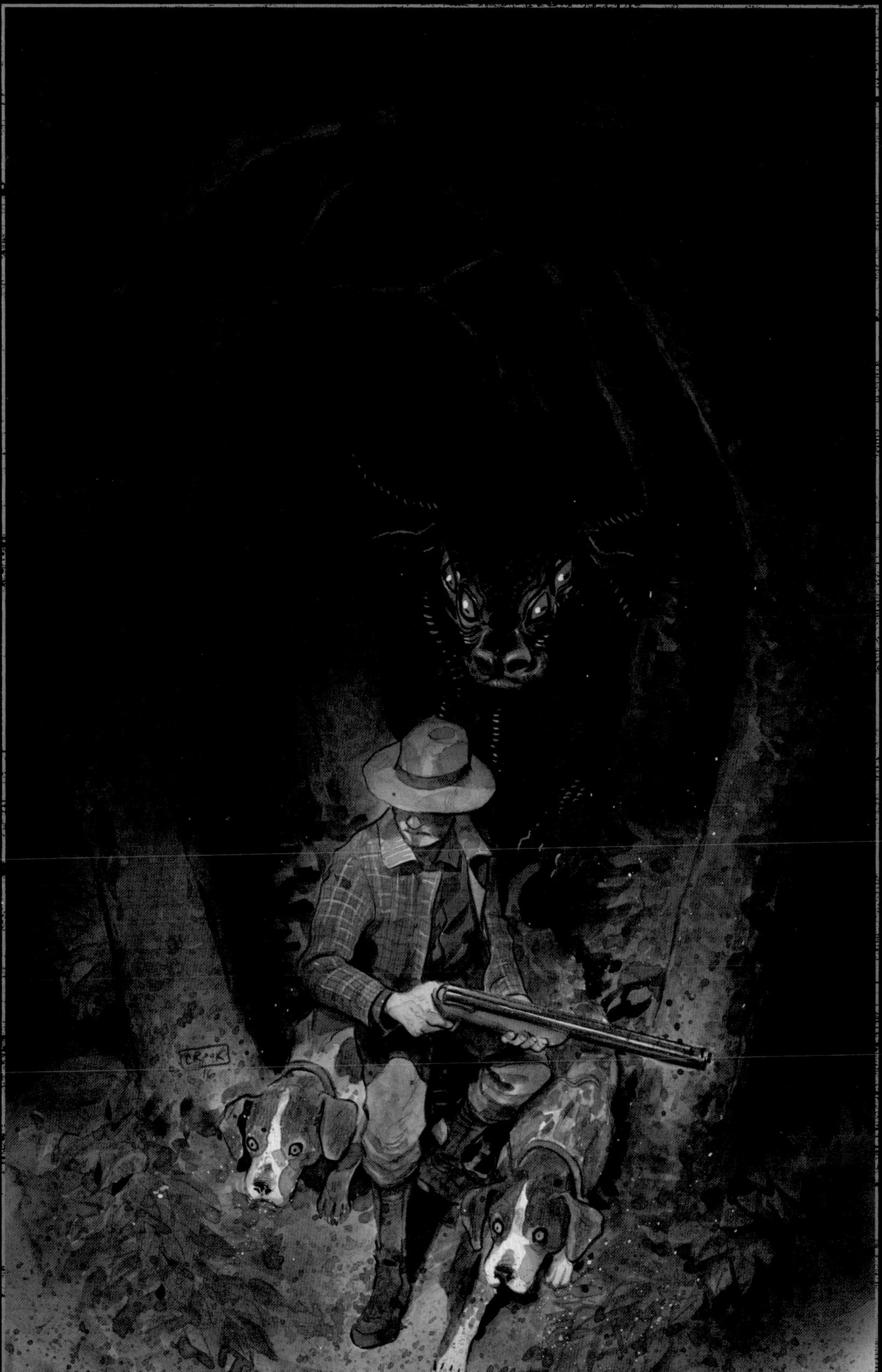

FOUR

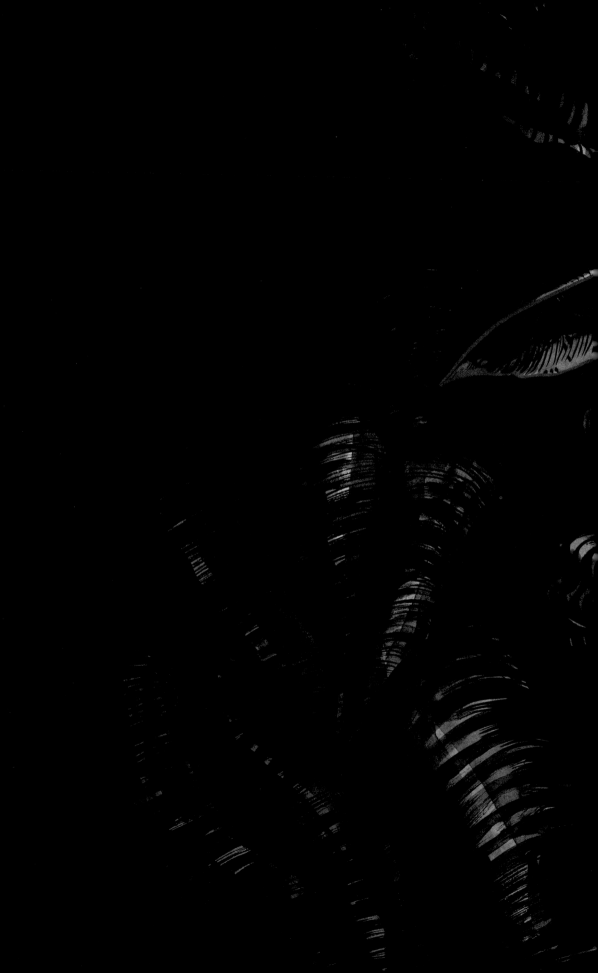

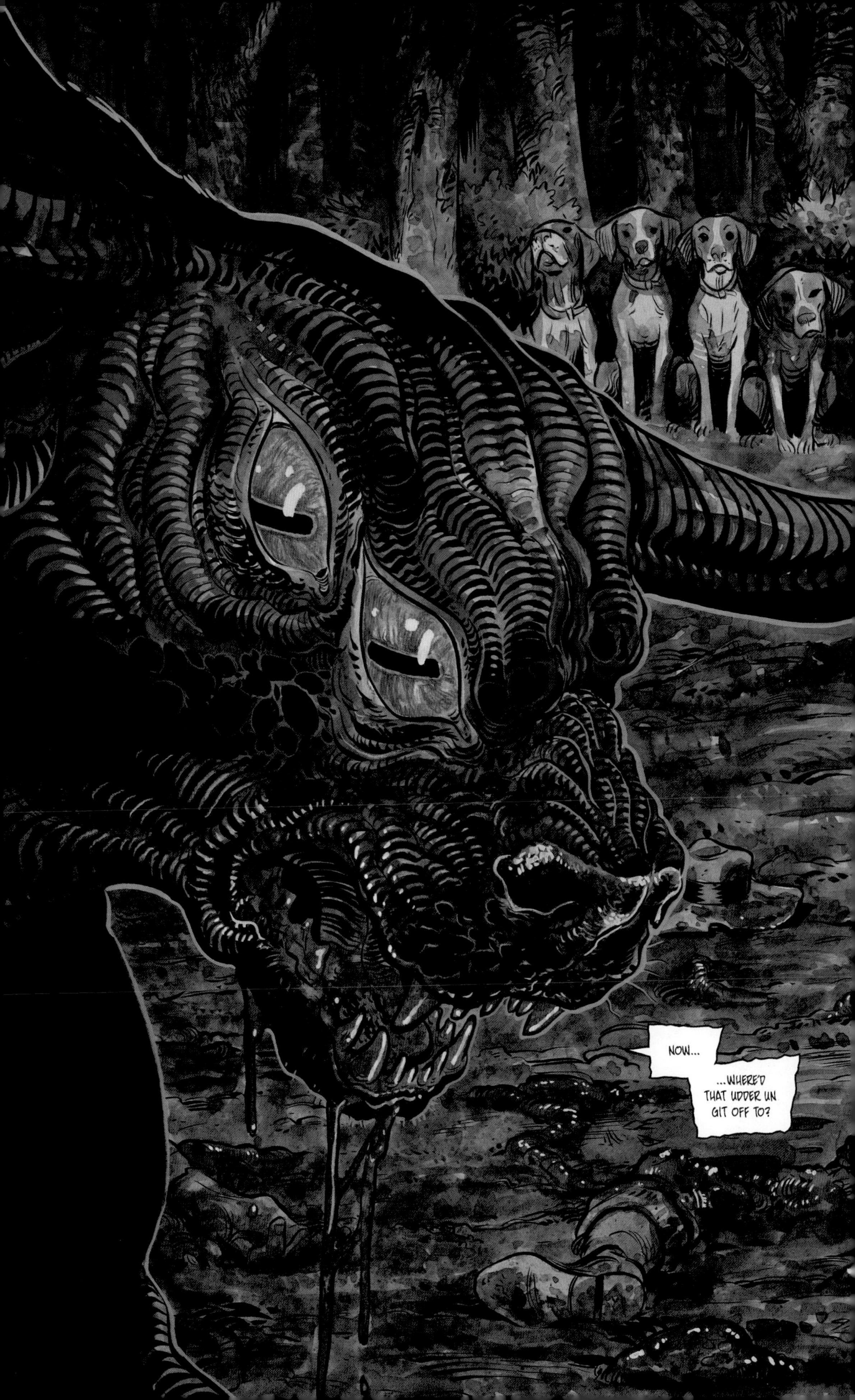
NOW...
...WHERE'D THAT UDDER UN GIT OFF TO?

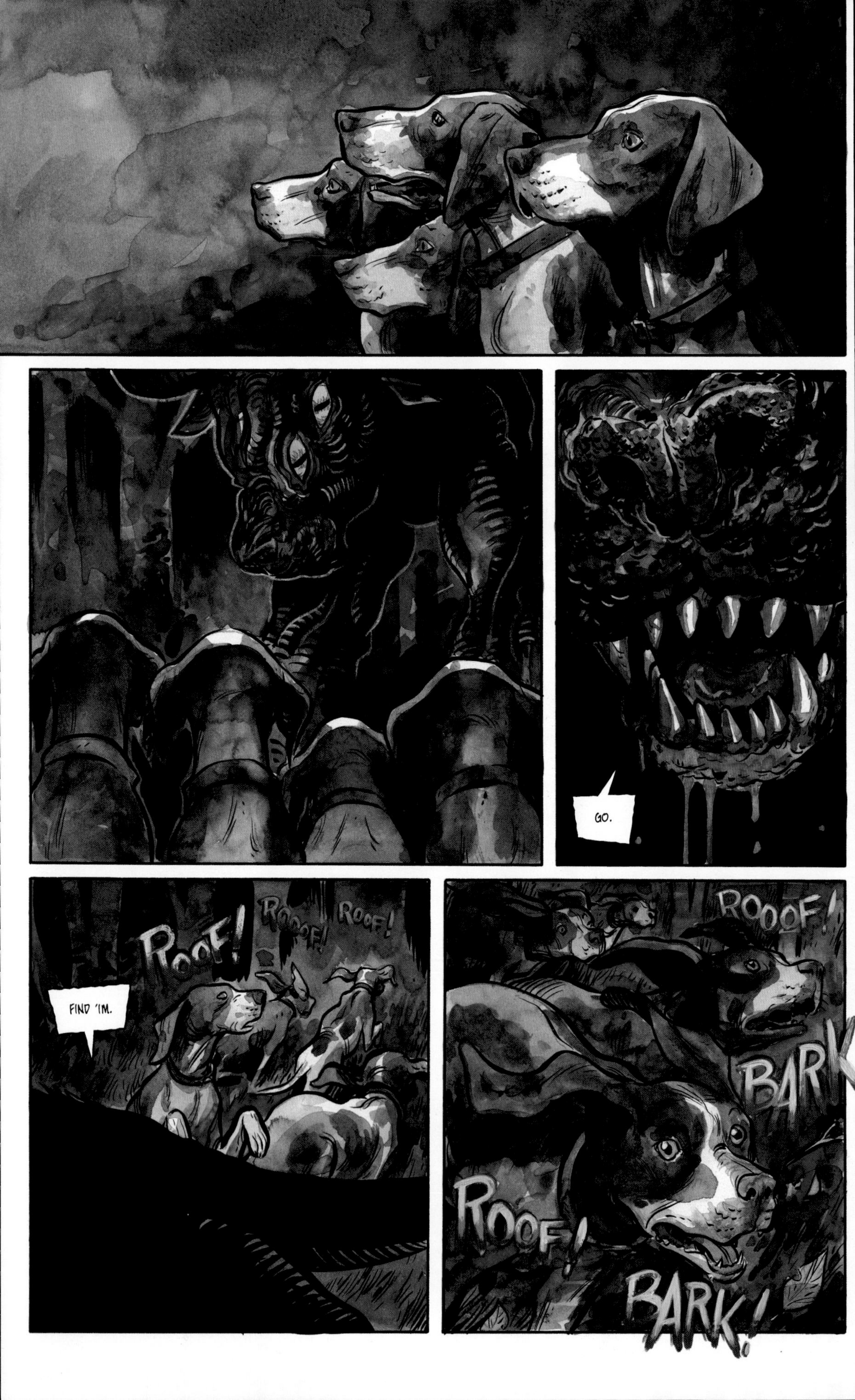
GO.
FIND 'IM.
ROOF!
ROOOF!
ROOF!
ROOOF!
BARK
ROOF!
BARK!

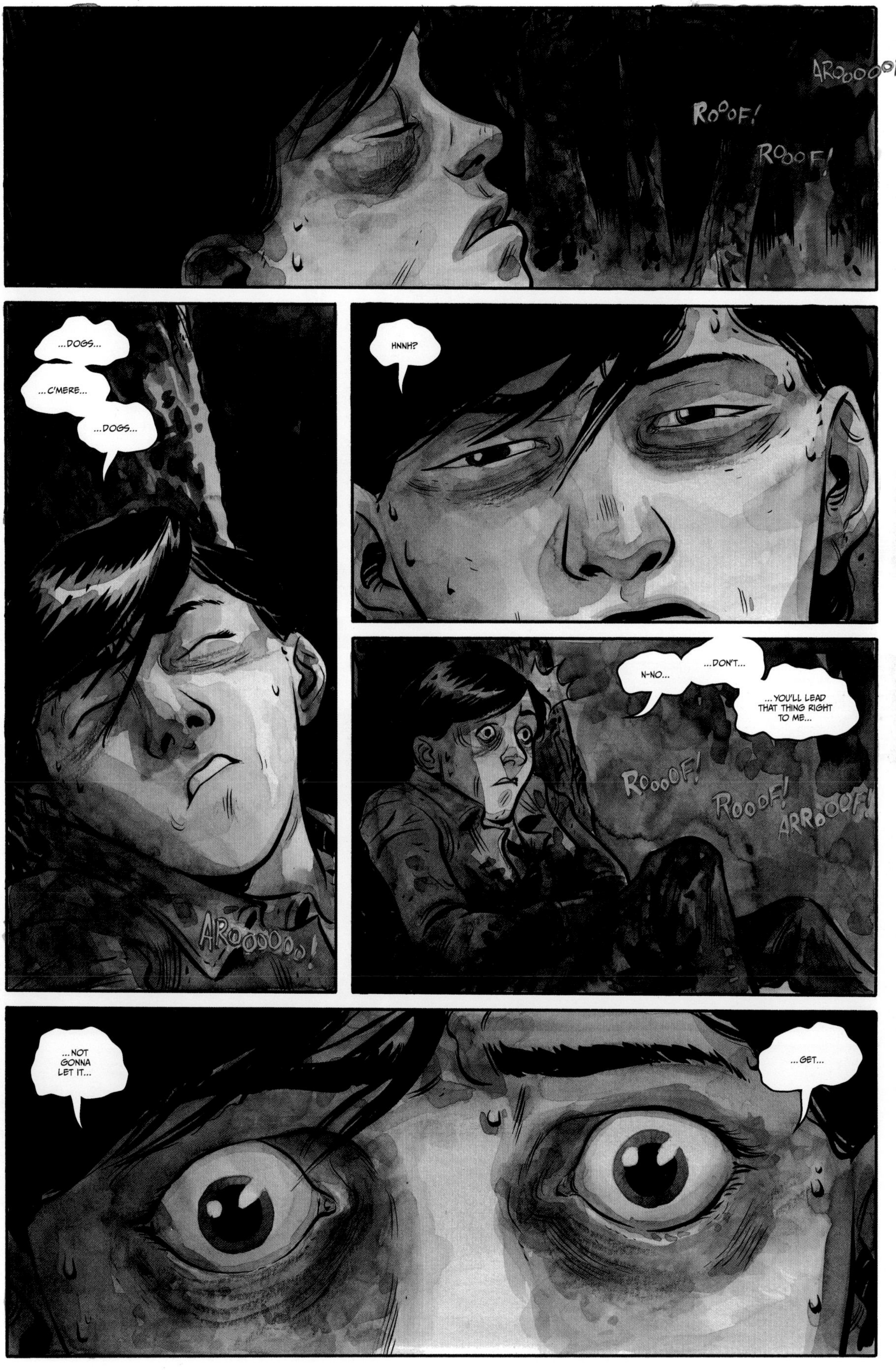
AROOOOOO!
ROOOF!
ROOOF!
...DOGS...
...C'MERE...
...DOGS...
AROOOOOO!
HNNH?
N-NO...
...DON'T...
...YOU'LL LEAD THAT THING RIGHT TO ME...
ROOOOF!
ROOOF!
ARROOOF!
...NOT GONNA LET IT...
...GET...

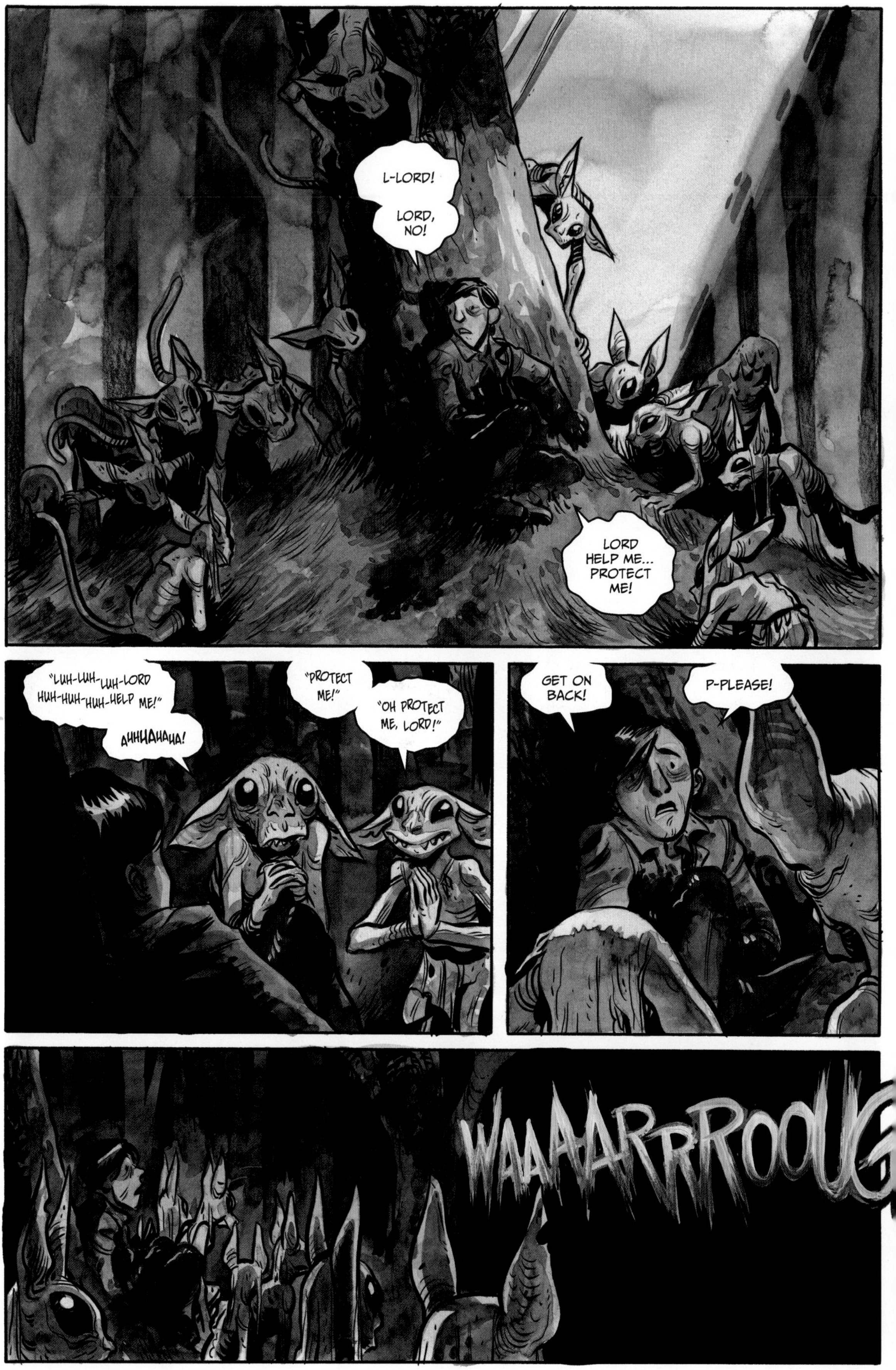
L-LORD!
LORD, NO!
LORD HELP ME... PROTECT ME!
"LUH-LUH-LUH-LORD HUH-HUH-HUH-HELP ME!"
AHHHAHAHA!
"PROTECT ME!"
"OH PROTECT ME, LORD!"
GET ON BACK!
P-PLEASE!
WAAAARRROOUG

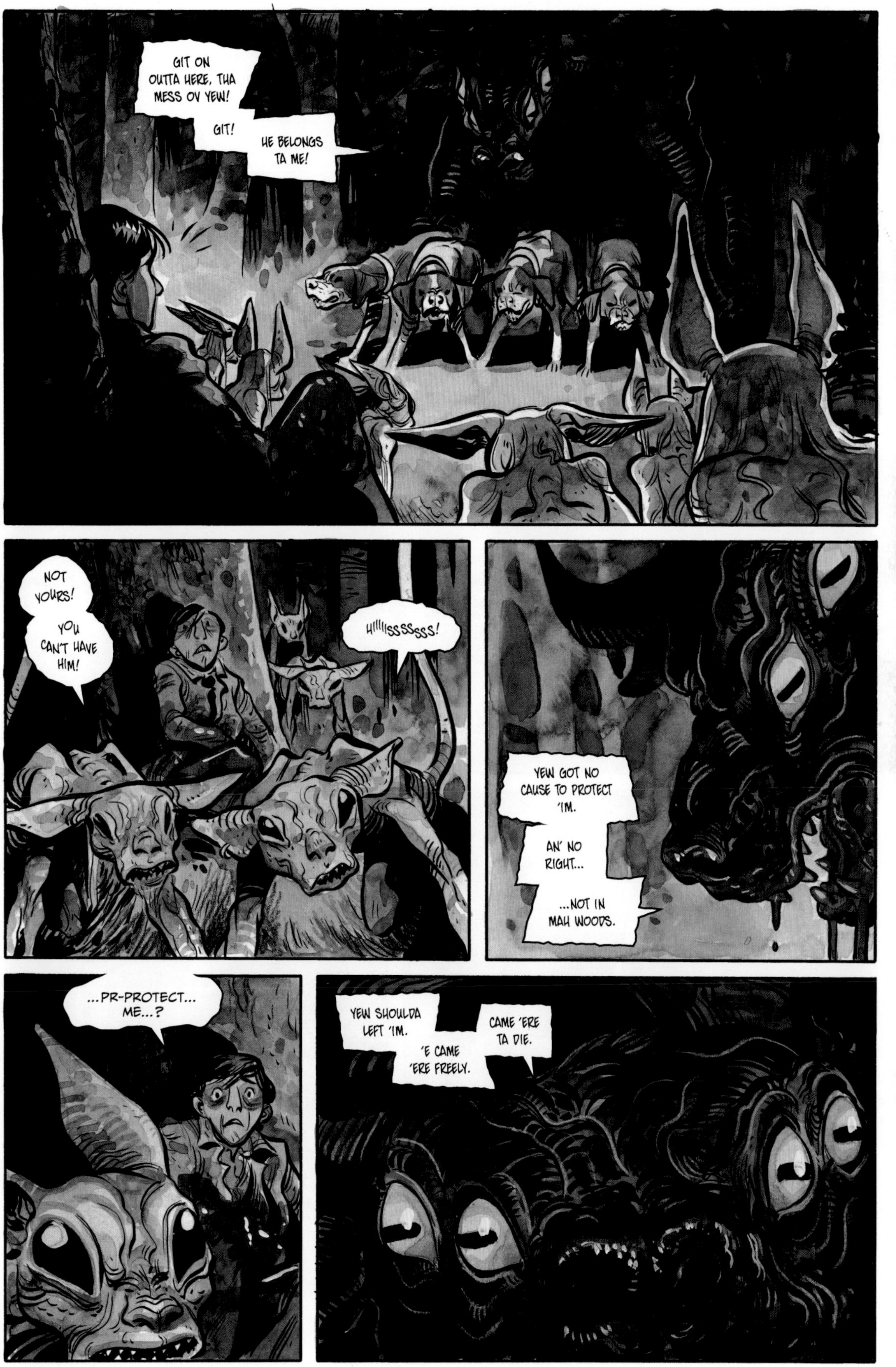
GIT ON OUTTA HERE, THA MESS OV YEW!
GIT!
HE BELONGS TA ME!
NOT YOURS!
YOU CAN'T HAVE HIM!
HIIIIISSSSSSS!
YEW GOT NO CAUSE TO PROTECT 'IM.
AN' NO RIGHT...
...NOT IN MAH WOODS.
...PR-PROTECT... ME...?
YEW SHOULDA LEFT 'IM.
'E CAME 'ERE FREELY.
CAME 'ERE TA DIE.

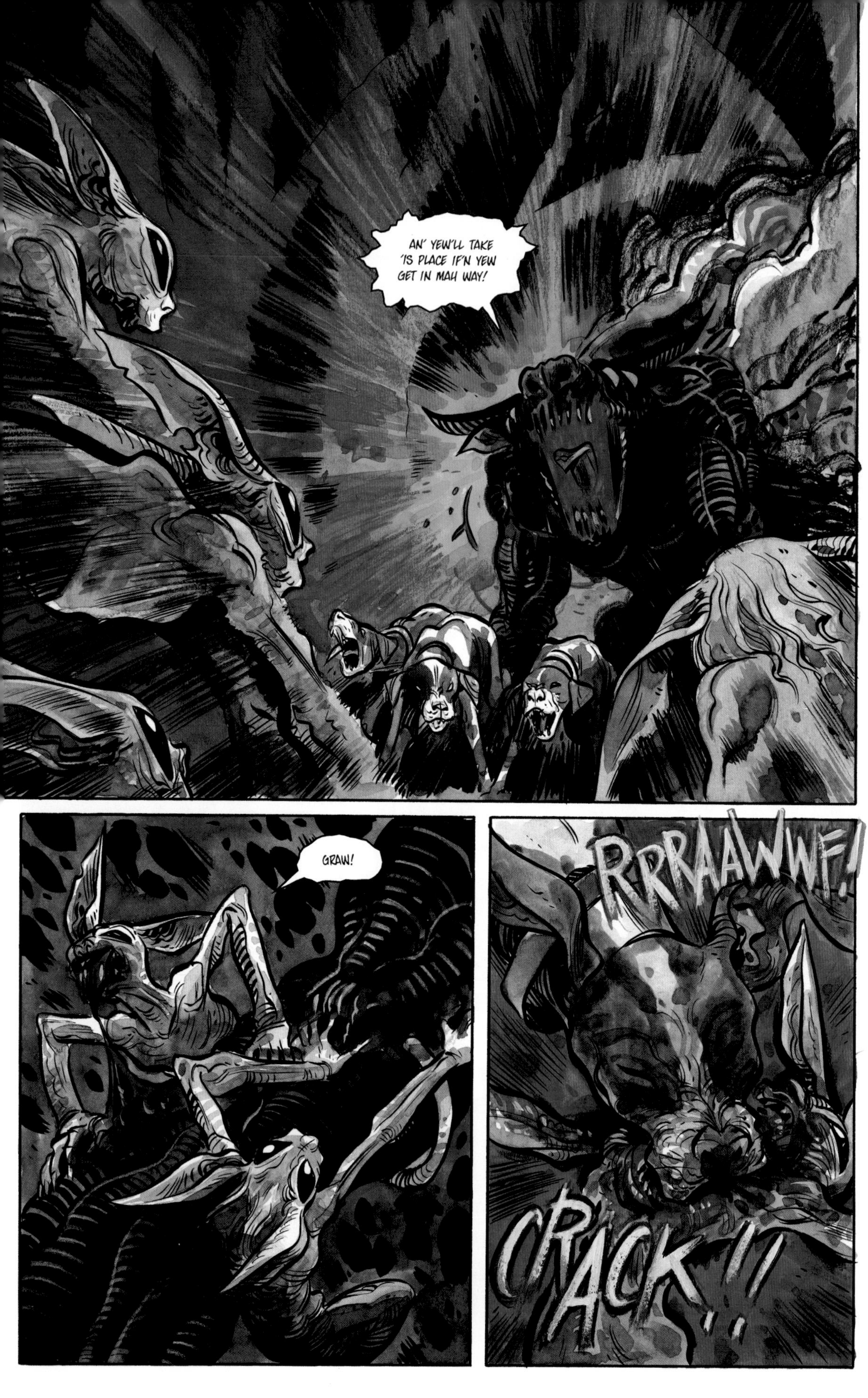
AN' YEW'LL TAKE 'IS PLACE IF'N YEW GET IN MAH WAY!
GRAW!
RRRAAWWF!
CRACK!!

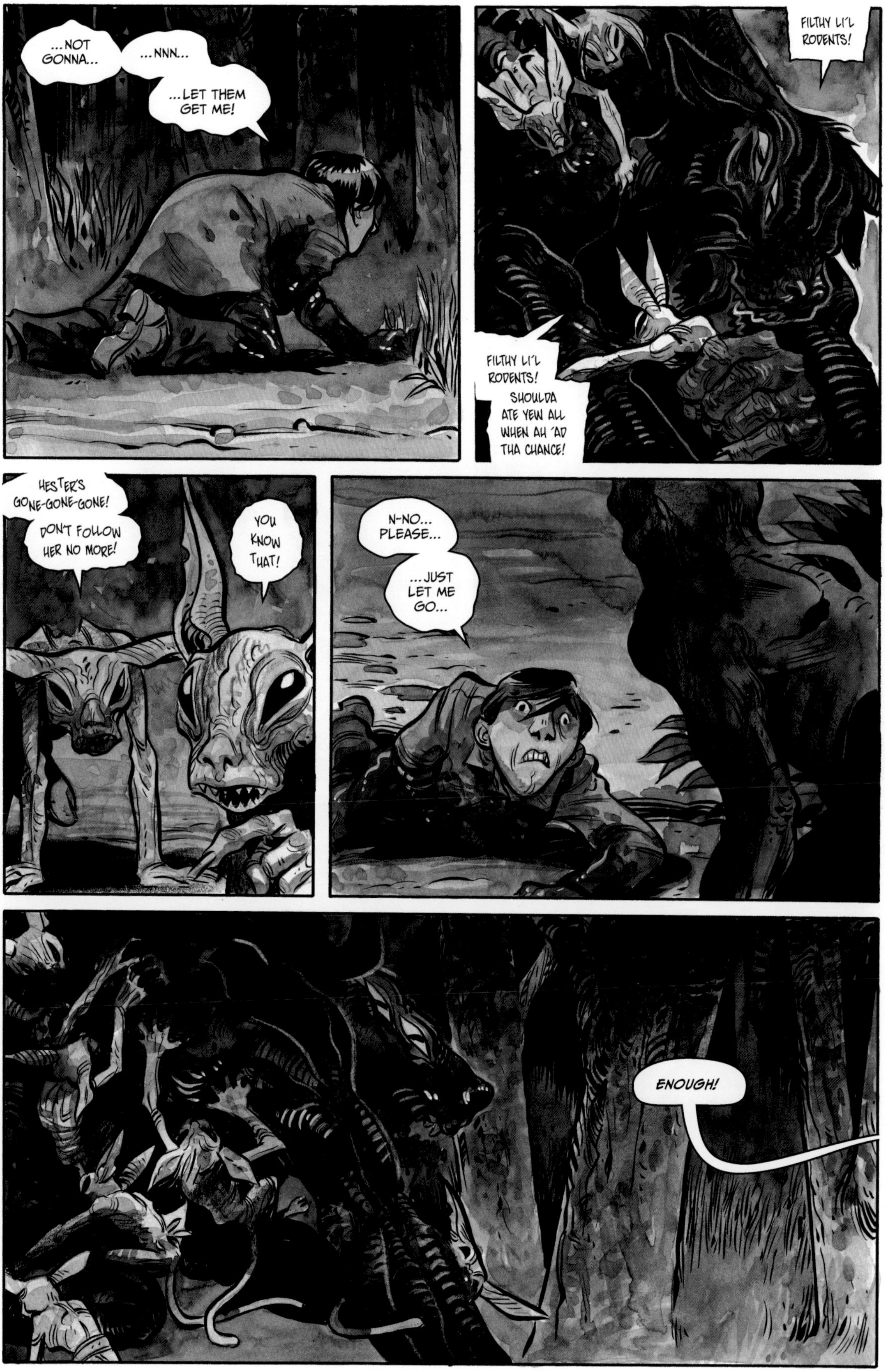
...NOT GONNA...
...NNN...
...LET THEM GET ME!
FILTHY LI'L RODENTS!
FILTHY LI'L RODENTS!
SHOULDA ATE YEW ALL WHEN AH 'AD THA CHANCE!
HESTER'S GONE-GONE-GONE!
DON'T FOLLOW HER NO MORE!
YOU KNOW THAT!
N-NO... PLEASE...
...JUST LET ME GO...
ENOUGH!

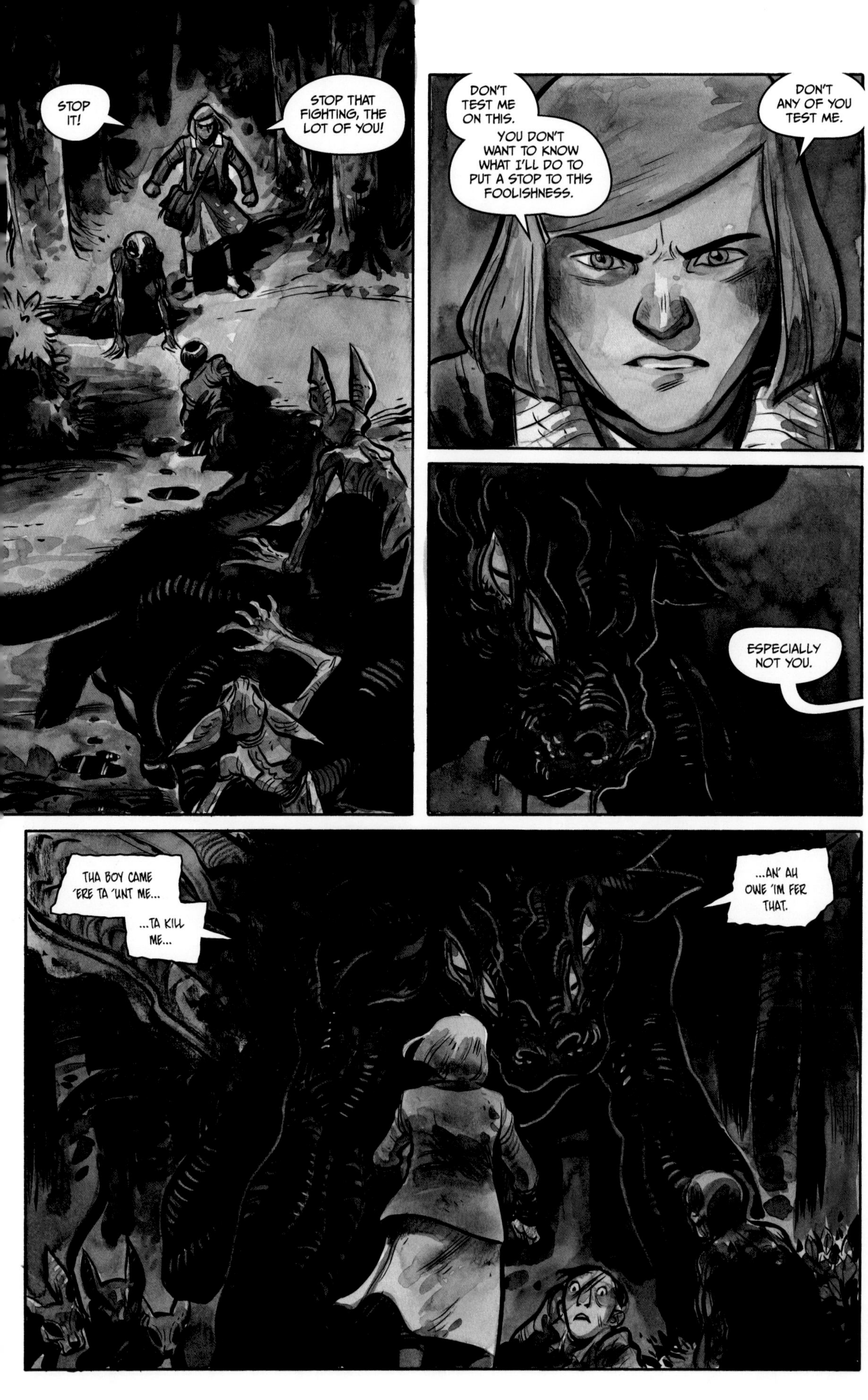
STOP IT!
STOP THAT FIGHTING, THE LOT OF YOU!
DON'T TEST ME ON THIS.
YOU DON'T WANT TO KNOW WHAT I'LL DO TO PUT A STOP TO THIS FOOLISHNESS.
DON'T ANY OF YOU TEST ME.
ESPECIALLY NOT YOU.
THA BOY CAME 'ERE TA 'UNT ME...
...TA KILL ME...
...AN' AH OWE 'IM FER THAT.

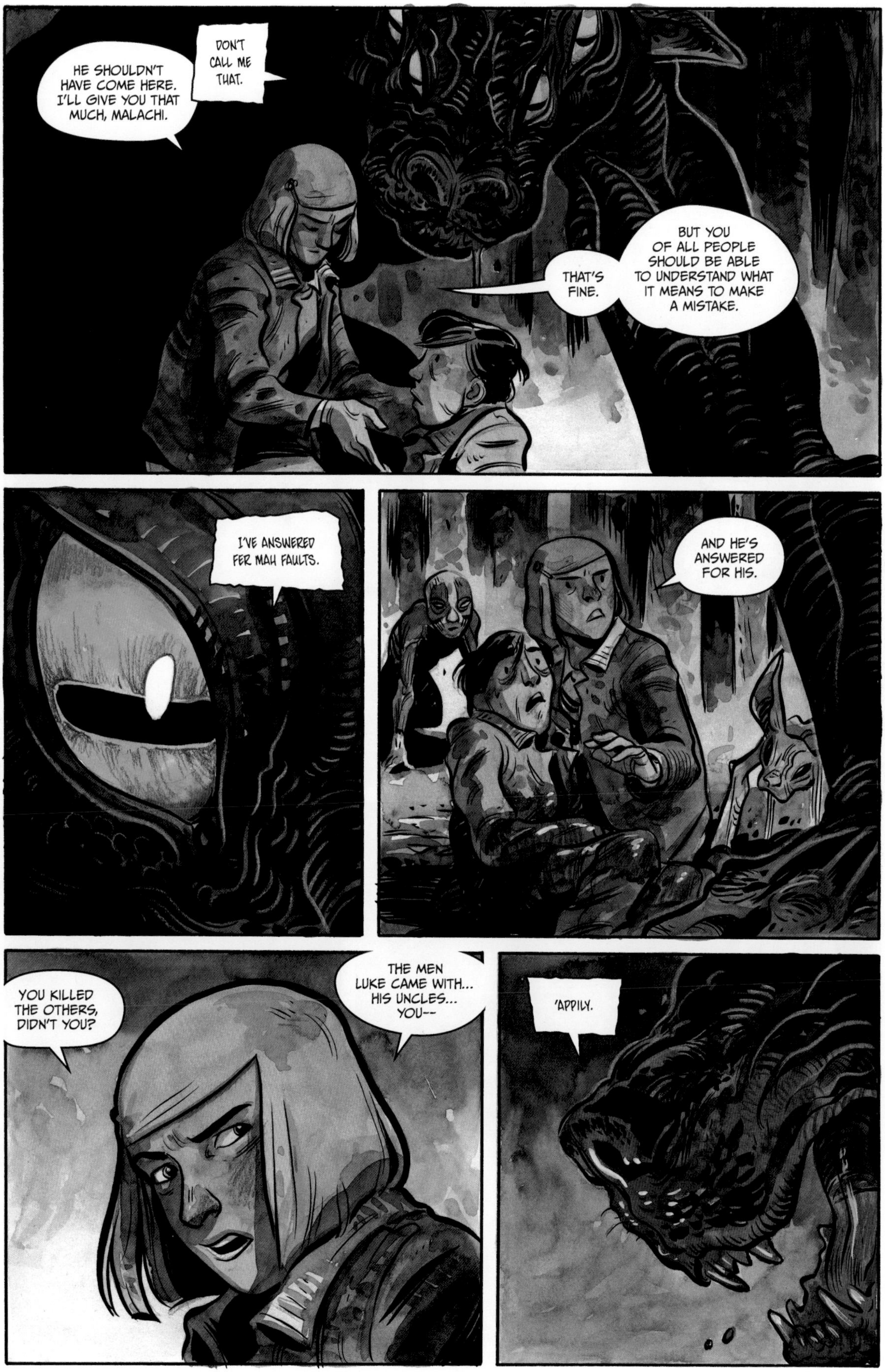
HE SHOULDN'T HAVE COME HERE. I'LL GIVE YOU THAT MUCH, MALACHI.
DON'T CALL ME THAT.
THAT'S FINE.
BUT YOU OF ALL PEOPLE SHOULD BE ABLE TO UNDERSTAND WHAT IT MEANS TO MAKE A MISTAKE.
I'VE ANSWERED FER MAH FAULTS.
AND HE'S ANSWERED FOR HIS.
YOU KILLED THE OTHERS, DIDN'T YOU?
THE MEN LUKE CAME WITH... HIS UNCLES... YOU--
'APPILY.

UNNNNN--

IT'S ALL RIGHT, LUKE.

YOU'RE GOING TO BE ALL RIGHT.

AGHH--

I KNOW IT HURTS.

JUST...

JUST CLOSE YOUR EYES.

JUST TRY TO STAY CALM, ALL RIGHT?

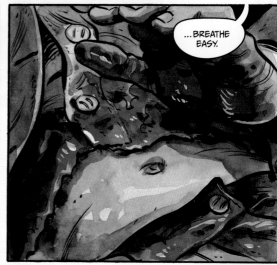

...BREATHE EASY.

YEW GIT 'IM OUTTA 'ERE, EMMY.

YEW WANT TA SAVE 'IM, THAT'S ON YEW.

BUT 'E'D BEST NOT FIND 'IMSELF 'ERE AGAIN.

AN' THA DOGS STAY WIT' ME.

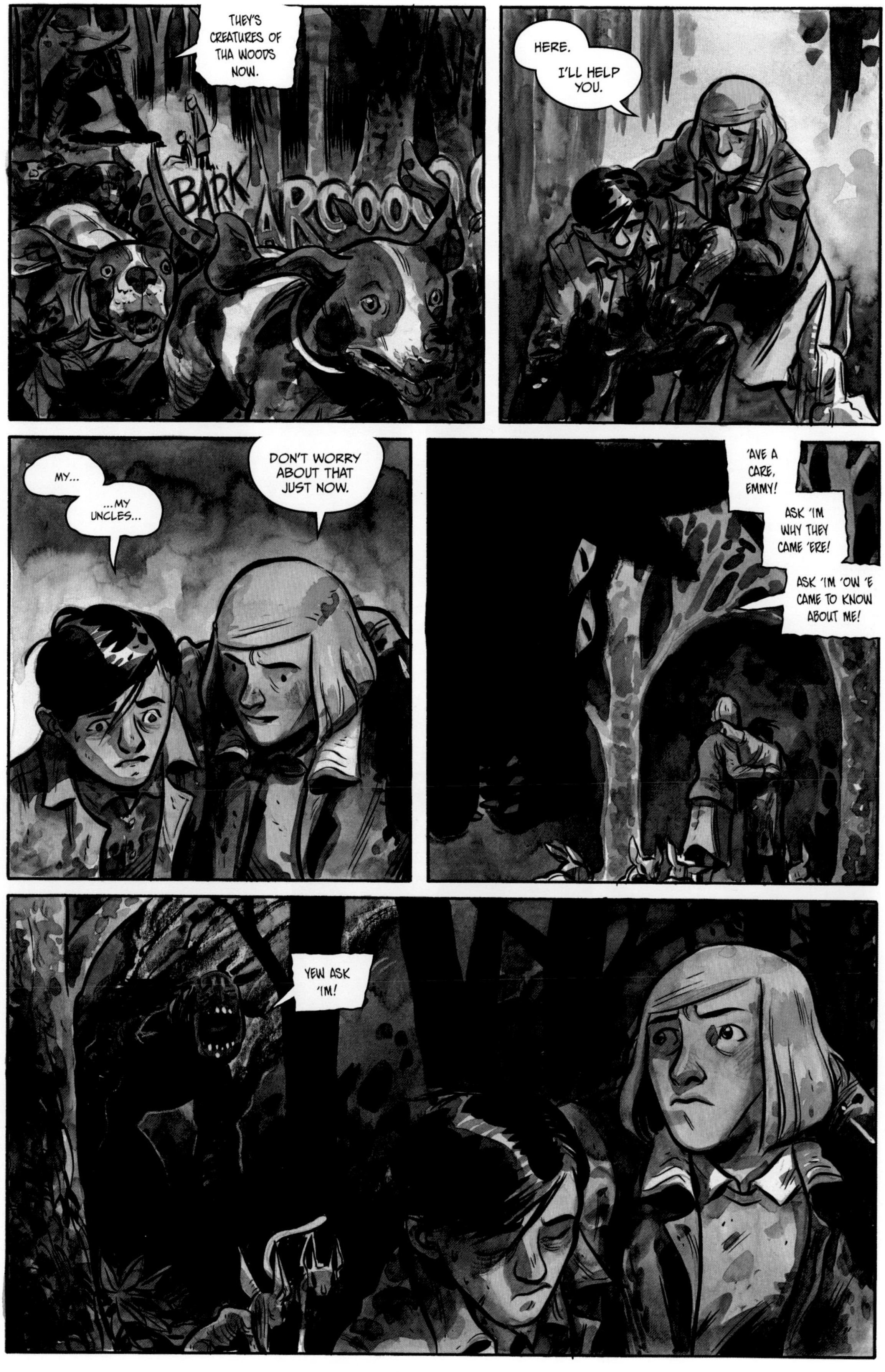
THEY'S CREATURES OF THA WOODS NOW.
BARK
ARGOOO
HERE.
I'LL HELP YOU.
MY...
...MY UNCLES...
DON'T WORRY ABOUT THAT JUST NOW.
'AVE A CARE, EMMY!
ASK 'IM WHY THEY CAME 'ERE!
ASK 'IM 'OW 'E CAME TO KNOW ABOUT ME!
YEW ASK 'IM!

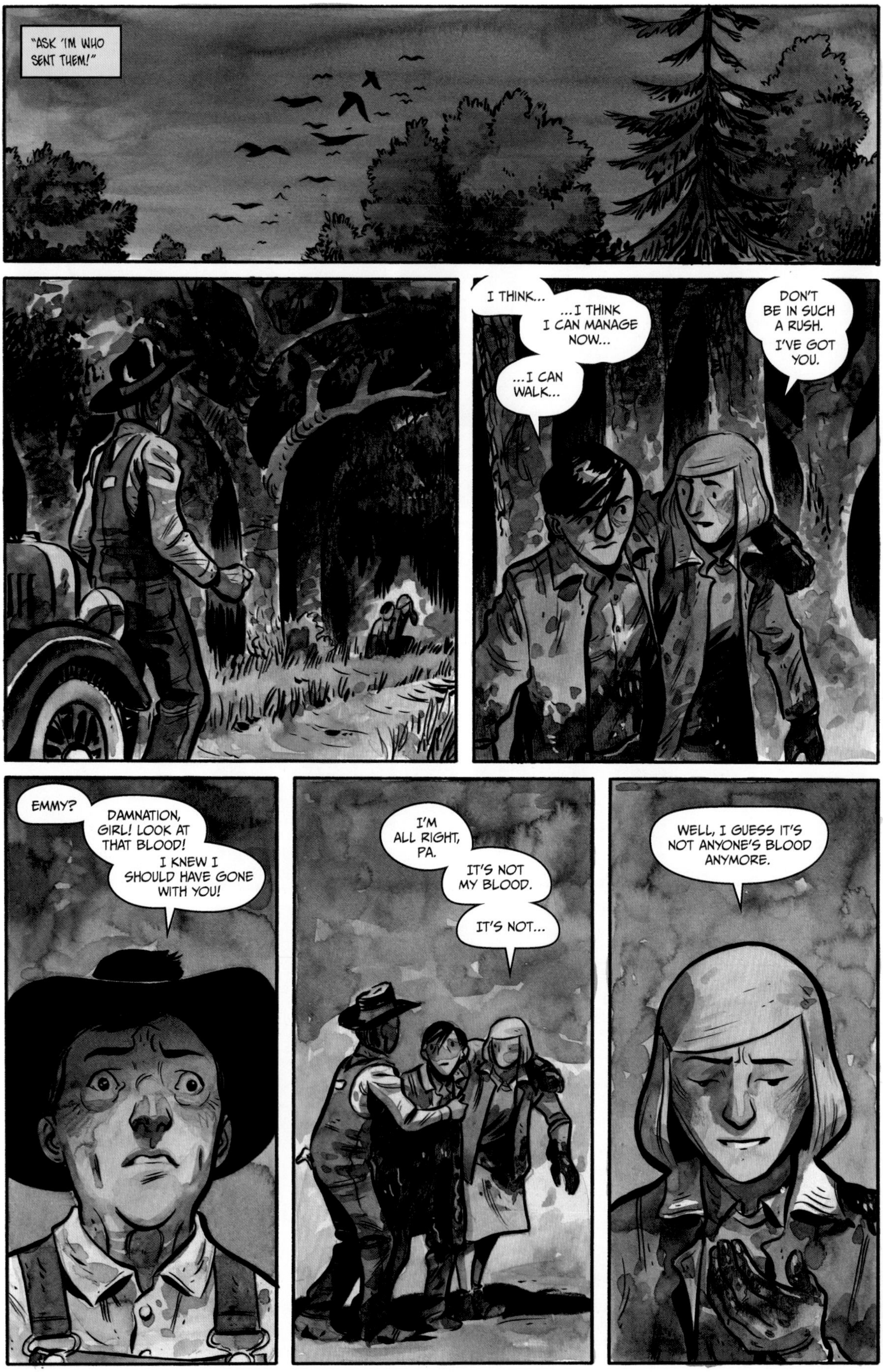
"ASK 'IM WHO SENT THEM!"
I THINK...
...I THINK I CAN MANAGE NOW...
...I CAN WALK...
DON'T BE IN SUCH A RUSH.
I'VE GOT YOU.
EMMY?
DAMNATION, GIRL! LOOK AT THAT BLOOD!
I KNEW I SHOULD HAVE GONE WITH YOU!
I'M ALL RIGHT, PA.
IT'S NOT MY BLOOD.
IT'S NOT...
WELL, I GUESS IT'S NOT ANYONE'S BLOOD ANYMORE.

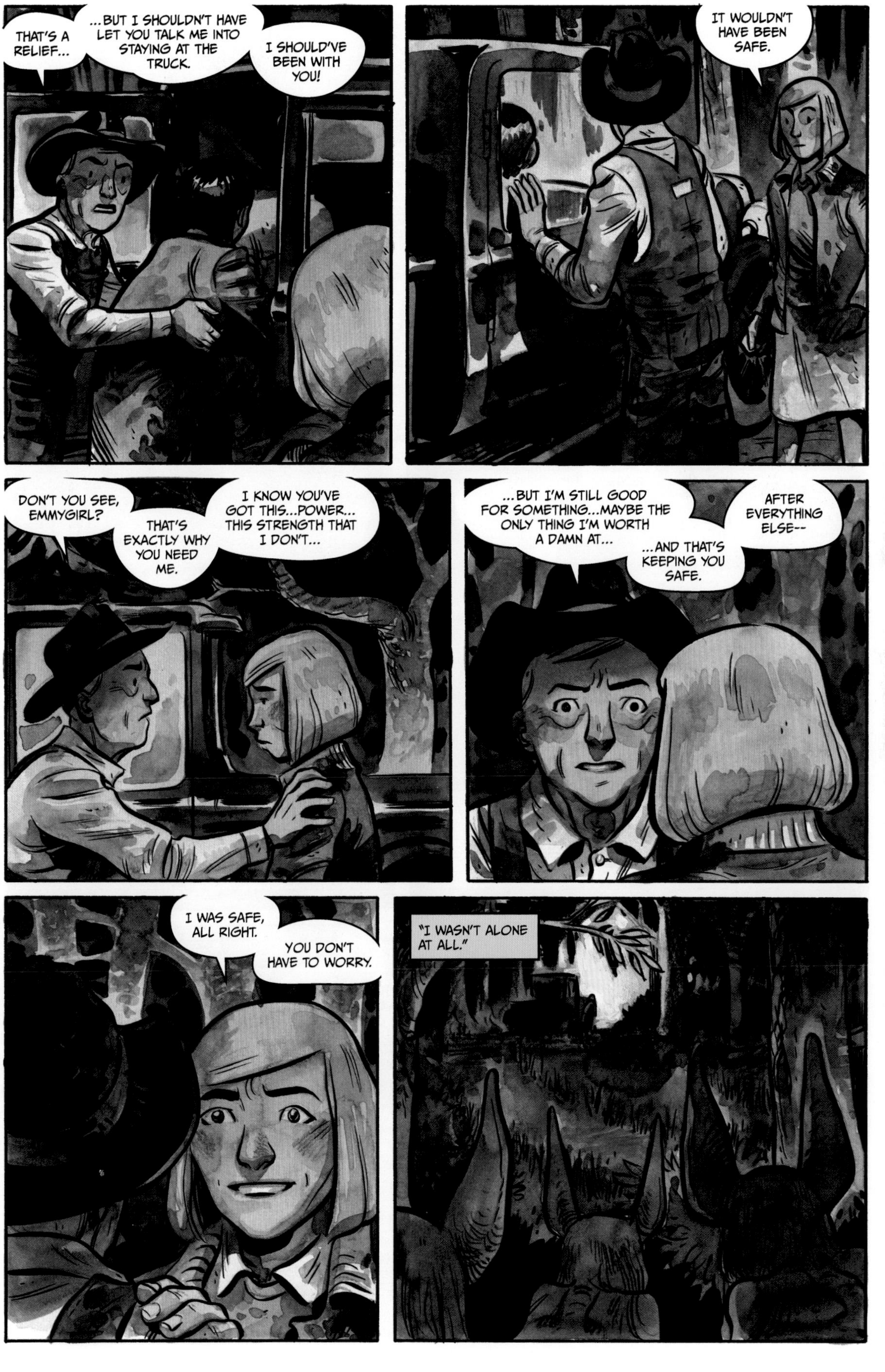
THAT'S A RELIEF...
...BUT I SHOULDN'T HAVE LET YOU TALK ME INTO STAYING AT THE TRUCK.
I SHOULD'VE BEEN WITH YOU!
IT WOULDN'T HAVE BEEN SAFE.
DON'T YOU SEE, EMMYGIRL?
THAT'S EXACTLY WHY YOU NEED ME.
I KNOW YOU'VE GOT THIS...POWER... THIS STRENGTH THAT I DON'T...
...BUT I'M STILL GOOD FOR SOMETHING...MAYBE THE ONLY THING I'M WORTH A DAMN AT...
...AND THAT'S KEEPING YOU SAFE.
AFTER EVERYTHING ELSE--
I WAS SAFE, ALL RIGHT.
YOU DON'T HAVE TO WORRY.
"I WASN'T ALONE AT ALL."

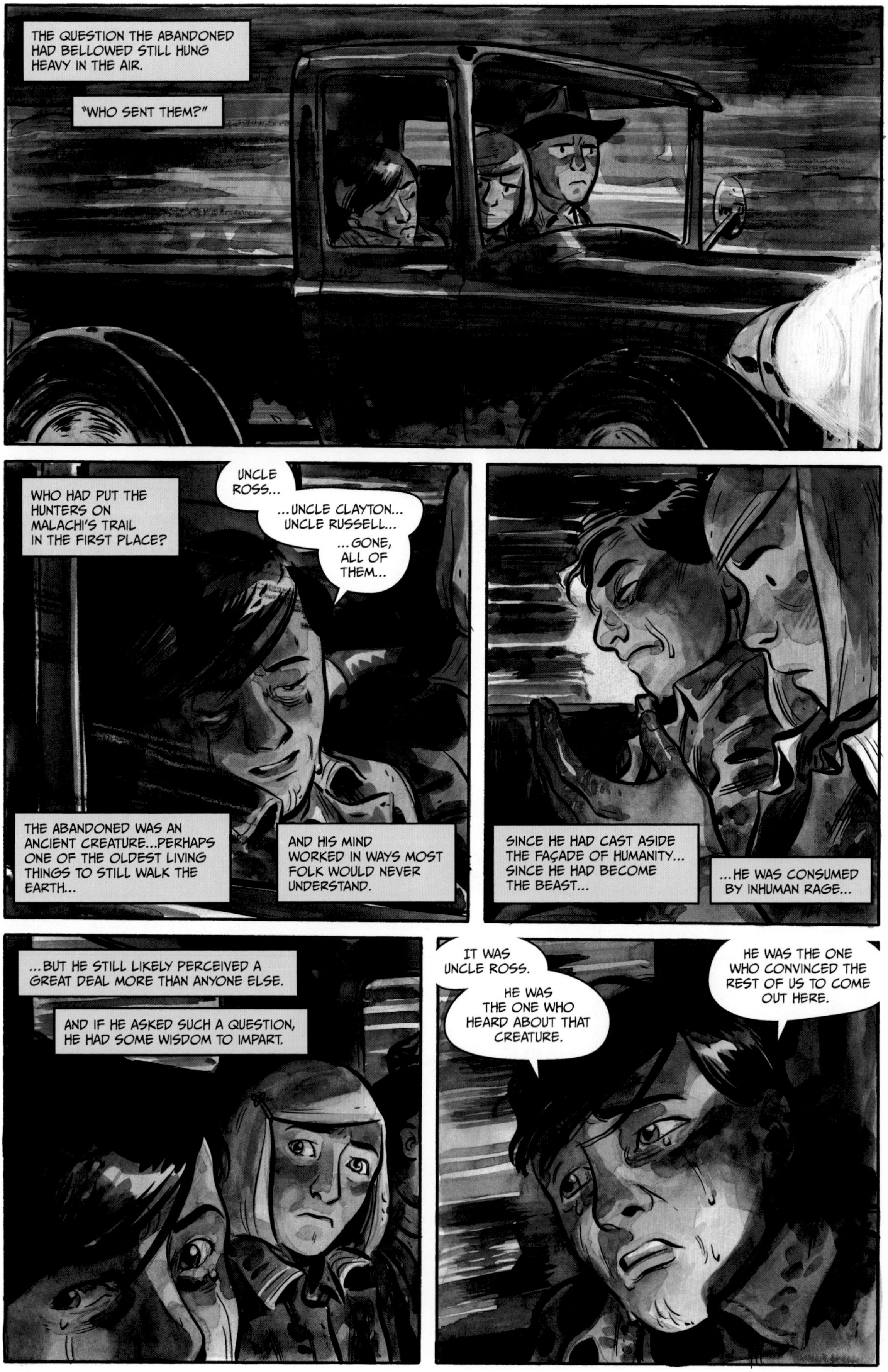
THE QUESTION THE ABANDONED HAD BELLOWED STILL HUNG HEAVY IN THE AIR.
"WHO SENT THEM?"
WHO HAD PUT THE HUNTERS ON MALACHI'S TRAIL IN THE FIRST PLACE?
UNCLE ROSS...
...UNCLE CLAYTON... UNCLE RUSSELL...
...GONE, ALL OF THEM...
THE ABANDONED WAS AN ANCIENT CREATURE...PERHAPS ONE OF THE OLDEST LIVING THINGS TO STILL WALK THE EARTH...
AND HIS MIND WORKED IN WAYS MOST FOLK WOULD NEVER UNDERSTAND.
SINCE HE HAD CAST ASIDE THE FAÇADE OF HUMANITY... SINCE HE HAD BECOME THE BEAST...
...HE WAS CONSUMED BY INHUMAN RAGE...
...BUT HE STILL LIKELY PERCEIVED A GREAT DEAL MORE THAN ANYONE ELSE.
AND IF HE ASKED SUCH A QUESTION, HE HAD SOME WISDOM TO IMPART.
IT WAS UNCLE ROSS.
HE WAS THE ONE WHO HEARD ABOUT THAT CREATURE.
HE WAS THE ONE WHO CONVINCED THE REST OF US TO COME OUT HERE.

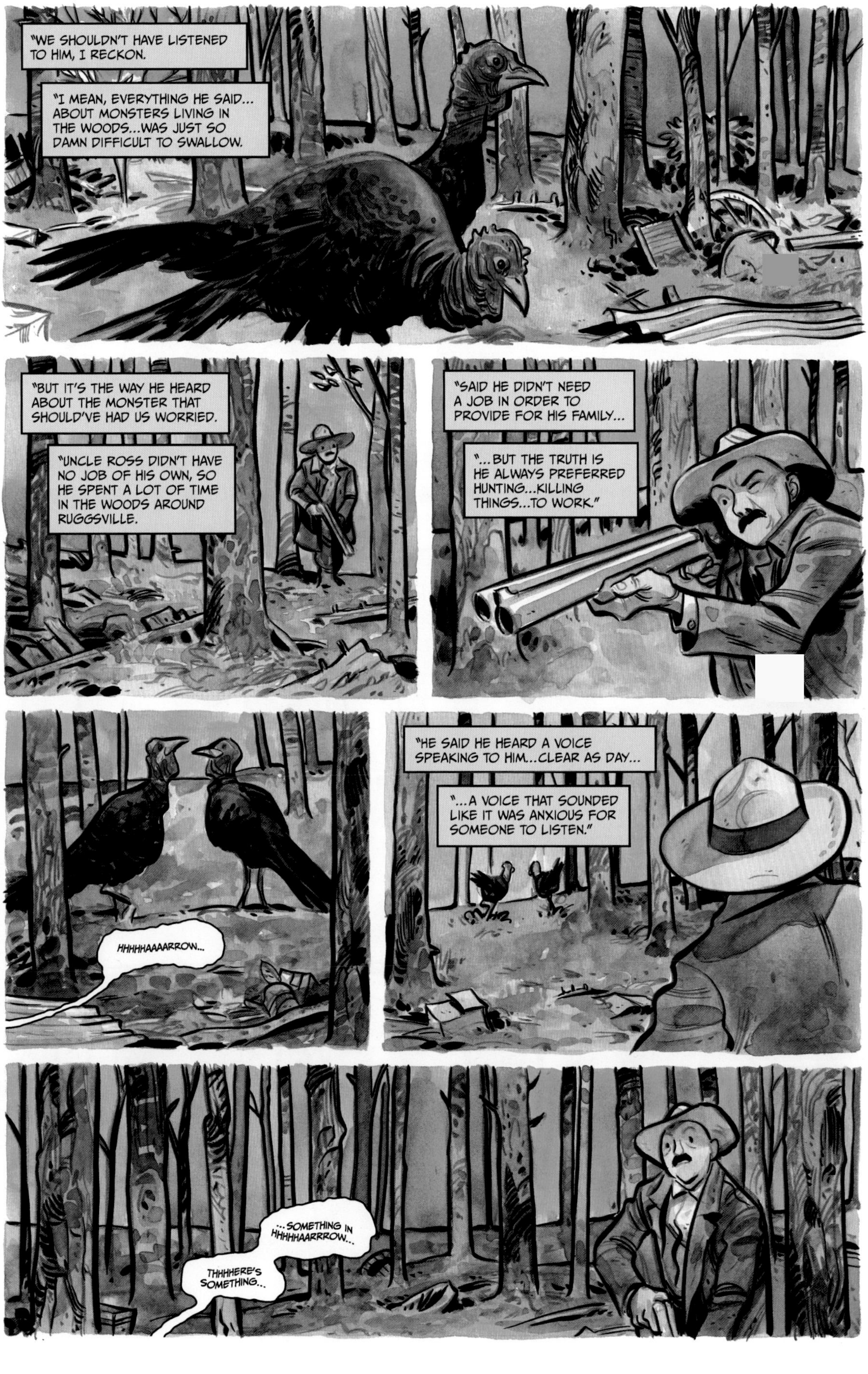
"WE SHOULDN'T HAVE LISTENED TO HIM, I RECKON.
"I MEAN, EVERYTHING HE SAID... ABOUT MONSTERS LIVING IN THE WOODS...WAS JUST SO DAMN DIFFICULT TO SWALLOW.
"BUT IT'S THE WAY HE HEARD ABOUT THE MONSTER THAT SHOULD'VE HAD US WORRIED.
"UNCLE ROSS DIDN'T HAVE NO JOB OF HIS OWN, SO HE SPENT A LOT OF TIME IN THE WOODS AROUND RUGGSVILLE.
"SAID HE DIDN'T NEED A JOB IN ORDER TO PROVIDE FOR HIS FAMILY...
"...BUT THE TRUTH IS HE ALWAYS PREFERRED HUNTING...KILLING THINGS...TO WORK."
HHHHHAAAARROW...
"HE SAID HE HEARD A VOICE SPEAKING TO HIM...CLEAR AS DAY...
"...A VOICE THAT SOUNDED LIKE IT WAS ANXIOUS FOR SOMEONE TO LISTEN."
THHHHERE'S SOMETHING...
...SOMETHING IN HHHHHAARRROW...

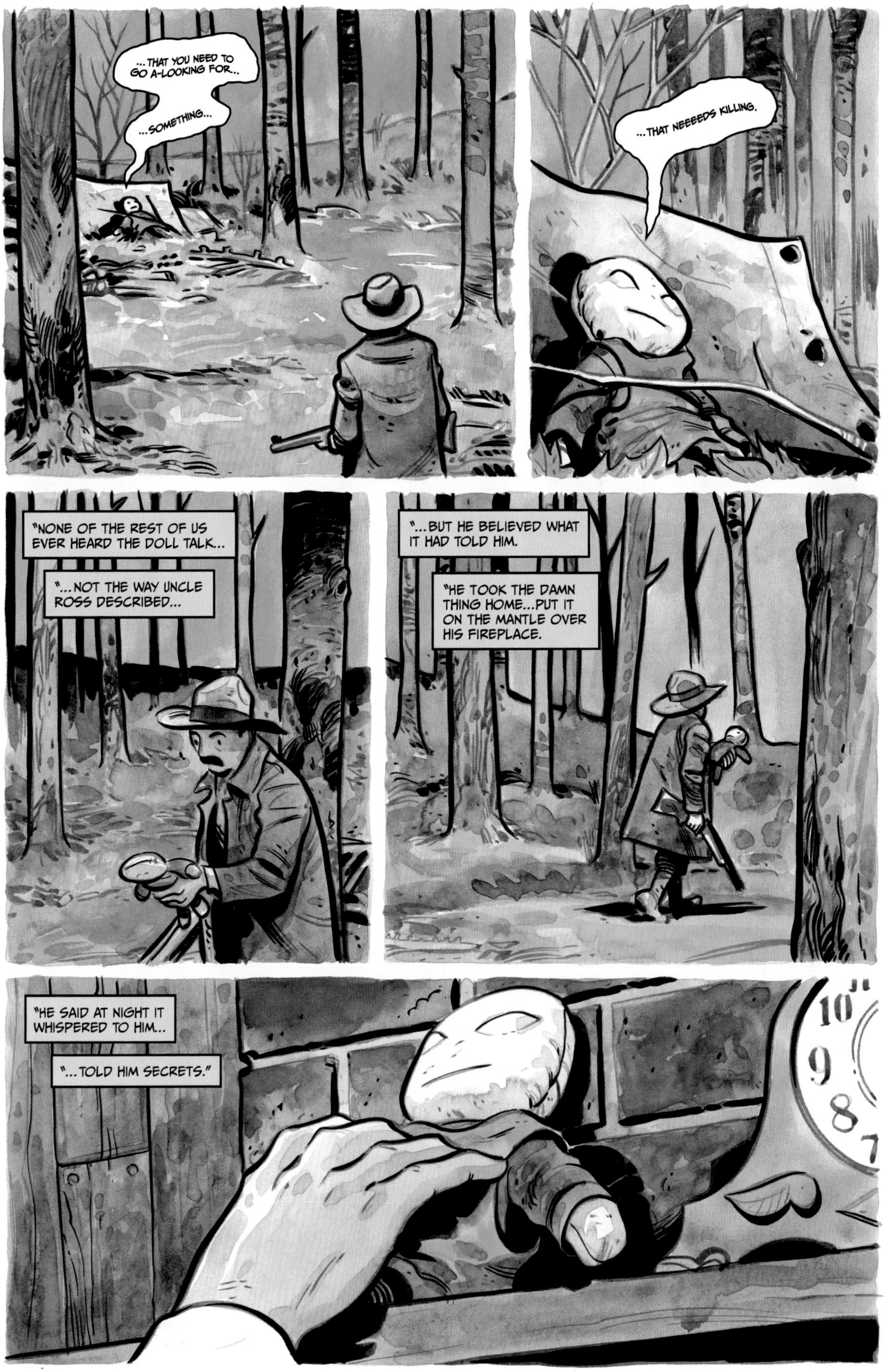
...THAT YOU NEED TO GO A-LOOKING FOR...
...SOMETHING...
...THAT NEEEEDS KILLING.
"NONE OF THE REST OF US EVER HEARD THE DOLL TALK...
"...NOT THE WAY UNCLE ROSS DESCRIBED...
"...BUT HE BELIEVED WHAT IT HAD TOLD HIM.
"HE TOOK THE DAMN THING HOME...PUT IT ON THE MANTLE OVER HIS FIREPLACE.
"HE SAID AT NIGHT IT WHISPERED TO HIM...
"...TOLD HIM SECRETS."

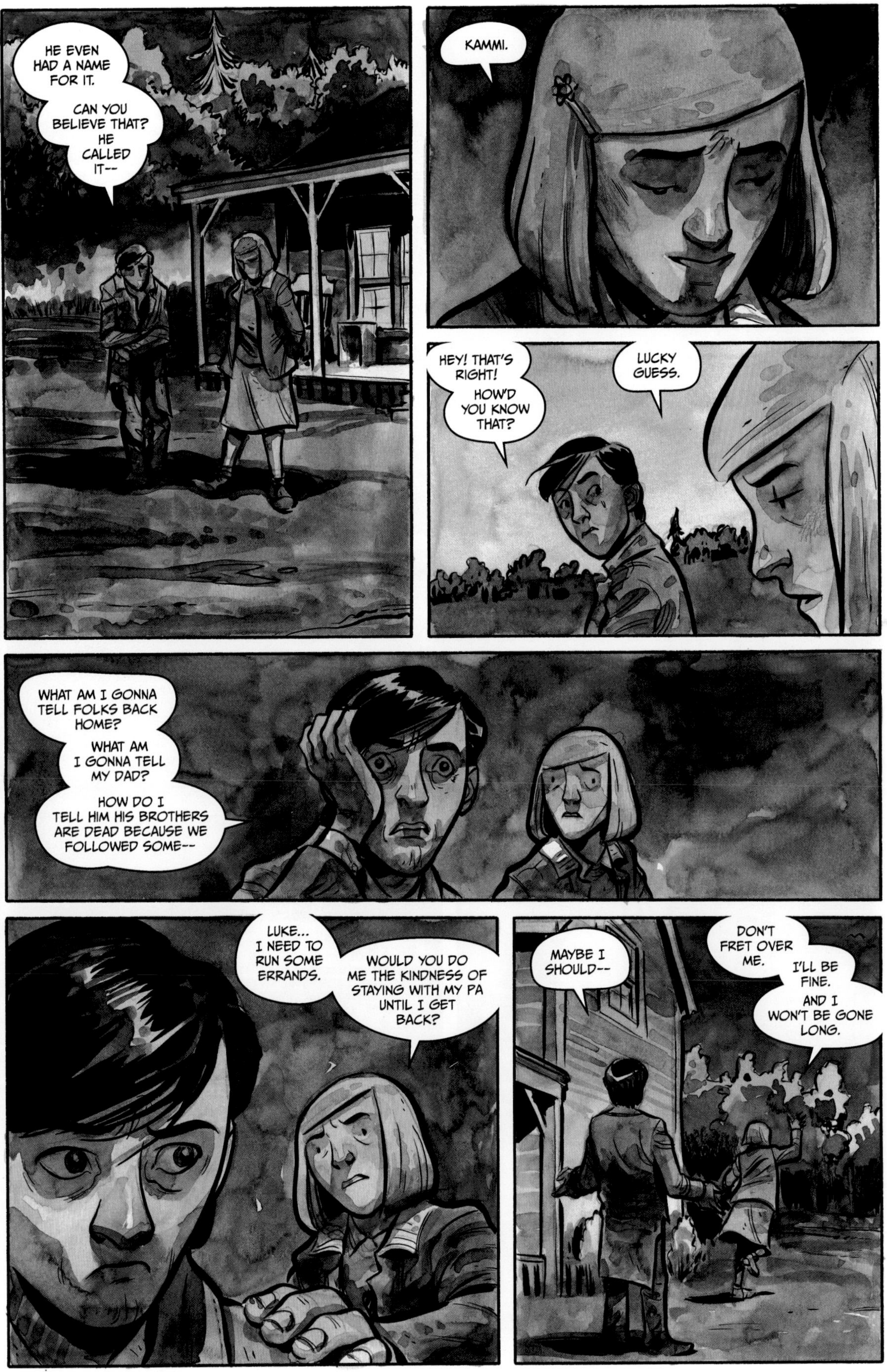
HE EVEN HAD A NAME FOR IT.
CAN YOU BELIEVE THAT? HE CALLED IT--
KAMMI.
HEY! THAT'S RIGHT!
HOW'D YOU KNOW THAT?
LUCKY GUESS.
WHAT AM I GONNA TELL FOLKS BACK HOME?
WHAT AM I GONNA TELL MY DAD?
HOW DO I TELL HIM HIS BROTHERS ARE DEAD BECAUSE WE FOLLOWED SOME--
LUKE... I NEED TO RUN SOME ERRANDS.
WOULD YOU DO ME THE KINDNESS OF STAYING WITH MY PA UNTIL I GET BACK?
MAYBE I SHOULD--
DON'T FRET OVER ME.
I'LL BE FINE.
AND I WON'T BE GONE LONG.

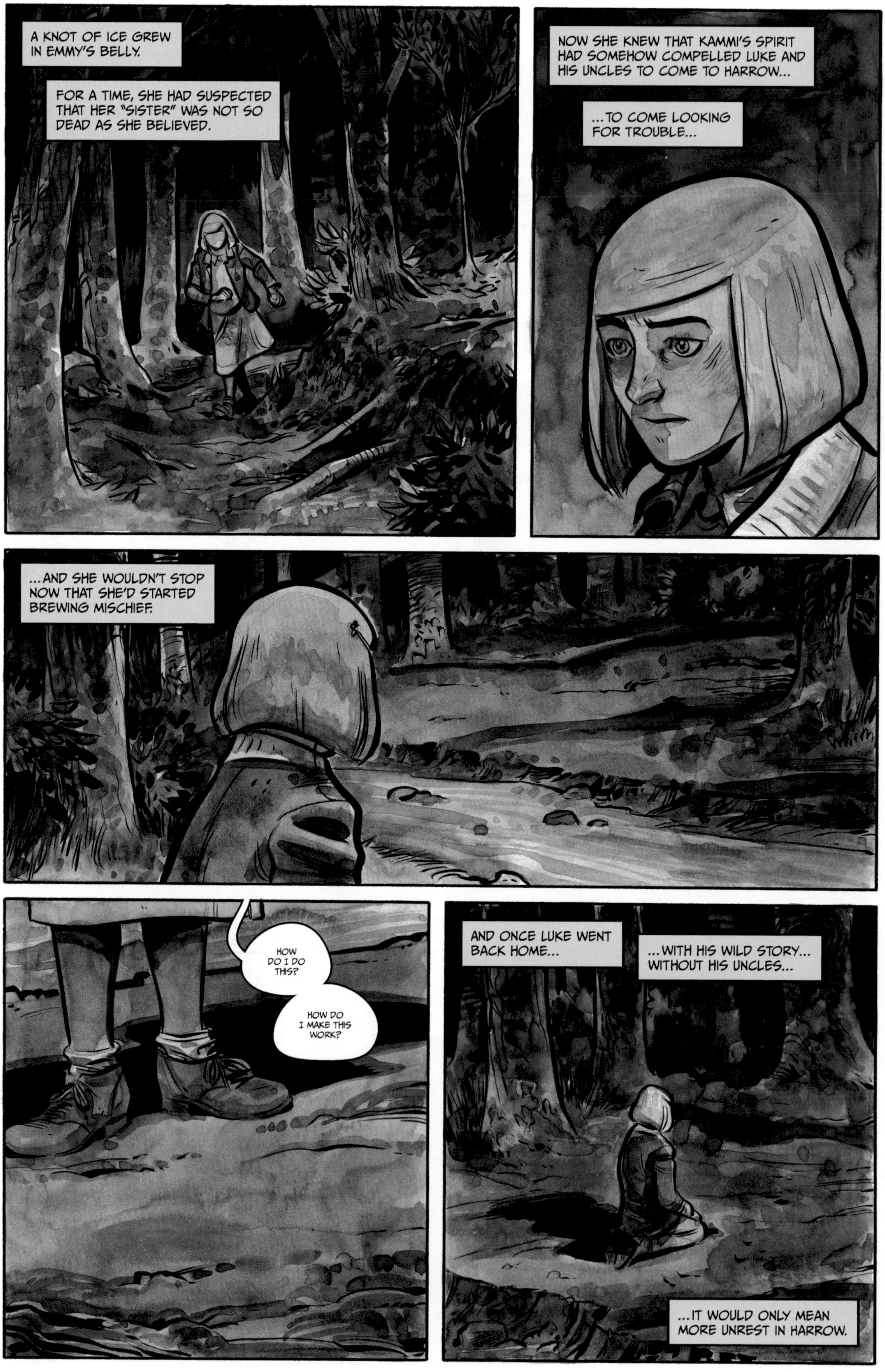
A KNOT OF ICE GREW IN EMMY'S BELLY.
FOR A TIME, SHE HAD SUSPECTED THAT HER "SISTER" WAS NOT SO DEAD AS SHE BELIEVED.
NOW SHE KNEW THAT KAMMI'S SPIRIT HAD SOMEHOW COMPELLED LUKE AND HIS UNCLES TO COME TO HARROW...
...TO COME LOOKING FOR TROUBLE...
...AND SHE WOULDN'T STOP NOW THAT SHE'D STARTED BREWING MISCHIEF.
HOW DO I DO THIS?
HOW DO I MAKE THIS WORK?
AND ONCE LUKE WENT BACK HOME...
...WITH HIS WILD STORY... WITHOUT HIS UNCLES...
...IT WOULD ONLY MEAN MORE UNREST IN HARROW.

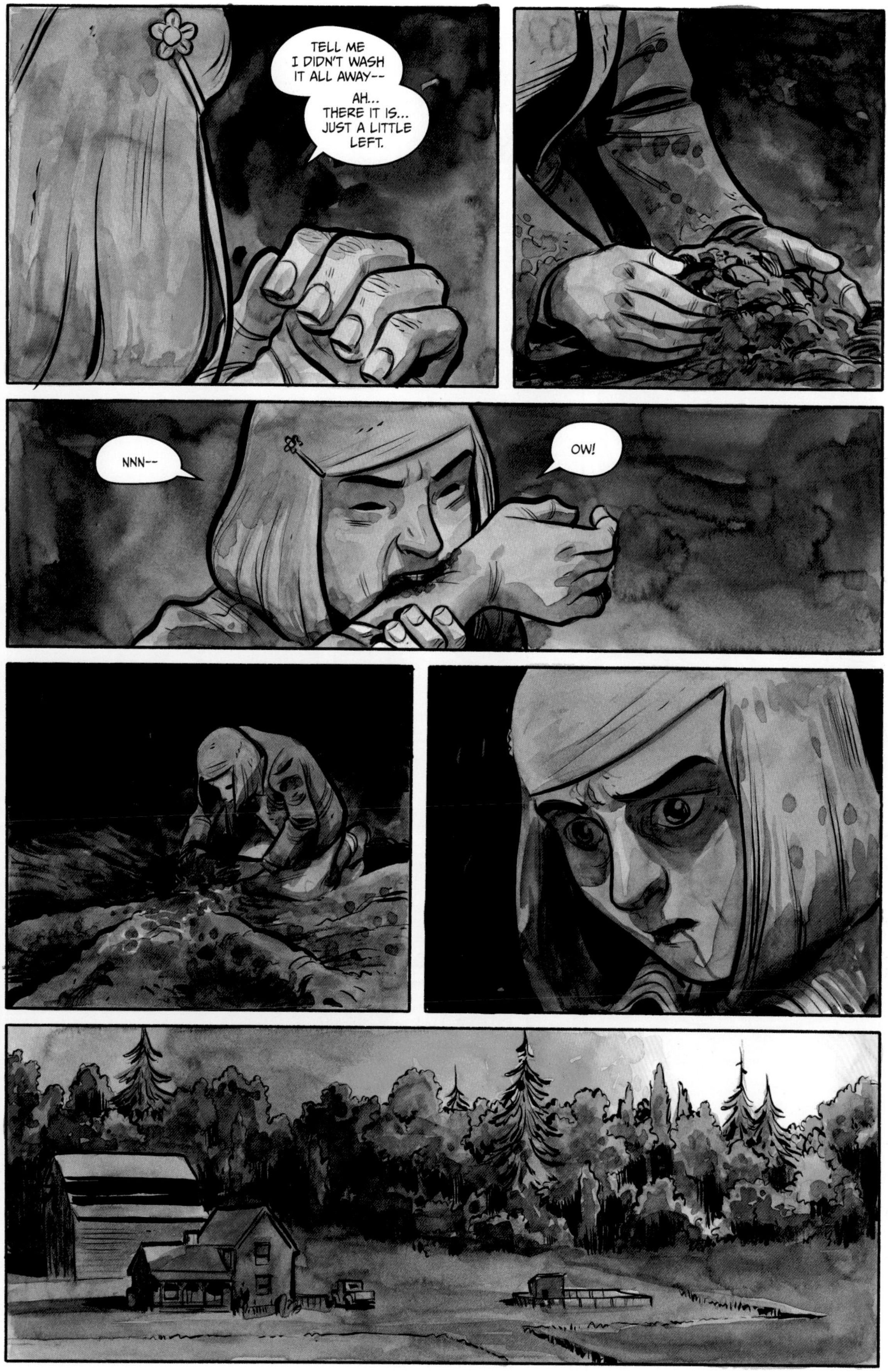
TELL ME I DIDN'T WASH IT ALL AWAY--
AH... THERE IT IS... JUST A LITTLE LEFT.
NNN--
OW!

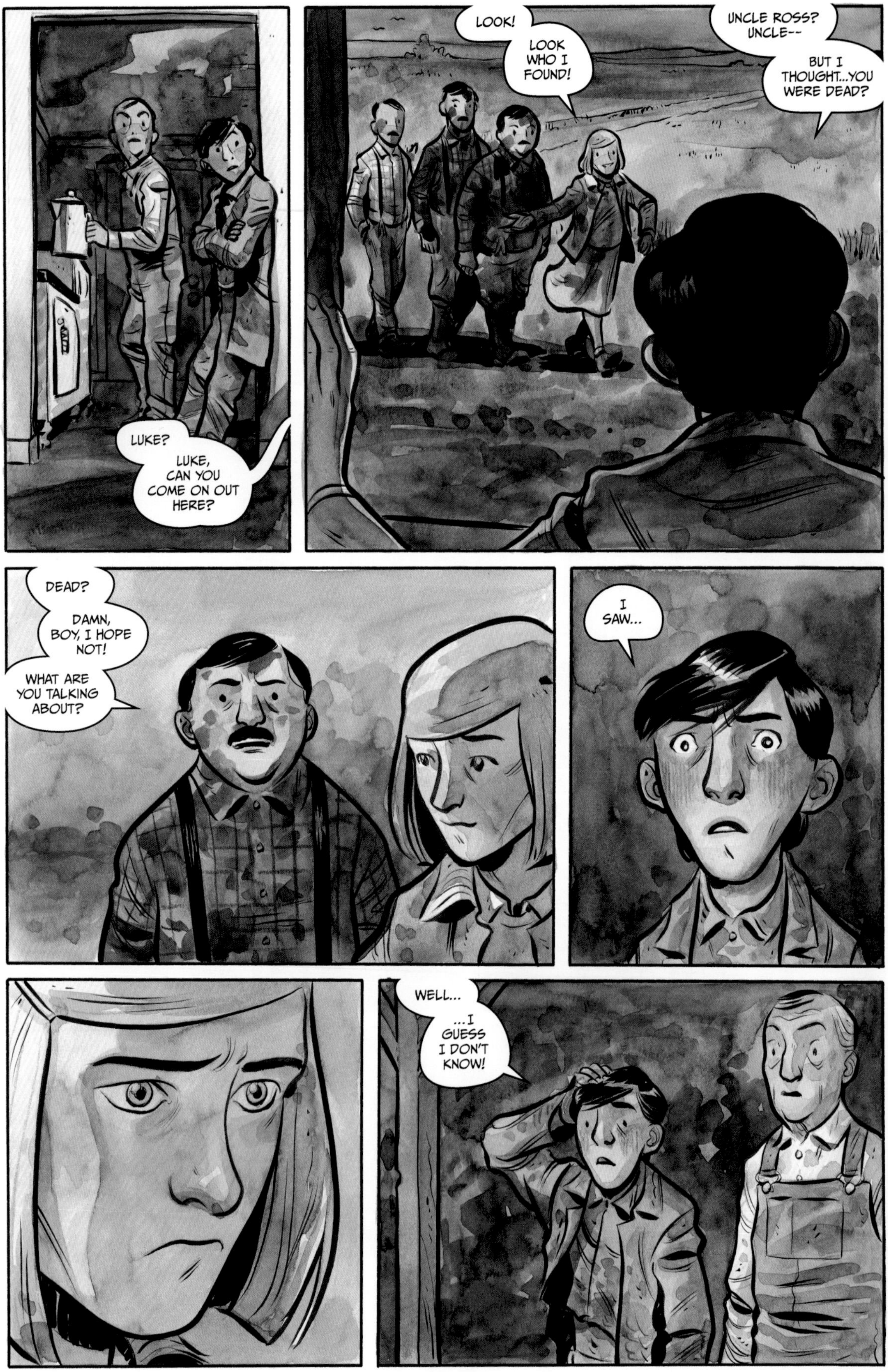
LUKE?
LUKE, CAN YOU COME ON OUT HERE?
LOOK!
LOOK WHO I FOUND!
UNCLE ROSS? UNCLE--
BUT I THOUGHT...YOU WERE DEAD?
DEAD?
DAMN, BOY, I HOPE NOT!
WHAT ARE YOU TALKING ABOUT?
I SAW...
WELL...
...I GUESS I DON'T KNOW!

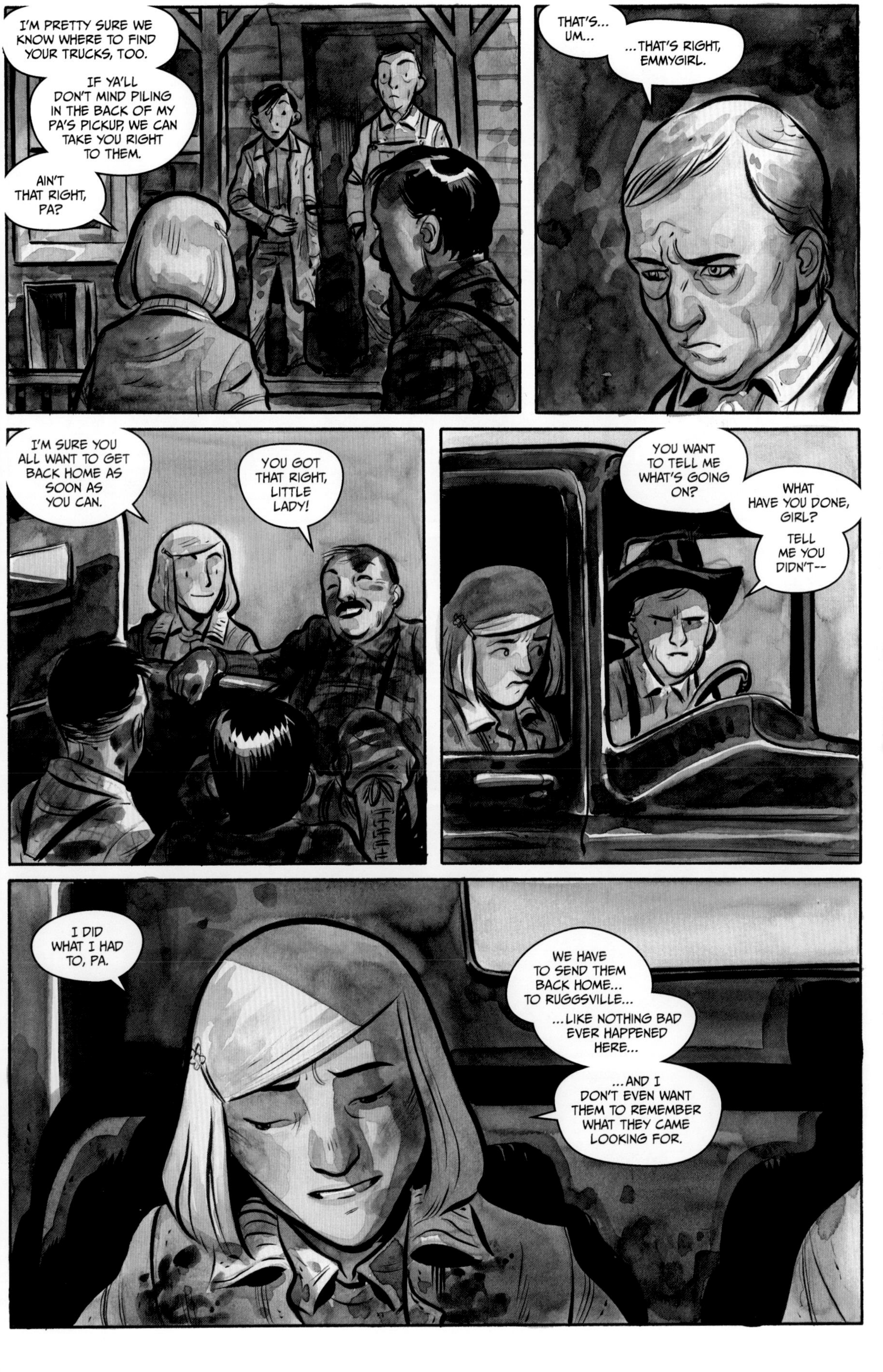
I'M PRETTY SURE WE KNOW WHERE TO FIND YOUR TRUCKS, TOO.
IF YA'LL DON'T MIND PILING IN THE BACK OF MY PA'S PICKUP, WE CAN TAKE YOU RIGHT TO THEM.
AIN'T THAT RIGHT, PA?
THAT'S... UM...
...THAT'S RIGHT, EMMYGIRL.
I'M SURE YOU ALL WANT TO GET BACK HOME AS SOON AS YOU CAN.
YOU GOT THAT RIGHT, LITTLE LADY!
YOU WANT TO TELL ME WHAT'S GOING ON?
WHAT HAVE YOU DONE, GIRL?
TELL ME YOU DIDN'T--
I DID WHAT I HAD TO, PA.
WE HAVE TO SEND THEM BACK HOME... TO RUGGSVILLE...
...LIKE NOTHING BAD EVER HAPPENED HERE...
...AND I DON'T EVEN WANT THEM TO REMEMBER WHAT THEY CAME LOOKING FOR.

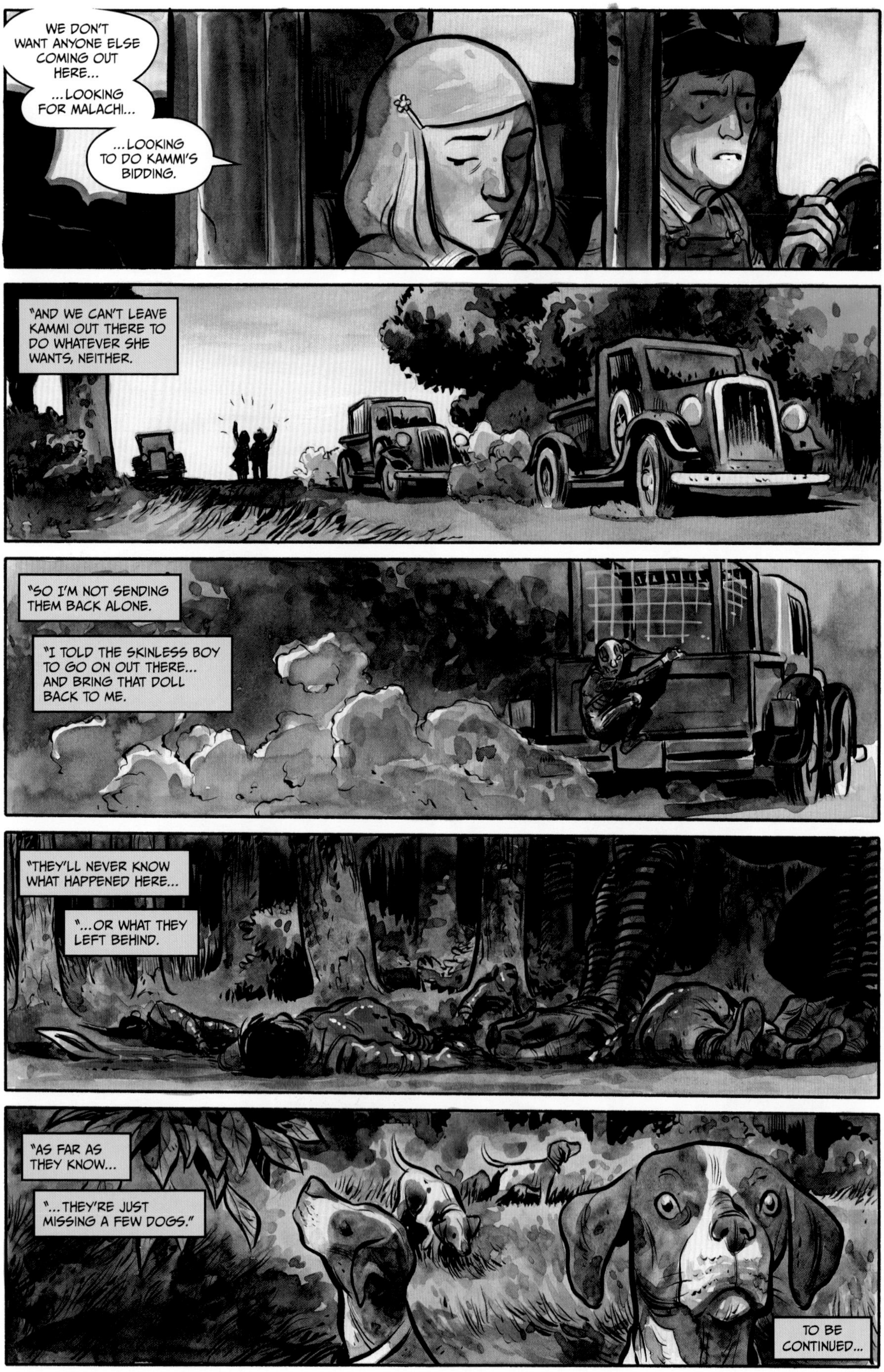
WE DON'T WANT ANYONE ELSE COMING OUT HERE...
...LOOKING FOR MALACHI...
...LOOKING TO DO KAMMI'S BIDDING.
"AND WE CAN'T LEAVE KAMMI OUT THERE TO DO WHATEVER SHE WANTS, NEITHER.
"SO I'M NOT SENDING THEM BACK ALONE.
"I TOLD THE SKINLESS BOY TO GO ON OUT THERE... AND BRING THAT DOLL BACK TO ME.
"THEY'LL NEVER KNOW WHAT HAPPENED HERE...
"...OR WHAT THEY LEFT BEHIND.
"AS FAR AS THEY KNOW...
"...THEY'RE JUST MISSING A FEW DOGS."
TO BE CONTINUED...

HARROW
◄ SKETCHBOOK ►
COUNTY ™

LUKE

① ② ③

**NOTES BY
TYLER CROOK, CARLA SPEED McNEIL,
AND JENN MANLEY LEE**

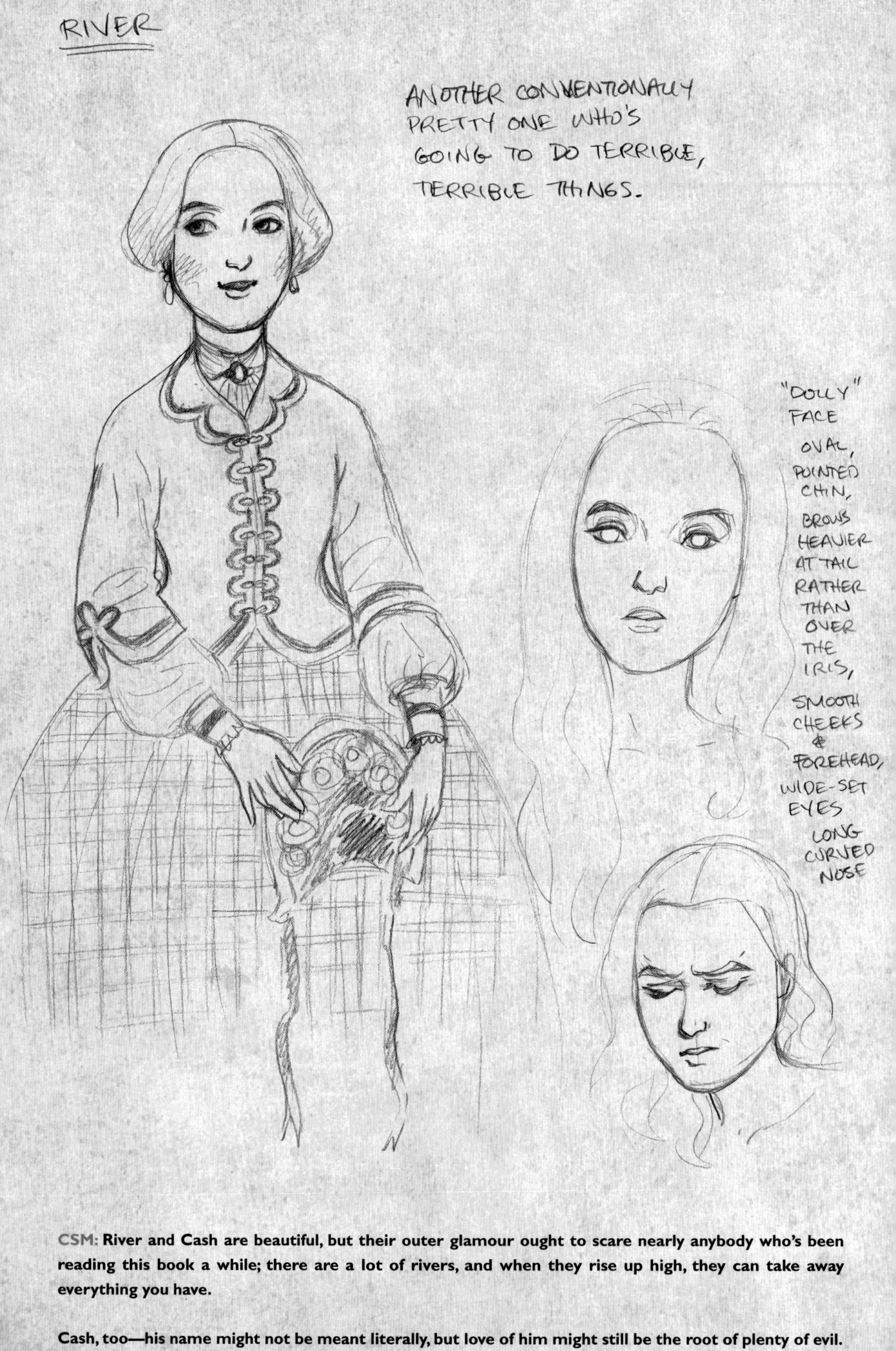
RIVER
ANOTHER CONVENTIONALLY PRETTY ONE WHO'S GOING TO DO TERRIBLE, TERRIBLE THINGS.
"DOLLY" FACE
OVAL, POINTED CHIN, BROWS HEAVIER AT TAIL RATHER THAN OVER THE IRIS, SMOOTH CHEEKS & FOREHEAD, WIDE-SET EYES
LONG CURVED NOSE

CSM: **River and Cash are beautiful, but their outer glamour ought to scare nearly anybody who's been reading this book a while; there are a lot of rivers, and when they rise up high, they can take away everything you have.**

Cash, too—his name might not be meant literally, but love of him might still be the root of plenty of evil.

CASH

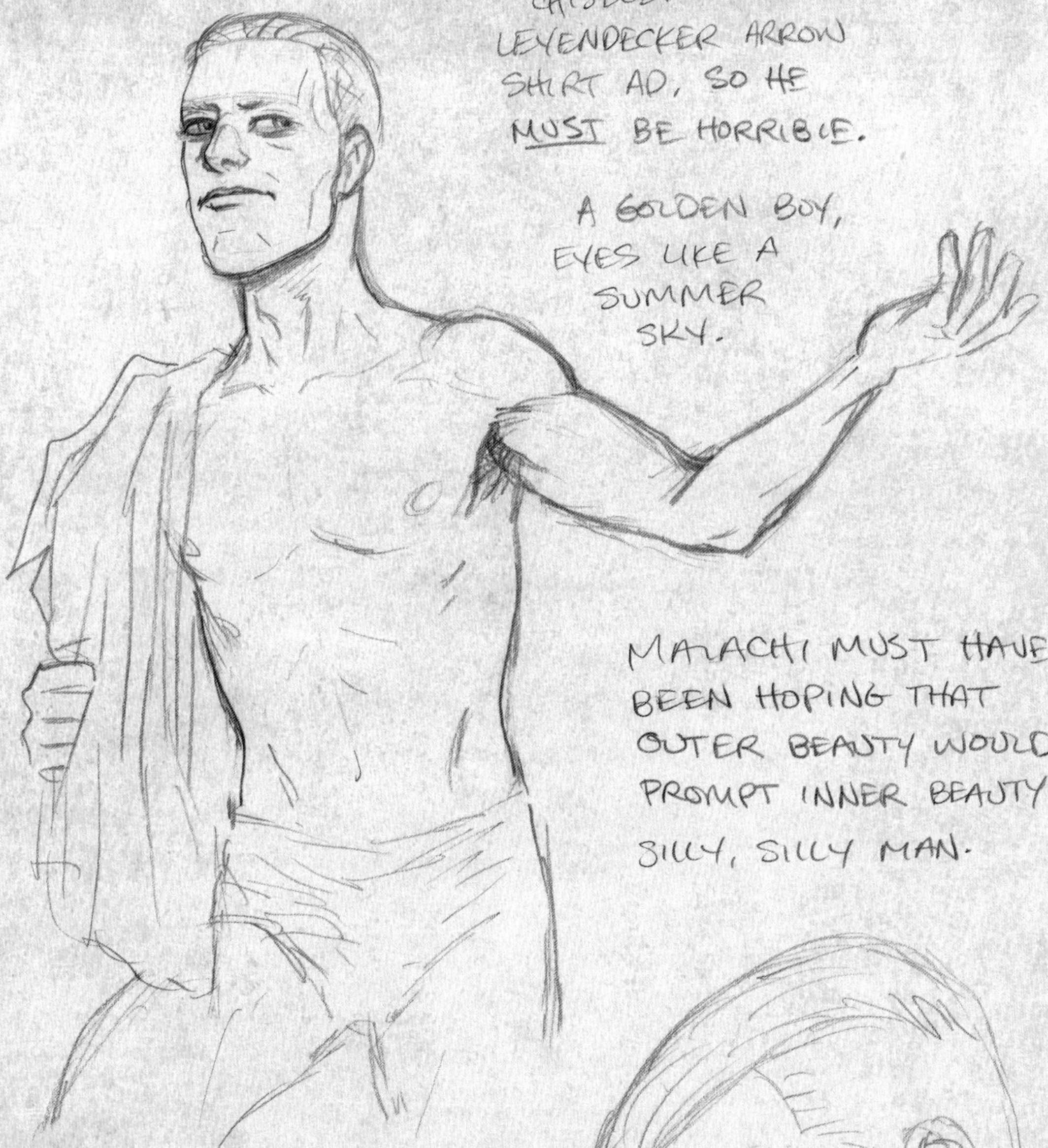

CHISELED LIKE A LEYENDECKER ARROW SHIRT AD, SO HE *MUST* BE HORRIBLE.

A GOLDEN BOY, EYES LIKE A SUMMER SKY.

MALACHI MUST HAVE BEEN HOPING THAT OUTER BEAUTY WOULD PROMPT INNER BEAUTY. SILLY, SILLY MAN.

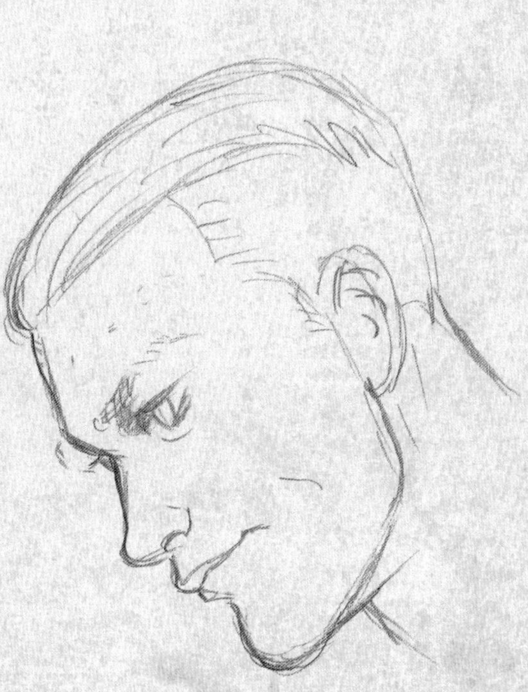

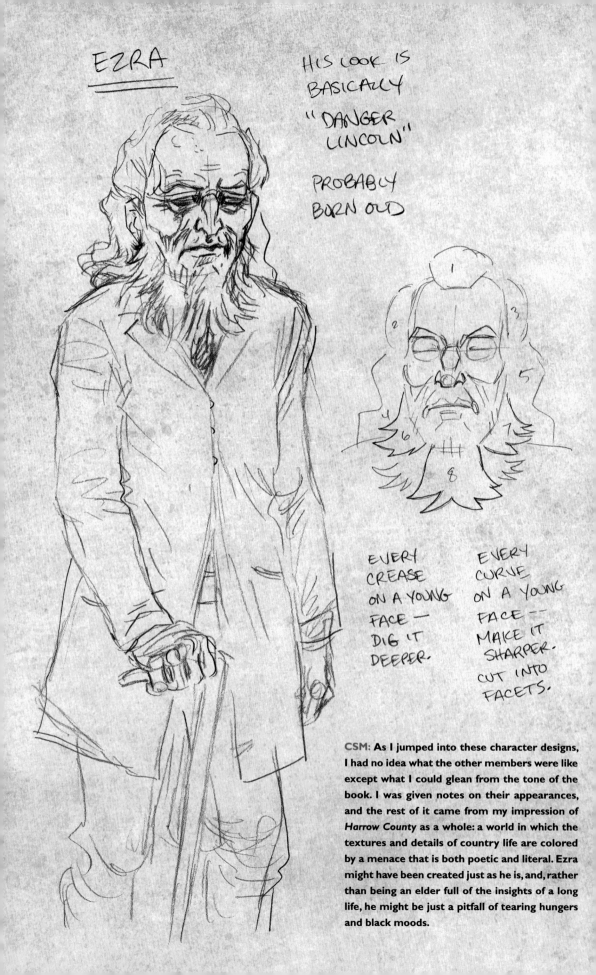

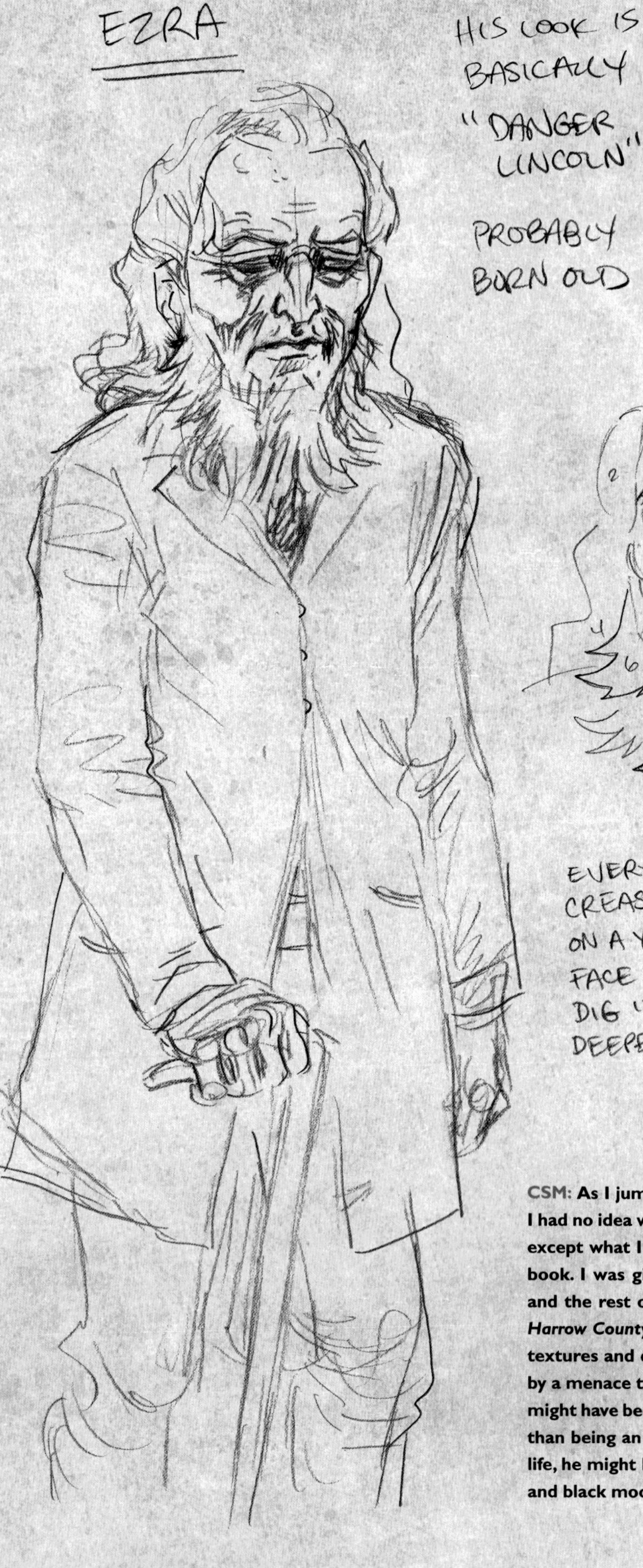
EZRA
HIS LOOK IS BASICALLY "DANGER LINCOLN"
PROBABLY BORN OLD

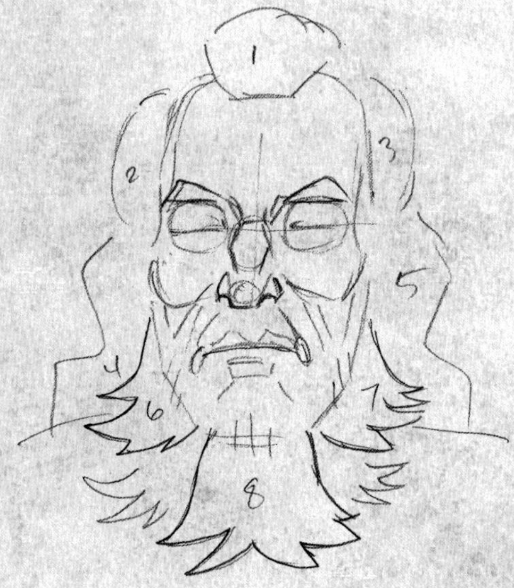
1
2
3
4
5
6
7
8
EVERY CREASE ON A YOUNG FACE — DIG IT DEEPER.
EVERY CURVE ON A YOUNG FACE — MAKE IT SHARPER. CUT INTO FACETS.

CSM: As I jumped into these character designs, I had no idea what the other members were like except what I could glean from the tone of the book. I was given notes on their appearances, and the rest of it came from my impression of *Harrow County* as a whole: a world in which the textures and details of country life are colored by a menace that is both poetic and literal. Ezra might have been created just as he is, and, rather than being an elder full of the insights of a long life, he might be just a pitfall of tearing hungers and black moods.

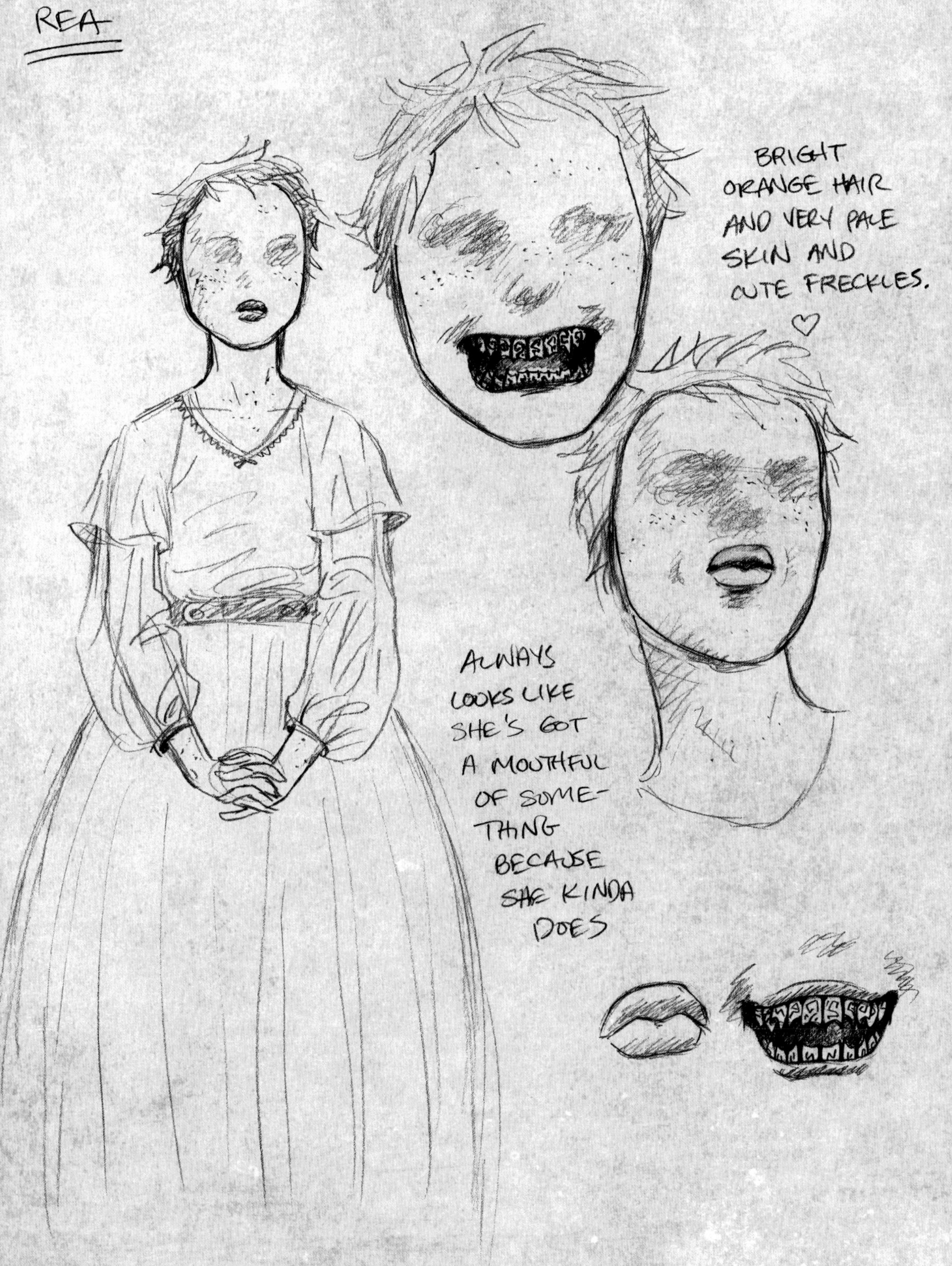
REA
BRIGHT ORANGE HAIR AND VERY PALE SKIN AND CUTE FRECKLES.
ALWAYS LOOKS LIKE SHE'S GOT A MOUTHFUL OF SOME-THING BECAUSE SHE KINDA DOES

CSM: Oddly, I'm more comfortable with Rea, who will not be easily able to hide her difference. The pretty ones scare me more . . . That's why I delved a bit into Clive Barker, one of our great fantasy-world builders, and borrowed the carved teeth of his hero Cabal. The shape of her teeth I took from a piranha, but—here's the funny part—I had to stick the pointy bits on, since the fish I was studying is actually a harmless eater of fallen fruit.

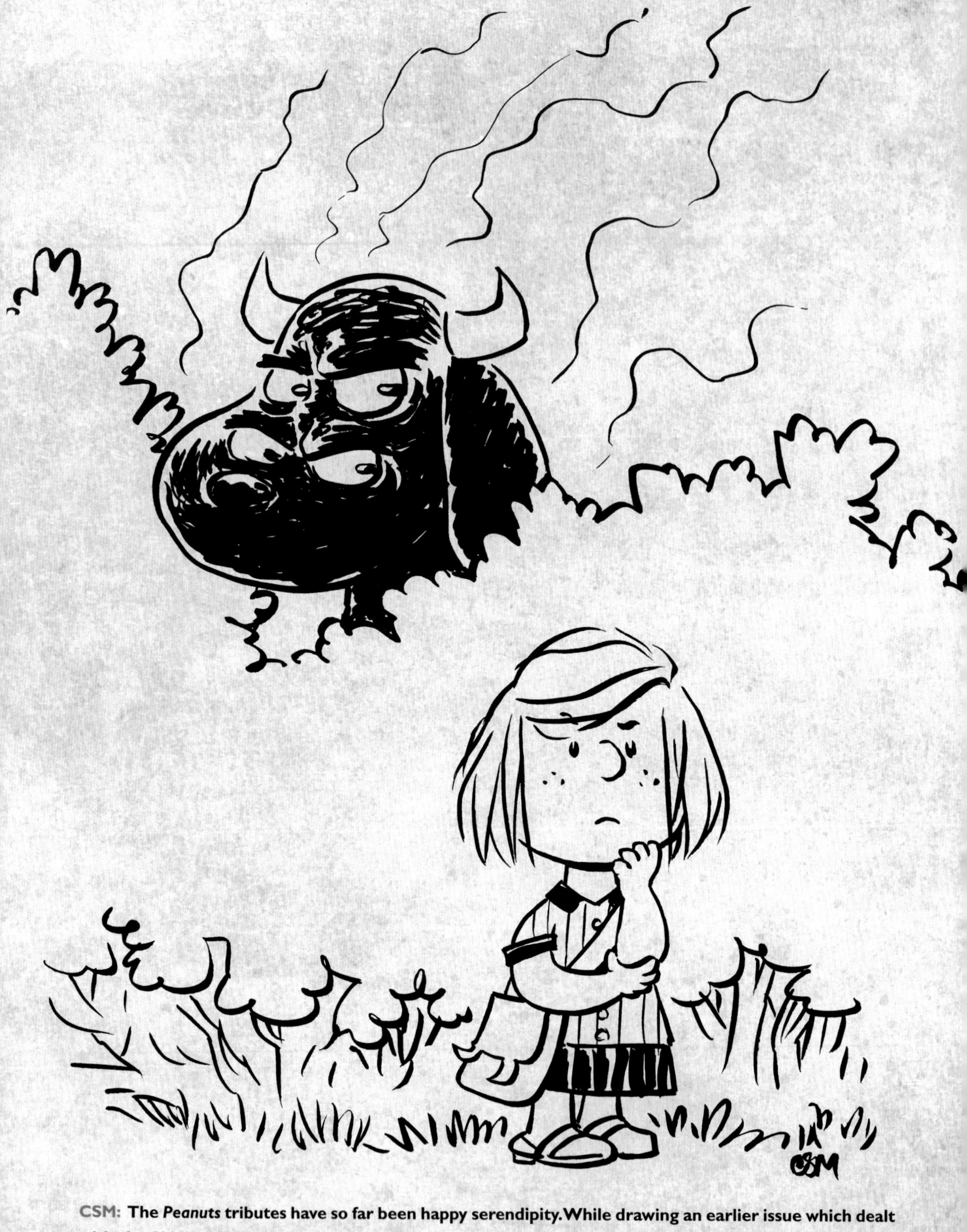
CSM

CSM: The *Peanuts* tributes have so far been happy serendipity. While drawing an earlier issue which dealt with the Skinless Boy carrying his skin around with him, it amused me to draw them as Linus van Pelt and his blanket, respectively, and with a skeletal Woodstock fluttering around just because. I thought it was just a funny one-off, a little pop-culture echo, until it occurred to me that Emmy's side part looked more like Peppermint Patty's unique forelock than I'd thought . . . and that left You Know Who to play You Know Who, because Charles Schulz didn't draw very many animals. Will I be able to add to the cast of crossovers? I have no idea. Depends on whether anyone takes up piano, I guess. Or if we have a baseball episode.

TC: It's like Charles Schulz returned from the dead and started exploring the horror of our everyday foibles and existential dread!

ART PROCESS

NOTES BY
JENN MANLEY LEE

It all starts when we get the script from Cullen.

HARROW COUNTY

ISSUE #17 SCRIPT

BY CULLEN BUNN

<u>PAGE 17 (Five Panels)</u>

PANEL 1
Cut to a gathering of people in a small town. They are dressed for the cold, but are happy and excited, gathering for an Old Christmas celebration. There are steaming oyster cook pots set up on the street, people gathered around awaiting food or seeking warmth. Men, women, children, and old folks are all here.

A few creepy things we should definitely see here:

Traditions of Old Christmas past also include beginning the festivities with fifes and drums playing eerie music at the crack of dawn to awaken natives.

Children and adults would put socks or homemade masks on their faces, dress in colorful clothing, and run around singing Christmas carols to their neighbors as they awaited the appearance of Old Buck.

I think we should see people playing their drums and some of them wearing creepy homemade masks.

CAPTION (The Abandoned):

"If'n ya know any folks from tha Outer Banks, ya might know that come January they celebrate **Ol' Christmas**.

"It's a tradition brought along by the first people to settle tha area...

"...steeped in tha **custom** and **superstation** of tha long-dead past.

PANEL 2
A Woman (not masked) is moving through the crowd. She is looking around, a little worried.

CAPTION (The Abandoned):

"Not cleanin' ashes from the hearth 'til tha night of tha celebration...

"...makin' meals fer haints...

"...roastin' oysters..."

WOMAN:

Has anyone seen my old man?

Has anyone seen Merl?

PANEL 3
The Woman, still seeking her husband, walks right past Malachi and Amaryllis, who stand amongst the crowd.

CAPTION (The Abandoned):

"...and gatherin' with them you love."

WOMAN:

He was out fishing, but he should be back by now.

Has anyone seen him?

PANEL 4
A couple of masked children come by, both of them carrying little baskets full of maple candies. One of the children is offering a piece of candy to Amaryllis, and she takes it, smiling sweetly.

AMARYLLIS:

Oh, thank you kindly.

CAPTION (Abandoned):

"Children pass out homemade maple candies to strangers...

PANEL 5
Amaryllis is delighted as she takes the piece of candy and bites into it. Malachi is looking off in another direction.

CAPTION (Abandoned):

"...never sure if'n spirits walked amongst 'em durin' tha merriment."

AMARYLLIS:

Mm.

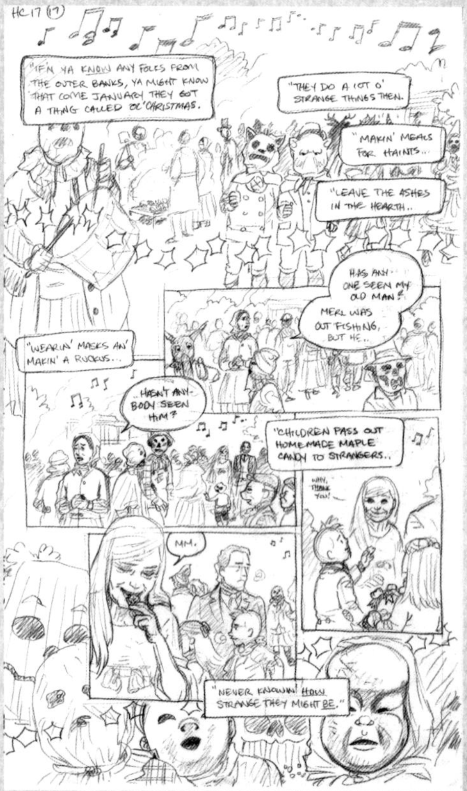
HC17 (17)
"IF'N YA KNOW ANY FOLKS FROM THE OUTER BANKS, YA MIGHT KNOW THAT COME JANUARY THEY GOT A THING CALLED OL' CHRISTMAS.
"THEY DO A LOT O' STRANGE THINGS THEN.
"MAKIN' MEALS FOR HAINTS...
"LEAVE THE ASHES IN THE HEARTH..
HAS ANY-ONE SEEN MY OLD MAN?
MERL WAS OUT FISHING, BUT HE..
"WEARIN' MASKS AN' MAKIN' A RUCKUS...
..HASN'T ANY-BODY SEEN HIM?
"CHILDREN PASS OUT HOMEMADE MAPLE CANDY TO STRANGERS..
WHY, THANK YOU!
MM.
"NEVER KNOWIN' HOW STRANGE THEY MIGHT BE."

1. Pencils

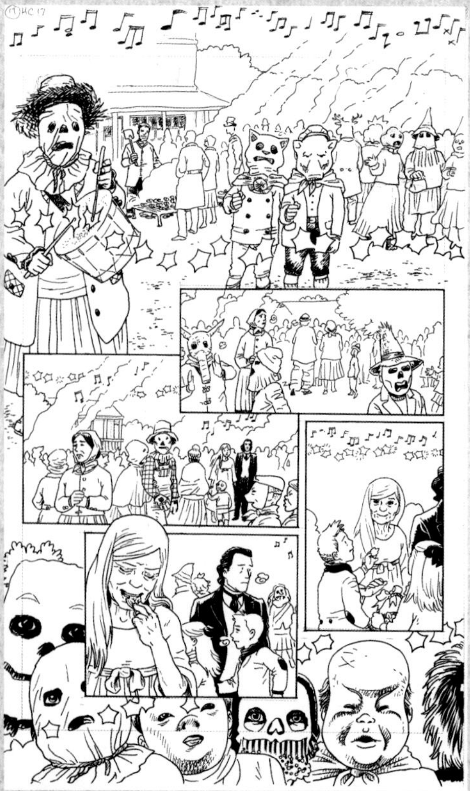

2. Inks

1. Pencils

After getting the script, Carla lays out and pencils the page. She always letters at this stage, whether or not she is doing final lettering. This not only makes it easier to review how well the layout works but also establishes the flow and ensures there is enough room for the words (always important).

Often Carla will make script suggestions through her pencil lettering. Here she proposed a rewording of the last line—the caption box in lower right—changing it from "never sure if'n spirits walked amongst 'em durin' tha merriment" to "never knowin' how strange they might be." Cullen and Tyler seem to have liked the change, as it made its way into the final page.

2. Inks

Once the pencils are approved, if there are no major changes, Carla uses a light box to create tighter art on Bristol board, which she then inks.

3. Flat Colors

After I get ahold of Carla's high-resolution scan, I create a layered Photoshop file and clean up the line art. Then I eliminate all white areas, so I just have the black line art on its own layer. This makes it easier to apply color and other effects to the art.

In flatting, I create separate layers for background art and figures, letting the background flood beneath to ensure no unintentional white gaps in the art. For this page I have two sets of these, a set for the top panels and another set for those that flood beneath.

I chose a limited palette for these flashback scenes, starting with the colors of a sepia photograph, adding grays and muted greens to help suggest cold winter days. The red is used as a focusing accent and bright yellow as an occasional highlight.

When establishing a new palette, I'll often run the fully flatted page past Carla to make sure that's the coloring she sees for the characters (I don't always get notes) and the color scheme strikes the right mood.

3. Flat Colors

4. Textures and Effects

I start by applying color to the line art, either to accentuate or soften it as needed.

Next, I apply broad texture effects to the flat art, by both adding and removing color from the flats using a layer mask. In both cases I use brushes from Kyle Webster's watercolor brushes for Photoshop. I try to keep it loose and uneven in application to further suggest a watercolor approach.

Finally I create a "borderless" effect to the panels, painting broad, ragged lines over the panel borders to conform with the panel treatment Tyler established for flashbacks in earlier issues of *Harrow County*.

5. Rendering and Lettering

Generally for rendering, I use a Multiply layer on top of the flat art in order to shade and a Screen layer to apply highlights. I do that here, but I also paint directly on the flat layers, such as the clouds in the sky. I also add tints for reddened cheeks and noses, do some cleanup, and, in this instance, mess things up a bit.

After my colors are approved by Carla and all, the page goes to Tyler for lettering, gets blessed by Daniel and Cullen, and then goes to print.

4. Textures and Effects

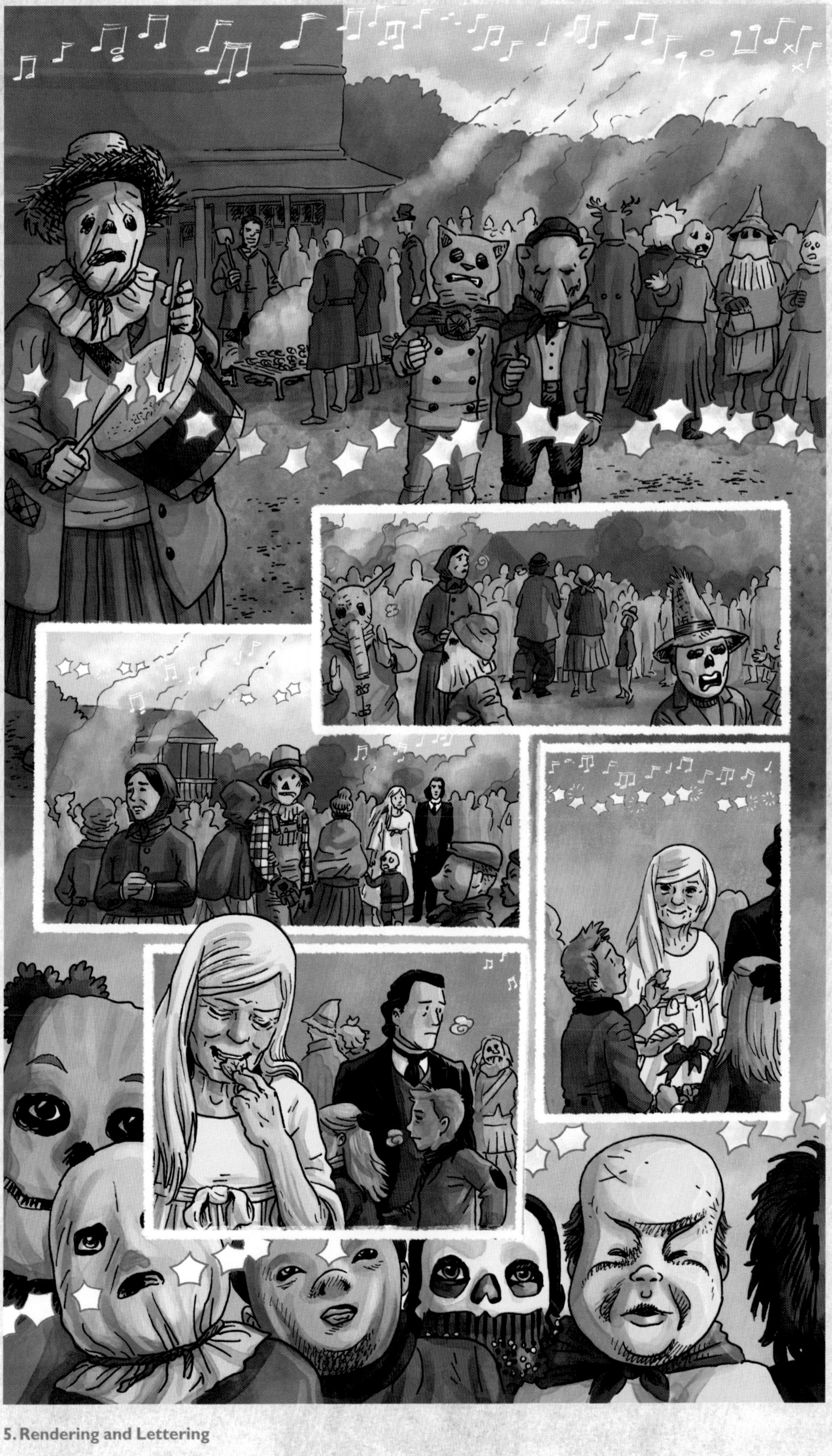

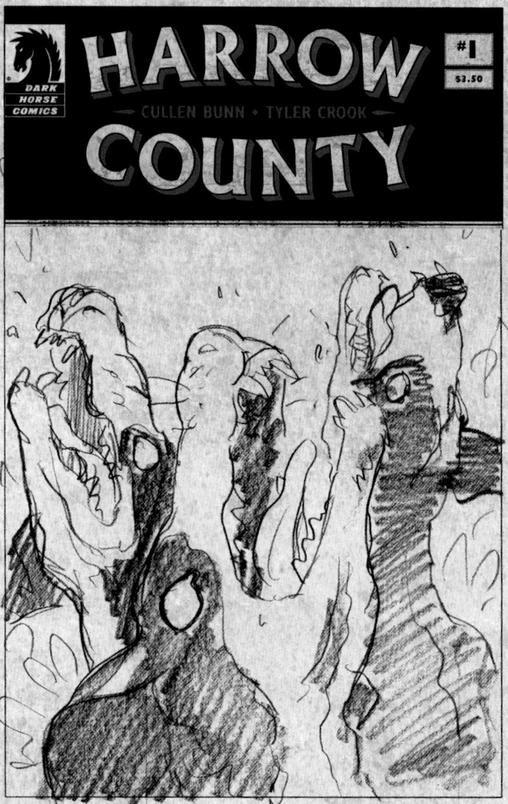
DARK HORSE COMICS
HARROW
CULLEN BUNN • TYLER CROOK
COUNTY
#1
$3.50
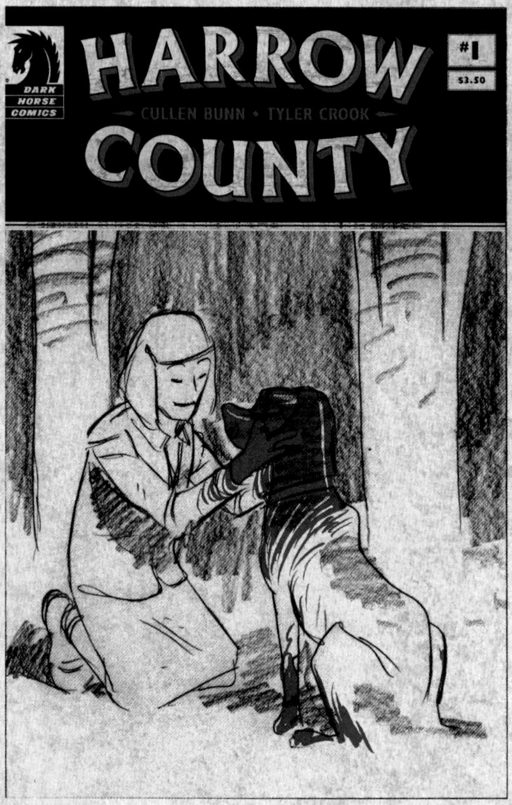
DARK HORSE COMICS
HARROW
CULLEN BUNN • TYLER CROOK
COUNTY
#1
$3.50
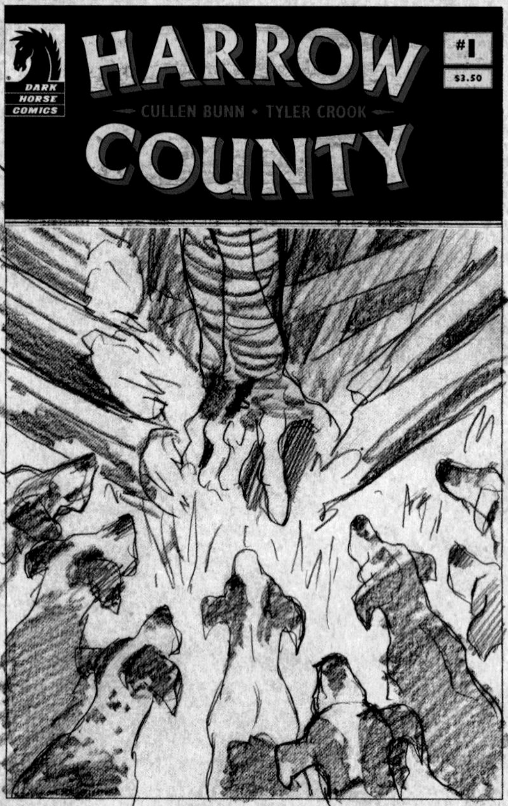
DARK HORSE COMICS
HARROW
CULLEN BUNN • TYLER CROOK
COUNTY
#1
$3.50
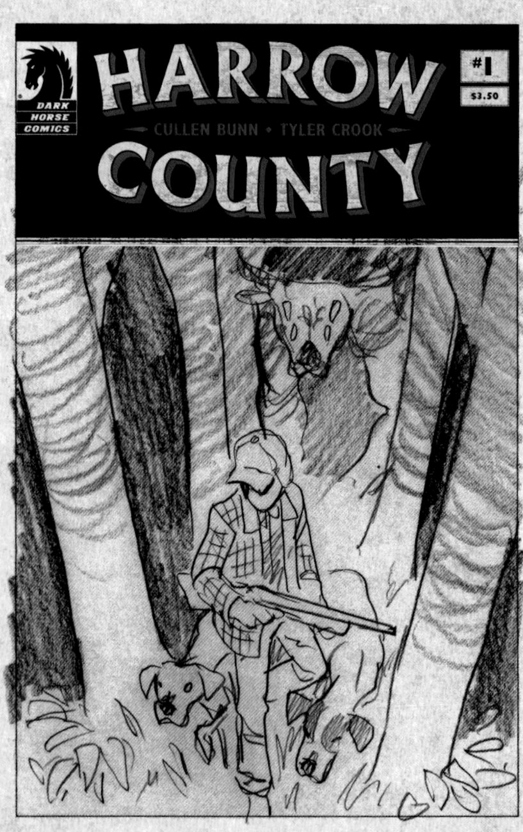
DARK HORSE COMICS
HARROW
CULLEN BUNN • TYLER CROOK
COUNTY
#1
$3.50

TC: These are the sketches I did for the cover of #19. I really liked the first one (just three dog heads). The idea of them putting their heads up like they are going to howl but not howling kind of freaked me out. I liked the idea enough that I asked Cullen to include it in issue #20.

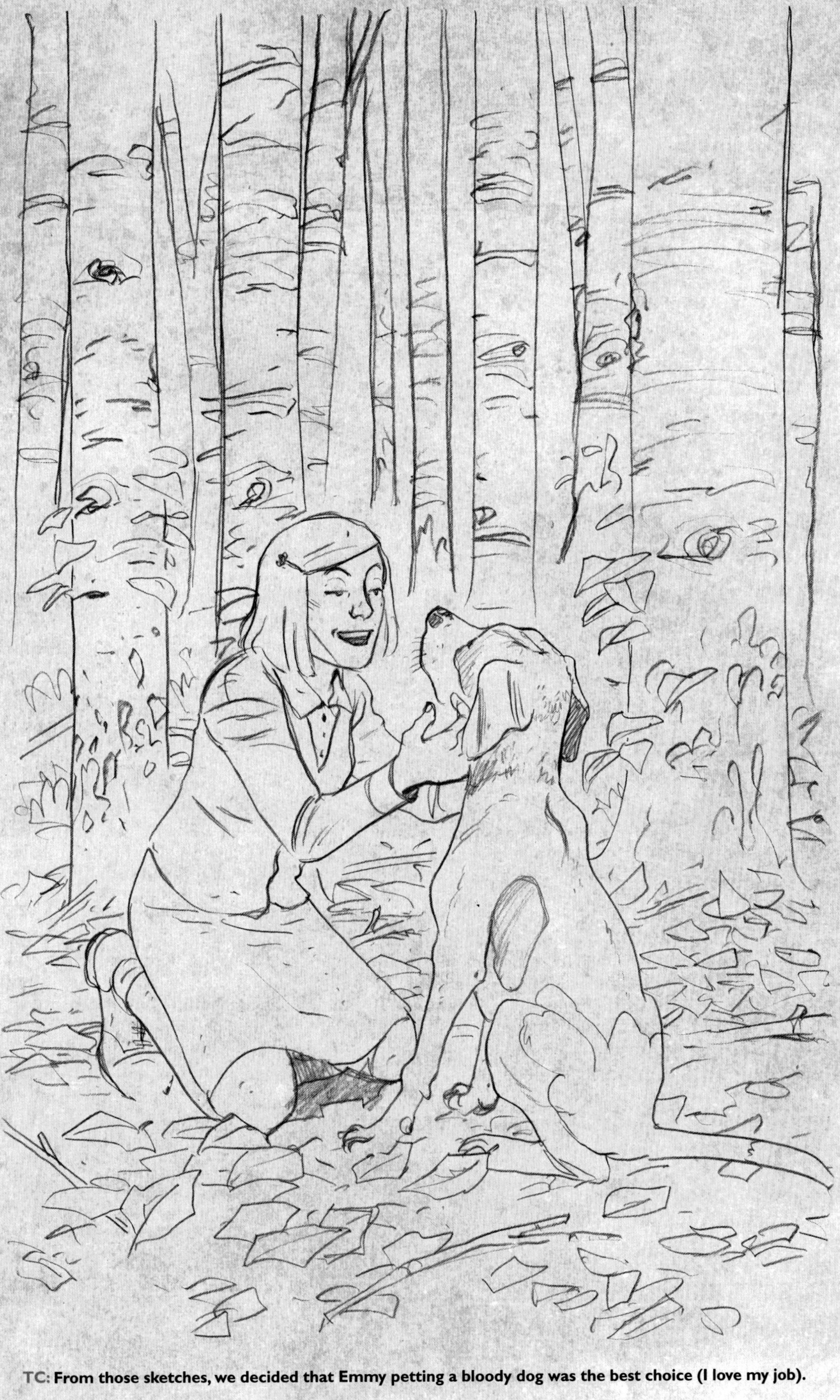

TC: From those sketches, we decided that Emmy petting a bloody dog was the best choice (I love my job).

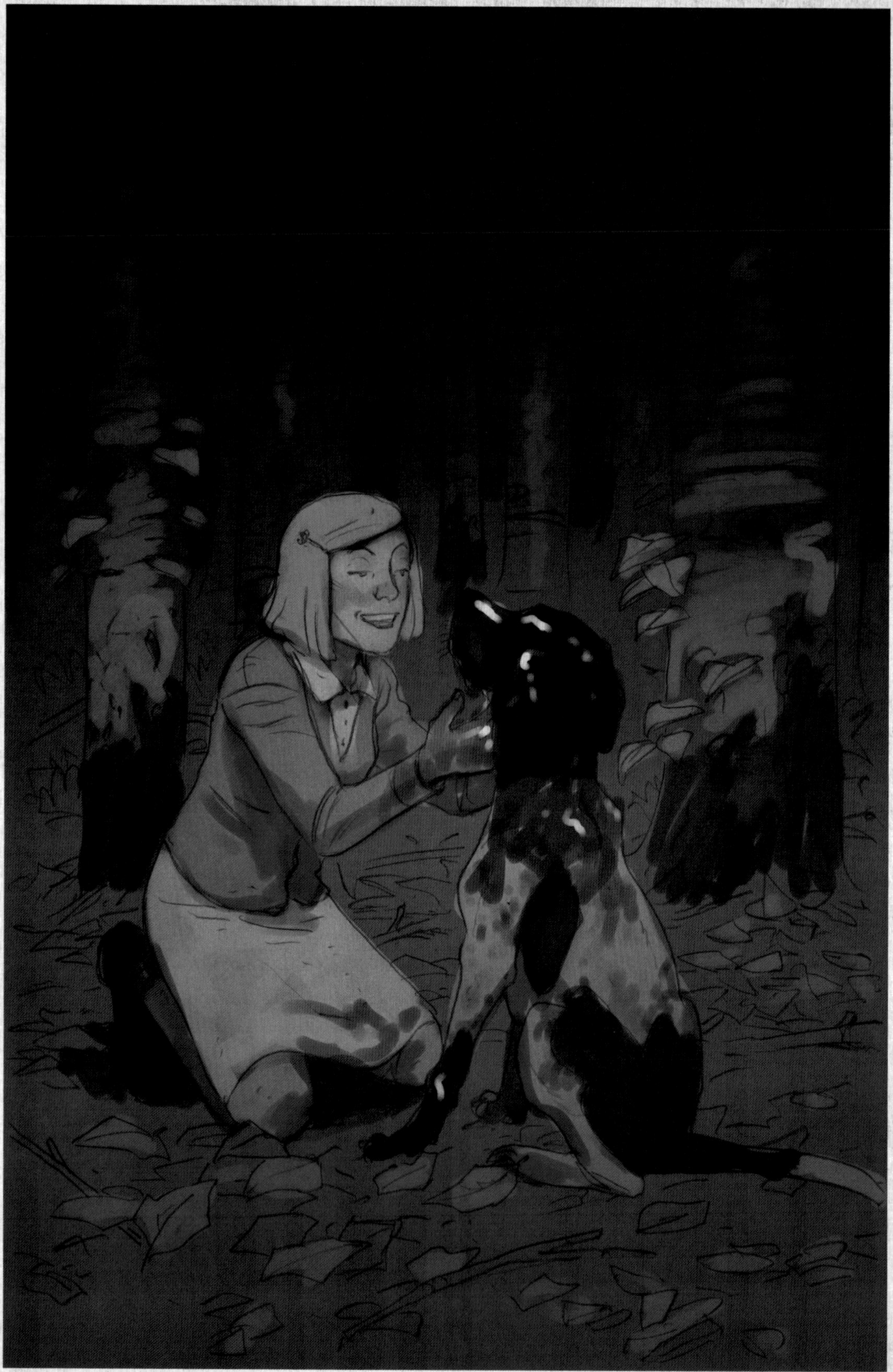

TC: I don't always do this, but for this cover I decided that I needed to do a color comp to work out the mood that I wanted. It's not exactly what I ended up doing, but it was enough to get me started.

PAINTING PROCESS

NOTES BY
TYLER CROOK

With the initial sketch done, I started on the final pencil drawing. I blocked in the major shapes and larger details in red pencil.

Then I used a regular graphite lead to do the "tight" drawing. First I focused on the main figures.

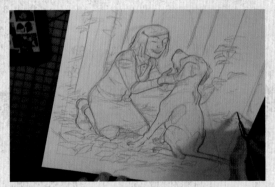

Then I worked out the background details.

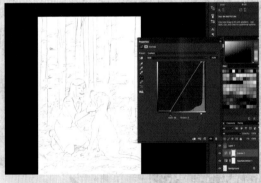

I scanned the image into Photoshop and removed the red pencils and then tinted the drawing so I could print it on my nice paper.

Here's the cleaned-up pencils printed on 11 x 17 Strathmore Mixed Media paper. This is my favorite paper for watercolor.

Usually I'll ink the drawing with brown ink, but I wanted a softer feel for this cover, so I skipped that step and went straight to painting.

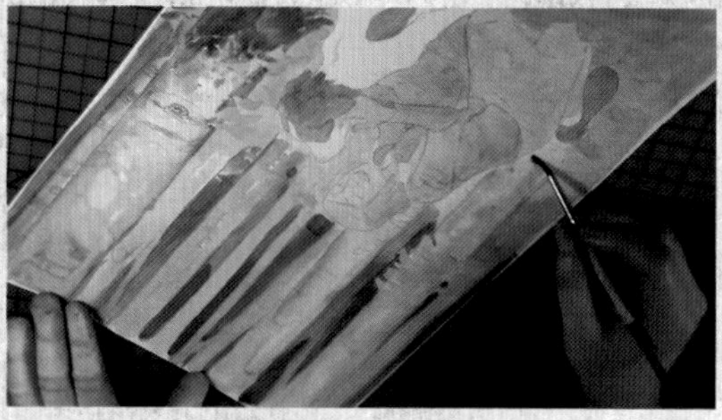

I used inexpensive synthetic brushes and professional-grade watercolor paint to lay in the basic colors.

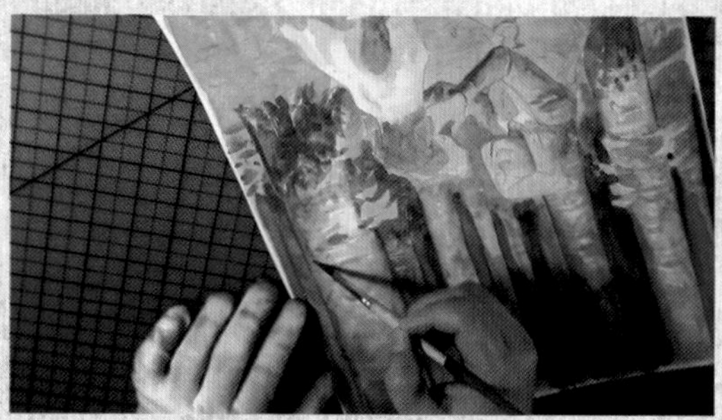

The background starts to get darker as I define the shapes of the tree trunks.

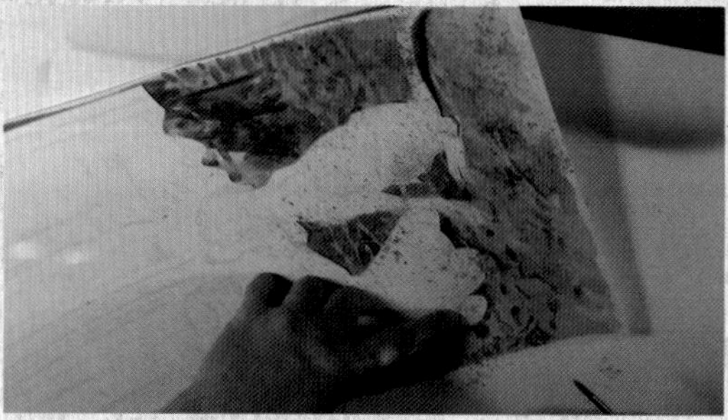

That way I can splatter paint on to the background without affecting the figures. Here I'm still masking off the trees because I want to splatter them with different colors.

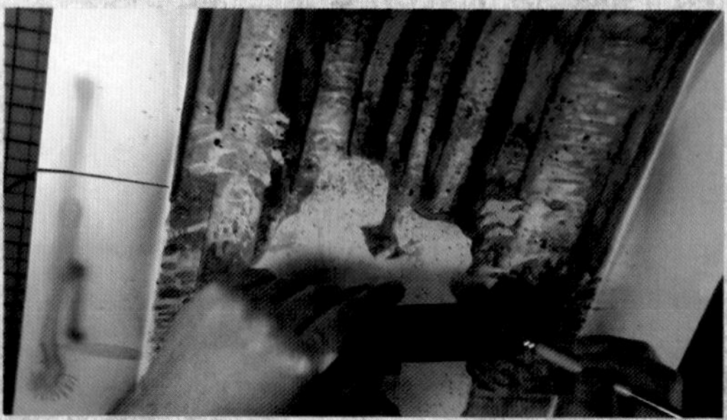

Using a brush and a putty knife, I splattered paint on the background to build up a natural-looking bark texture.

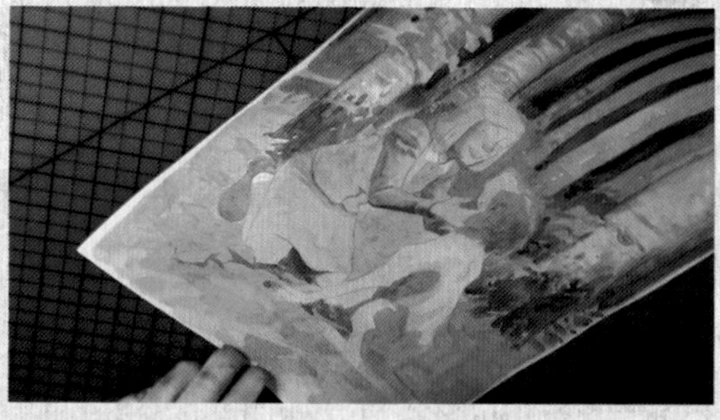

Watercolor is a transparent medium, so I can build layers of color until I get the result I want.

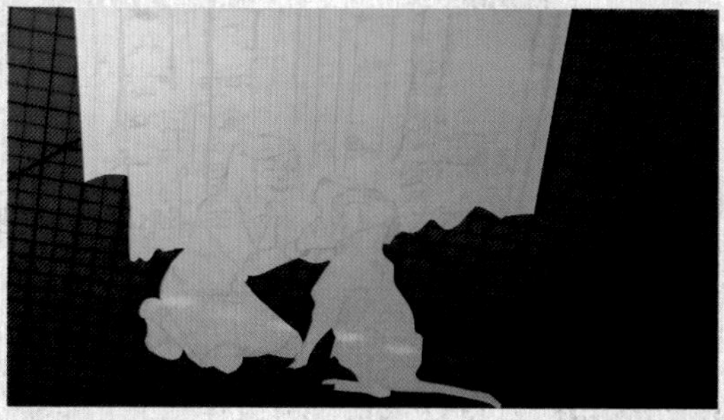

On a separate piece of paper, I printed out the pencil drawing and cut out the main figures. I used this to mask off the figures.

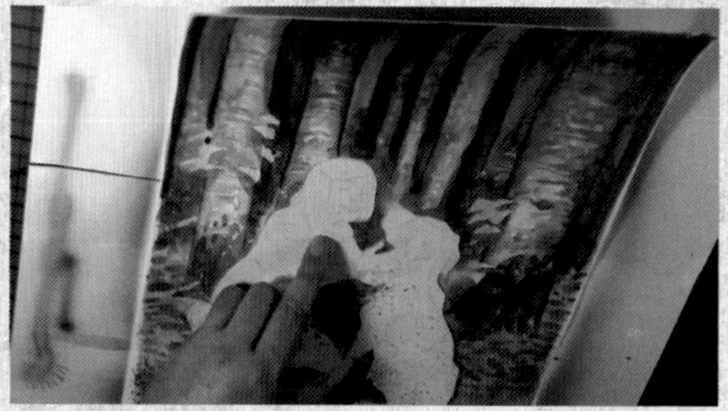

The accuracy of the mask isn't super critical, so I just hold it down with my fingers.

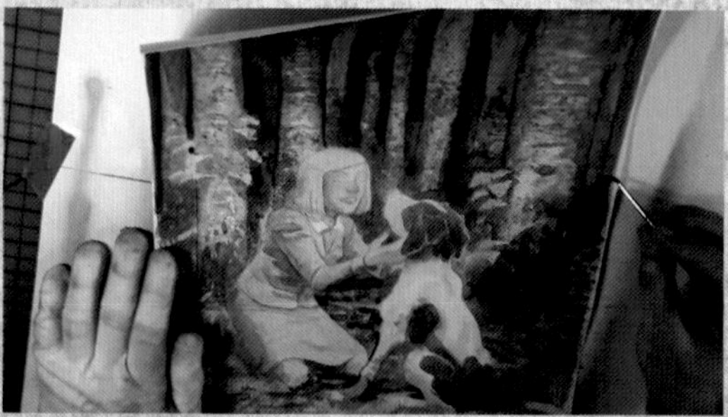

I continued to build up the colors and define the shapes.

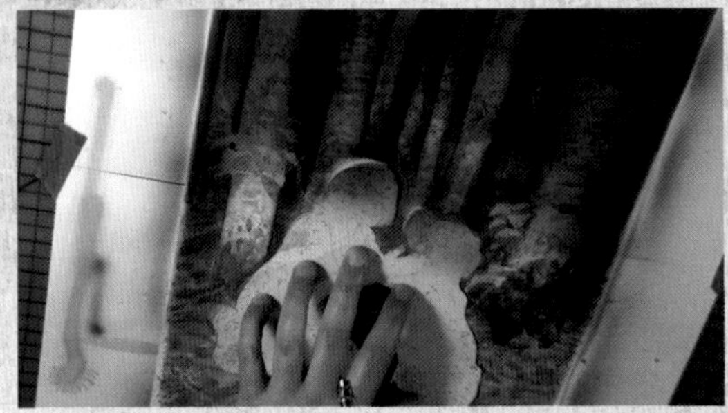

I used the mask to cover the figures while I used an airbrush to darken the background. I love how the airbrush softens the light and shadows.

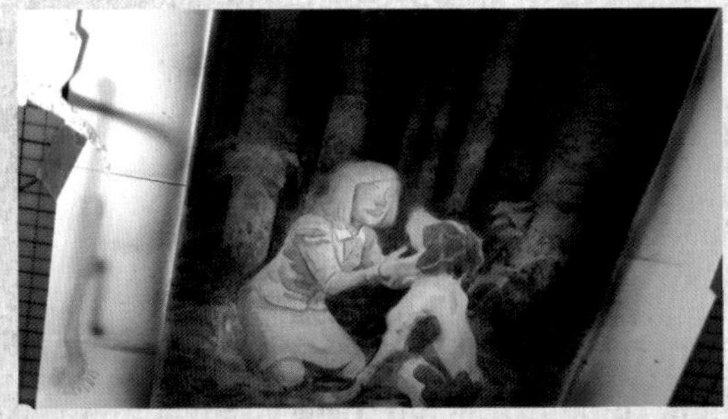

I used the airbrush to lay down some yellow tones on the figures and the foreground, too.

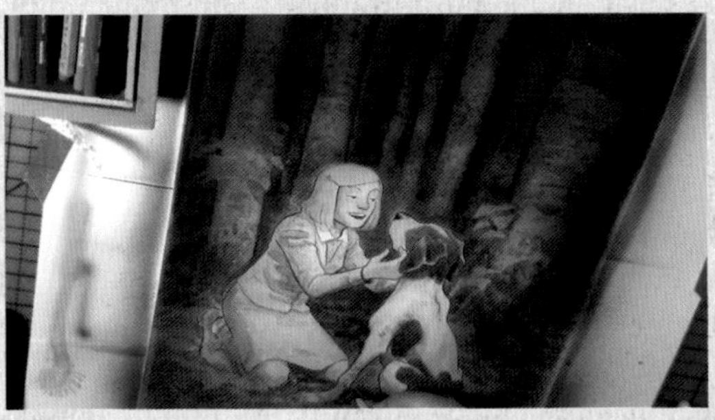

At this point, I decided that the image was looking a little too soft, so I started going in with colored pencil to define some of the forms and details.

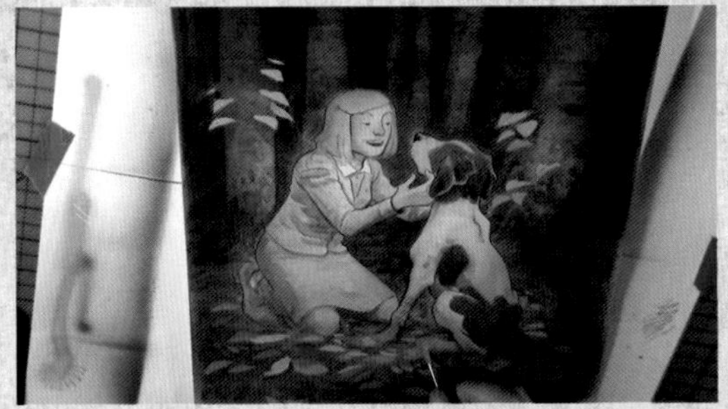

I used gouache, an opaque watercolor paint, to build up the forms of the leaves on the ground and on the tree trunks.

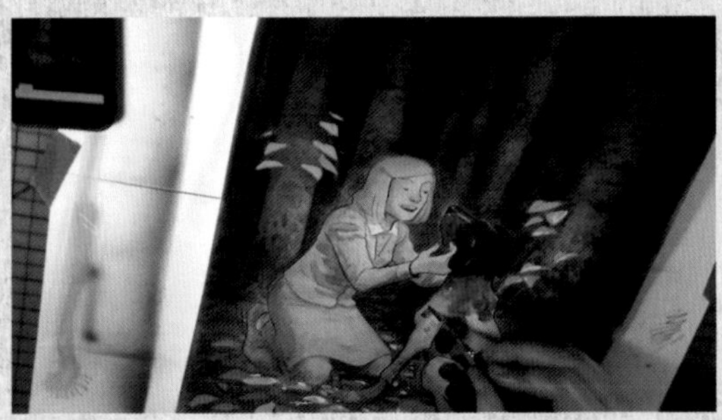

Finally, time for the blood! I switched back to regular watercolor paint and built up a few layers of red on the dog's head, as well as a little on Emmy's dress and hands.

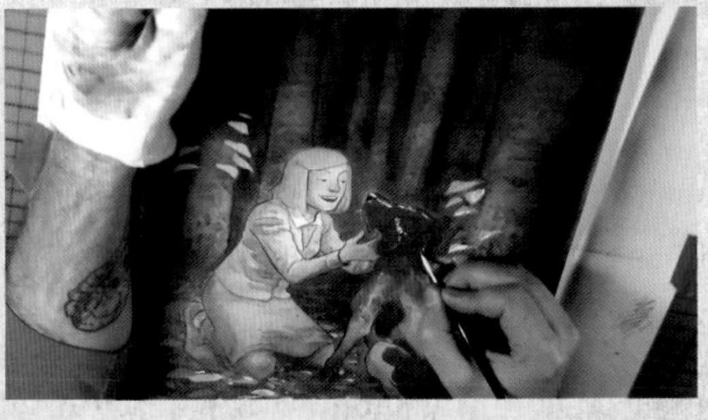

To make the blood look nice and wet, I added some specular highlights with white gouache.

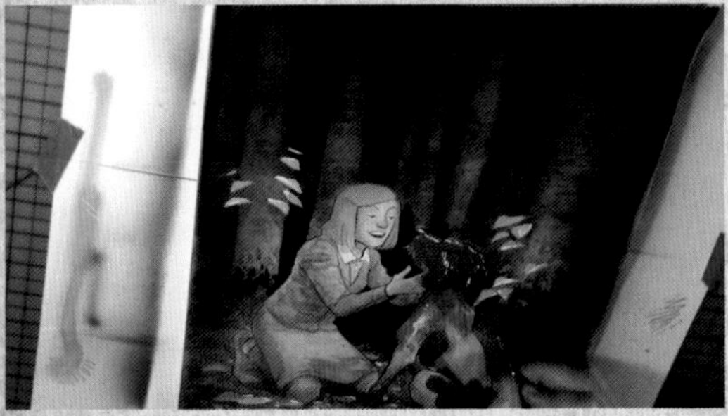

I entered the final stretch using black gouache to define the blackest blacks of the image, making sure that all the forms were clear and well defined.

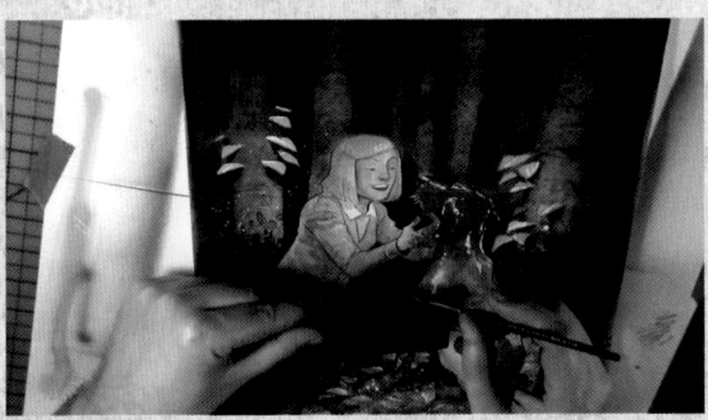

Finally, I did a little more splattering across the whole painting to add texture and some surface interest to the image.

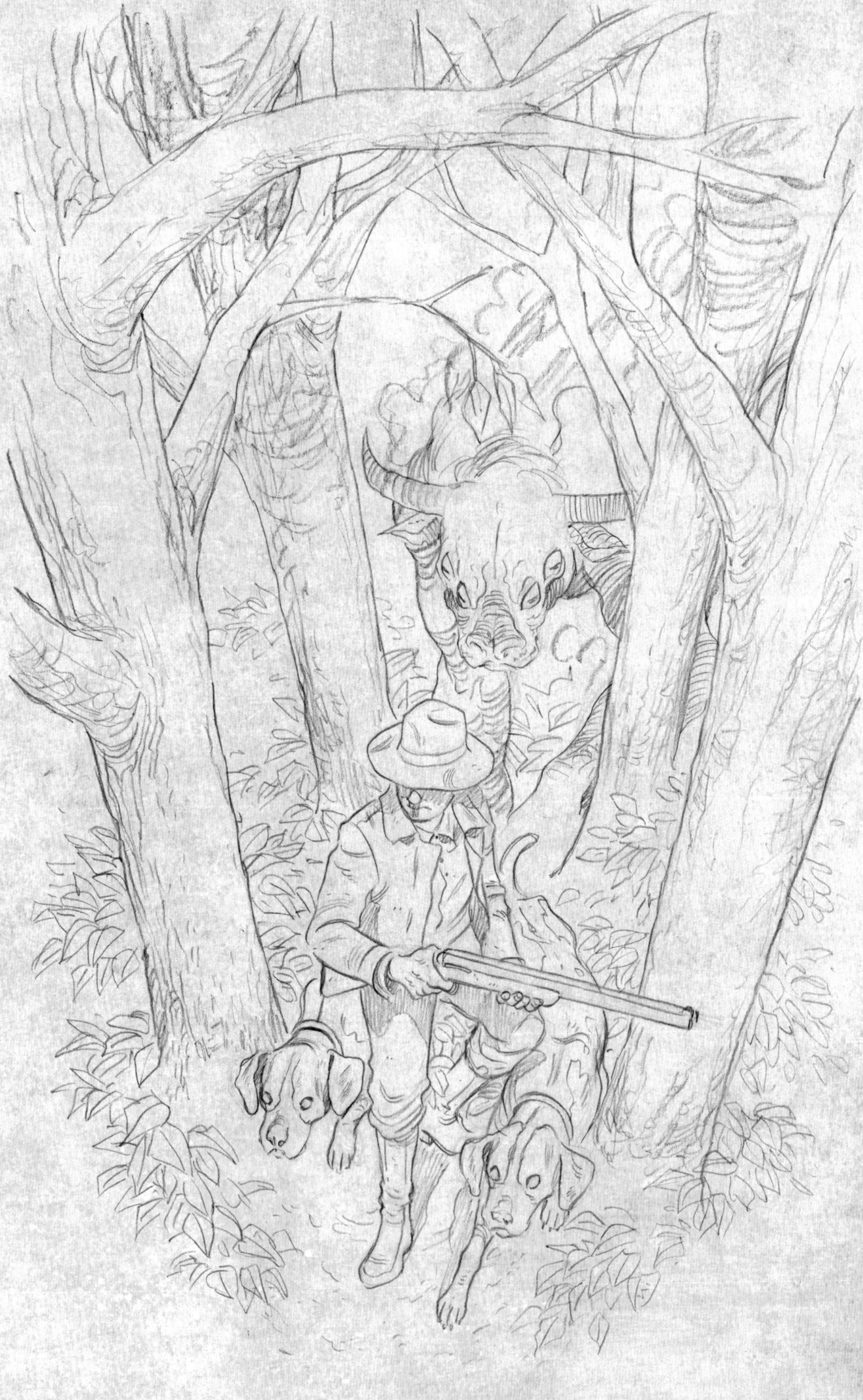

TC: Here's the pencil drawing for the cover of #20. You might recognize it—I originally pitched this idea for the cover of #19. It ended up being one of my favorite covers of the whole series (so far).

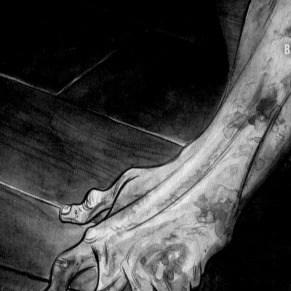

MORE TITLES FROM
TYLER CROOK,
CULLEN BUNN, AND DARK HORSE

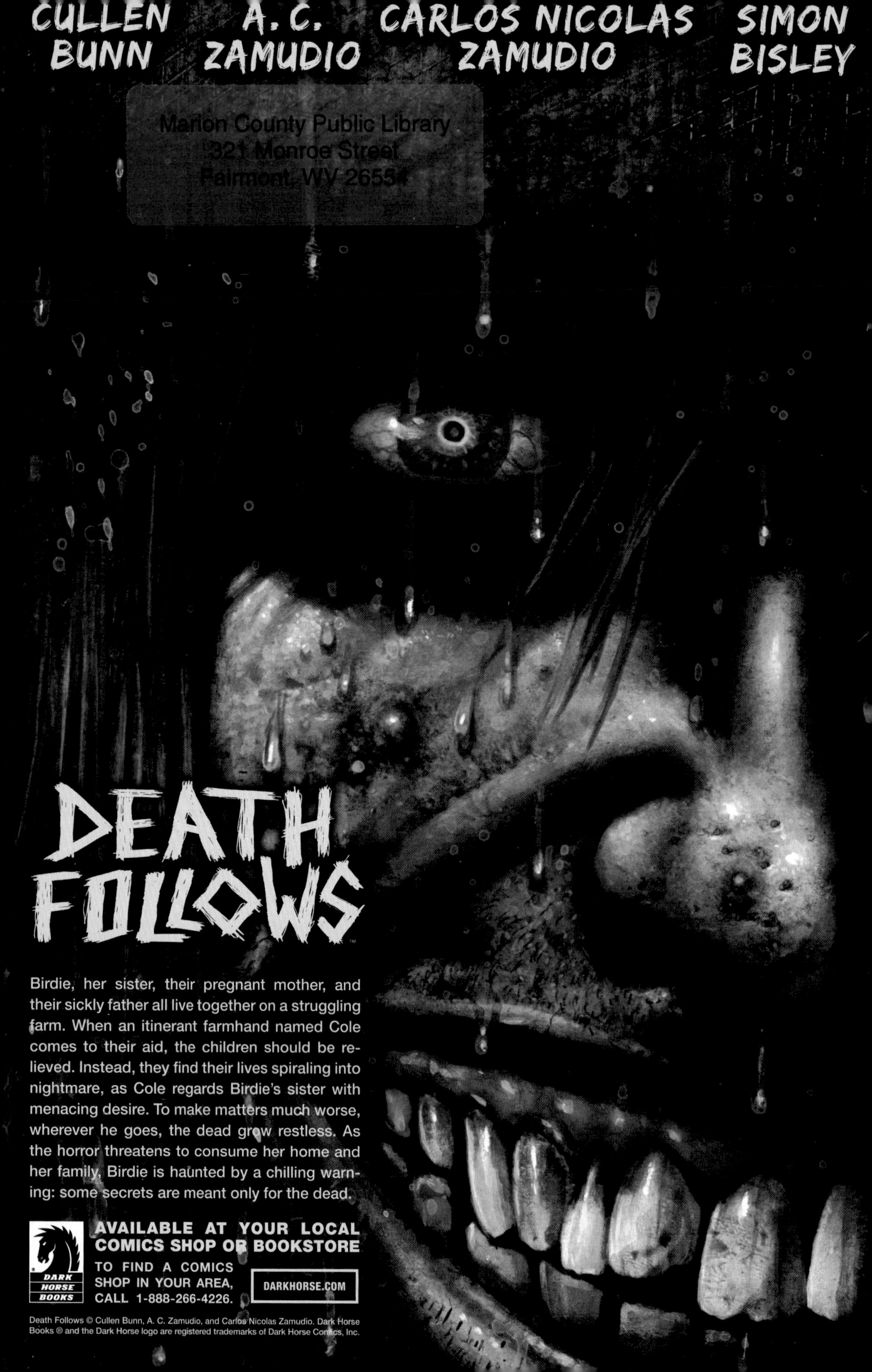
CULLEN BUNN
A. C. ZAMUDIO
CARLOS NICOLAS ZAMUDIO
SIMON BISLEY
Marion County Public Library
321 Monroe Street
Fairmont, WV 26554
DEATH FOLLOWS™
Birdie, her sister, their pregnant mother, and their sickly father all live together on a struggling farm. When an itinerant farmhand named Cole comes to their aid, the children should be relieved. Instead, they find their lives spiraling into nightmare, as Cole regards Birdie's sister with menacing desire. To make matters much worse, wherever he goes, the dead grow restless. As the horror threatens to consume her home and her family, Birdie is haunted by a chilling warning: some secrets are meant only for the dead.
DARK HORSE BOOKS
AVAILABLE AT YOUR LOCAL COMICS SHOP OR BOOKSTORE
TO FIND A COMICS SHOP IN YOUR AREA, CALL 1-888-266-4226.
DARKHORSE.COM
Death Follows © Cullen Bunn, A. C. Zamudio, and Carlos Nicolas Zamudio. Dark Horse Books ® and the Dark Horse logo are registered trademarks of Dark Horse Comics, Inc.